P9-EAO-360

SHAKESPEAREAN FILMS/ SHAKESPEAREAN DIRECTORS

Media and Popular Culture
A Series of Critical Books

SERIES EDITOR
David Thorburn
Director of Film and Media Studies and
Professor of Literature,
Massachusetts Institute of Technology

In recent years a new, interdisciplinary scholarship devoted to popular culture and modern communications media has appeared. This emerging intellectual field aims to move beyond inherited conceptions of "mass society" by recognizing the complexity and diversity of the so-called mass audience and its characteristic cultural experiences. The new scholarship on media and popular culture conceives communication as a complex, ritualized experience in which "meaning" or significance is constituted by an intricate, contested collaboration among institutional, ideological, and cultural forces.

Intended for students and scholars as well as the serious general reader, **Media and Popular Culture** will publish original interpretive studies devoted to various forms of contemporary culture, with emphasis on media texts, audiences, and institutions. Aiming to create a fruitful dialogue between recent strains of feminist, semiotic, and marxist cultural study and older forms of humanistic and social-scientific scholarship, the series will be open to many methods and theories and committed to a discourse that is intellectually rigorous yet accessible and lucid.

Communication as Culture
Essays on Media and Society
JAMES W. CAREY

Myths of Oz
Reading Australian Popular Culture
JOHN FISKE, BOB HODGE, and GRAEME TURNER

Teenagers and Teenpics
The Juvenilization of American Movies in the 1950s
THOMAS DOHERTY

Comic Visions
Television Comedy and American Culture
DAVID MARC

Reporting the Counterculture
RICHARD GOLDSTEIN

Shakespearean Films/Shakespearean Directors
PETER S. DONALDSON

Forthcoming

British Cultural Studies
An Introduction
GRAEME TURNER

Sold Separately
Aspects of Children's Consumer Culture
ELLEN SEITER

Additional titles in preparation

SHAKESPEAREAN FILMS/ SHAKESPEAREAN DIRECTORS

Peter S. Donaldson

Boston
UNWIN HYMAN
London   Sydney   Wellington

Unwin Hyman, Inc.
8 Winchester Place, Winchester, Mass. 01890, USA

Published by the Academic Division of
Unwin Hyman Ltd
15/17 Broadwick Street, London W1V 1FP, UK

Allen & Unwin (Australia) Ltd,
8 Napier Street, North Sydney, NSW 2060, Australia

Allen & Unwin (New Zealand) Ltd in association with the
Port Nicholson Press Ltd,
Compusales Building, 75 Ghuznee Street, Wellington 1, New Zealand

First published in 1990

Library of Congress Cataloging in Publication Data

Donaldson, Peter Samuel, 1942–
  Shakespearean films/Shakespearean directors/Peter S. Donaldson.
  p. cm. — (Media and popular culture)
  Filmography: p.
  ISBN 0–04–445231–4. — ISBN 0–04–445230–6 (pbk.)
  1. Shakespeare, William, 1564–1616 — Film adaptations.   I. Title.
  II. Series.
  PR3093.D66   1990   89–21493
  791.43′657—dc20   CIP

British Library Cataloguing in Publication Data

Donaldson, Peter S. (Peter Samuel), *1942–*
  Shakespearean films/Shakespearean directors. – (Media
  and popular culture).
  1. Drama in English. Shakespeare, William. Adaptations:
  Cinema films
  I. Title   II. Series
  791.4375

  ISBN 0–04–445231–4
  ISBN 0–04–445230–6 pbk

Typeset in 10 on 12 point Palatino by
Nene Phototypesetters Ltd, Northampton
and printed in Great Britain by
Billing and Son Ltd, London and Worcester

This book is dedicated to
Don R. Lipsitt, M.D.

Contents

Series Editor's Preface   ix

Preface   xi

Acknowledgments   xvii

1   "Claiming from the Female:" Gender and
Representation in Laurence Olivier's *Henry V*   1
2   Olivier, Hamlet, and Freud   31
3   Surface and Depth: *Throne of Blood* as Cinematic
Allegory   69
4   Mirrors and M/Others: The Welles *Othello*   93
5   "Haply for I Am Black": Liz White's *Othello*   127
6   "Let Lips Do What Hands Do": Male Bonding, *Eros*,
and Loss in Zeffirelli's *Romeo and Juliet*   145
7   Disseminating Shakespeare: Paternity and Text
in Jean-Luc Godard's *King Lear*   189

Filmography   227

About the Author   231

Index   233

Series Editor's Preface

Although Shakespearean adaptations are an established topic in British and American scholarship, the nuanced, imaginative readings of seven Shakespearean films presented here constitute nonetheless a significant turning in the history of such inquiry.

Shakespeareans have looked at film versions of their poet before but usually in a grudging or at least a naive spirit, avid to defend the integrity of the literary text against despoliation by montage or camera angle or, more broadly, against world views deemed excessively contemporary. And film folk have written on Shakespearean adaptations, but often in ways that betray an insufficient sense of Renaissance culture and of Shakespeare's verbal and dramatic mastery.

Peter Donaldson's suggestive essays avoid both of these common pitfalls. A professional Shakespearean and scholar of the Renaissance, Donaldson is also open to contemporary strains of literary and cultural theory, especially to psychoanalytic argument. Most important, his readings attend to the visual texture of his material with the care and subtlety of the strongest film scholarship. This unusual mingling of historical, biographical, literary and cinematic perspectives confers a particular authority on his work.

A central implication of Donaldson's argument is that we must understand Shakespearean film as something of an independent subject. The accumulated pressure of prior commentary on Shakespeare and on Shakespearean performance as well as the by-now massive archive of film adaptations of his plays create a backdrop or screen against which we interpret and measure any particular film. A combination of biographical inquiry and close attention to visual texture can yield valuable insight into what living artists make of Shakespeare and into their often troubled connection to the cultural past.

The close study of movies made from Shakespeare thus offers a rare, perhaps unique perspective on the drama of cultural appropriation, that continuing process by which the cultural capital of the past is absorbed, resisted and transformed in the present. The Shakespearean text is not a fixed, immutable monument in Donaldson's always instructive readings, not the artifact of a society long dead, but a vital source of possibility and challenge, the site or ground on which contemporary artists define their modernity—and our own.

—David Thorburn

Preface

Many people have seen one or more Shakespeare films, but few are aware that there are literally hundreds of film and video productions of Shakespeare that span the entire period of film history, from earliest silents to the present, from independent 16mm productions to high-budget feature films, from close transcriptions of stage productions to loose postmodernist collages.[1] These productions constitute an immense potential archive for the study of Shakespeare, film history, and the processes of cultural change.

The study of Shakespearean film has been under way for some time: Robert Hamilton Ball's *Shakespeare on Silent Film* was published in 1968, and Jack Jorgens's excellent *Shakespeare on Film* appeared in 1977. The *Shakespeare on Film Newsletter* is now in its eleventh year, and, in addition to reviews, a substantial literature of journal articles and other scholarly contributions has evolved.[2] Courses (such as my own at MIT) entirely devoted to Shakespeare films are being taught at the university level, and some form of televised or film supplement to high school and university courses on Shakespeare has become common.

Shakespearean Films/Shakespearean Directors is meant to point some new directions for this rapidly developing field and to exemplify some of the ways in which students and teachers of film and literature can make best use of the possibilities for the study of Shakespeare created by the videocassette recorder and by newer technologies such as the laserdisc.

This book is primarily concerned not with the fidelity of the films it discusses to their Shakespearean originals, but rather with the process of appropriation by which the conventions and practices of the Elizabethan stage are refashioned in the contemporary medium of film, and by which the work of individual film artists is nourished and challenged by the task of adapting Shakespeare. I regard each film as the site of a cultural, artistic, and personal negotiation the contours of which may be mapped by careful analysis of visual figuration and imagery. Because Shakespeare's plays were intended to be performed on the bare platform stage of the English Renaissance theater, each director must invent a visual design to accompany or supplant the play text. And precisely because words and images, plays and films are so different, study of visual style can often reveal the implicit terms on which Shakespeare and contemporary directors meet.

The essays contained in this book draw to varying degrees on film theory, psychoanalysis, and biographical materials to explore the mix of conscious and unconscious motive and design operating in the work of cultural adaptation. The references I make to "the gaze" and to the construction of gender and subjectivity in cinema, to Baudry, Metz, Mulvey, and others will not surprise film scholars but may be new to Shakespeareans. My psychoanalytic paradigms are drawn, eclectically, from Freud, Heinz Kohut, and object relations theory and its feminist revisions. I use biography— especially directorial autobiography—in conjunction with psychological theory not to attempt to explain the work of directors by reference to their lives but to suggest how early and how deep an artist's engagement with Shakespeare can be. For several of the directors studied here Shakespeare's plays were formative (or pivotal) influences. It is not easy— perhaps not even possible—to specify when the work of adaptation begins. For other directors psychological issues arising in childhood, even at times specific images associated with early fears or traumas, are revived in the work of adaptation and contribute to its interest.

Shakespearean Films/Shakespearean Directors consists of close and detailed readings of seven films from a number of widely divergent cultural and cinematic traditions. Included are the first substantial studies of Liz White's independent African-American *Othello* and Jean-Luc Godard's deconstructive *King Lear*. Other chapters deal with more familiar films from new perspectives. Olivier's *Henry V* is read in relation to its translation of the convention of the "boy actress" into cinematic terms. Olivier's *Hamlet* is seen as a tragedy of narcissistic self-enclosure and as the artistic reprise of a childhood sexual trauma suffered by the director. Kurosawa's *Throne of Blood* is interpreted as an allegory of the relation between Western and Japanese cinematic practice. Orson Welles's *Othello* is approached through analogies between the film screen as mirror and the fantasies of maternal insufficiency that haunt its protagonist. Franco Zeffirelli's *Romeo and Juliet* is presented as an antipatriarchal, homoerotic reading of Shakespeare's play.

Central to these readings and rereadings of Shakespeare film is the idea that films are texts: replayable, repeatable, and subject to multiple interpretations. Harry Berger, Jr. has written interestingly about some differences between text and performance:

> Performance does not allow us the leisure to interrupt, challenge, or question. And since we can't flip the moments of a performance back and forth the way we can the pages of a book, we are prevented as spectators from carrying out our central interpretive operations that presuppose our ability to decelerate the text, to ignore sequence while accumulating synchronic or paradigmatic clusters of imagery and to dislocate and compare speeches.[3]

Film may be regarded as performance retextualized. Having a text means that what is written, inscribed, or recorded can be repeated and reexperienced in the modes that repetition makes possible. Surface meanings, manifest drifts of design may be resisted. Textualization, which might be thought of as *stabilizing* meaning, actually opens meaning to an uncircumscribable play of possibilities.

Shakespearean Films/Shakespearean Directors will focus on individual works of art and individual filmmakers and honor them. Yet, with Foucault, I do not believe in authors—or cinematic *auteurs*—in quite the old sense and have learned to value dissonance, irresolution, and contradiction in ways that exceed the old new critical, ultimately Coleridgean aesthetic of opposition and tension within organic unity. Texts are, in principle, open to a play of meaning both essential to the experience of art and impossible to constrict, foreclose, or prevision. Authors and *auteurs* cannot foresee the uses and misuses their words or images will subserve, and in fact live only in and through such wayward and secondary acts of reconstitution, performed by adaptors, translators, critics, students, readers.

All of these films have been richly rewarding to watch, to think about, and to study. I write in order to share the discoveries I have made in watching them. In each chapter I try to propose a clear interpretive hypothesis; to say what I think each film is doing and what it does with Shakespeare. However, one may ask: "Who is Shakespeare?"

The author is ... the ideological figure by which one marks the manner in which we fear the proliferation of meaning.
—Michel Foucault[4]

Mine is a heuristic *auteurism*, a skeptical bardolatry. If the ego is not even master of its own house, and if Althusser is right (he can be only partly right) that the impression of vivid, individual, lived experience is a sure sign of the workings of ideology, then Foucault's question (which is also Samuel Beckett's) may be asked of Shakespeare film: "Who is speaking?" Who is speaking, for instance, when Laurence Olivier utters Hamlet's lines (or those of the ghost of Hamlet's father)? "Shakespeare" is one answer, "Hamlet" another. But if the displacements this book attempts are successful, it will become as appropriate to answer "Freud" or "Ernest Jones," to cite two undoubted influences on Olivier's interpretation, or, in keeping with the more radical reversals of sequence and priority I hope for, to hear later voices, those of revisionist psychoanalysts and perhaps that of my own commentary, in Hamlet's wish to be remembered.

Notes

1 See Robert Hamilton Ball, *Shakespeare on Silent Film* (London: Allen and Unwin, 1968), and Barry Parker, *The Folger Shakespeare Filmography* (Washington, DC: Folger Shakespeare Library, 1979). The filmography now being prepared by Kenneth Roth-

well and Annabelle Meltzer for publication in 1990 by Neal Schuman (New York) is the most comprehensive source.

2   The last two years have seen a dramatic increase in the pace of scholarly publication. *Shakespeare Survey* devoted its 1987 issue to film, and in 1988 no fewer than three new and substantial books appeared: Anthony Davies, *Filming Shakespeare's Plays* (Cambridge: Cambridge University Press); Bernice Kliman, *Hamlet: Film, Television and Audio Performance* (Cranbury, NJ: Fairleigh Dickinson University Press); and J. C. Bulman and H. R. Coursen, eds., *Shakespeare on Television: An Anthology of Essays and Reviews* (Hanover, NH: University Press of New England). At the 1988 convention of the Shakespeare Association of America, five sessions were devoted to film or video, including a lecture/demonstration on "Two Versions of *King Lear*"; a workshop on "Using Shakespeare Videos in the Classroom"; and seminars on "Shakespeare on Film," "Shakespeare on Television: The Work of Elijah Moshinsky," and "Shakespeare and Television: The Work of Jane Howell." Some of these titles may suggest how television, particularly the rapid growth of the videocassette industry, has renewed both popular and scholarly interest in the older "classic" Shakespeare films, many of which are now available for purchase or rental on cassette. In addition, several Shakepeare titles are now available in the new laserdisc format, and very promising educational experiments have been undertaken in the educational use of computer-linked, interactive laserdiscs in teaching Shakespeare.

3   Harry Berger, Jr., "Text against Performance in Shakespeare: The Example of *Macbeth*," in *The Forms of Power and the Power of Forms in the Renaissance*, ed. Stephen Greenblatt (Norman: University of Oklahoma Press, 1982), 163 [= *Genre* 15, nos. 1–2 (Spring–Summer 1982): 51–2].

4   Michel Foucault, "What Is an Author?" in *Textual Strategies: Perspectives in Post-Structuralist Criticism*, ed. Josue V. Harari (Ithaca, NY: Cornell University Press, 1979), 159.

Acknowledgments

Shakespearean Films/Shakespearean Directors owes much to the help of family, friends, and colleagues. My wife and children have joined me in watching most of the films I write about and in the extended discussions the videocasette recorder and videodisc player make possible. My colleagues at MIT—especially William Paul and David Thorburn—have patiently fostered a Renaissance scholar's new interest in film. The Literature Section, the I. A. Kelly III fund, the Dean's Fund, and the Provost's Fund and MIT provided essential financial assistance for equipment and travel to archives.

Several scholarly organizations and journals provided a first forum for several of the chapters of this book: earlier versions of "Liz White's *Othello*" were published in *Shakespeare on Film Newsletter* and *Shakespeare Quarterly*; and "Olivier, Hamlet, and Freud" appeared first, in slightly different form, in *Cinema Journal*. A shortened version of my chapter on Franco Zeffirelli was presented to the Society for Cinema Studies; the *Henry V* chapter was presented at a conference at the University of Florida, Gainesville, sponsored by the Institute for the Psychological Study of the Arts; and the chapters on Liz White, Orson Welles, and Jean-Luc Godard began as papers for the Shakespeare Association of America. I am especially grateful to the participants in the 1987 SAA seminar on psychological approaches to Shakespeare and its codirectors, Janet Adelman and Richard Wheeler.

Archivists at the Harvard Film Archive, the University Film Study Center, the Library of Congress, and the Folger Shakespeare Library have given invaluable assistance. For help with technical aspects of this project I am grateful to Richard Bianchi and Antonio Tucci.

Thanks also to editors, archivists, respondents, panel

chairs, and others who have offered encouragement or criticism, especially Claire Kahane, David Leverenz, my good friend Joseph Westlund (always more consistently Kohutian than I), Bruce Mazlish, Chris Pomiecko, Briany Keith, Monica Kearney, Barabara Schulman, Ruth Perry, Charles Affron, Foster Hirsch, Bruce Kawin, Barbara Hodgdon, Lorne Buchman, Bernice Kliman, Kenneth Rothwell, Lauren M. Osborne, Laurie E. Osborne, David Halperin, Elio Frattaroli, M.D., Stephen Tapscott, Alice Donaldson, Emily Donaldson, Ethan Donaldson, John Caleb Donaldson, Linda Gregerson, Barbara Mowat, Steven Mullaney, Priscilla Forance, Lisa Freeman, Peggy McMahon, Liz White, Roberta Murphy, Miranda Haddad, Virginia Wexman, John Belton, Heather Dubrow, Alvin Kibel, and Ann Friedlaender.

Finally, thanks to my parents, John and Constance Donaldson. Their love of literature has been a precious gift.

"Claiming from the Female:" Gender and Representation in Laurence Olivier's Henry V

All of the essays in this book treat Shakespeare films as the work of individual filmmakers tracing, in visual image and style, the interplay between psychologically resonant source texts and the recurring themes and concerns of directors' artistic and personal lives. At the same time, each chapter tries to specify key aspects of the work of cultural and artistic mediation through which each filmmaker engages the text and makes the transition from the conventions of the Elizabethan theater to those of the contemporary cinema.

The present chapter examines two aspects of Laurence Olivier's 1944 film adaptation of Shakespeare's *Henry V*: its treatment of gender and its recasting, in cinematic terms, of Shakespeare's posing of the problem of representation. These are closely related: the transition from the practices of the Elizabethan stage, dramatized in the opening scenes of the film, to those of contemporary cinema involves, as one of its most significant features, a shift from the use of boys in women's parts to the use of actresses. This shift is central to Olivier's representational strategy and to his attempt to make good the ambitions of Elizabethan theater by cinematic means. It is also central to understanding the place of this Shakespearean adaptation in the director's artistic biography. Olivier himself had acted women's parts in Shakespeare as a child, and the film in some scenes recapitulates the role these performances played in the resolution of his own early conflicts about gender.

The prologue of Shakespeare's *Henry V* apologizes famously for the shortcomings of the Elizabethan theater, demanding "a kingdom for a stage." The public playhouse is a "cockpit," an "unworthy scaffold" too small to hold the "vasty fields of France," and too disreputable to present the heroic deeds of a godlike king. By calling attention to the disparity between theatrical representation and the historical reality it stands for, the play does not merely lament its limitations, however, but also initiates a double perspective on the action. The prologue of *Henry V* signals a discrepancy between self and role that guides our perception of the king's performative and self-divided character; it authorizes the "imaginations" of the spectators, who must complete what the stage cannot present; and it creates possibilities for alternative political readings of the play's ideological premises. The ill-repute of the theater—its manipulative, even tawdry devices—and the vacuity or emptiness that haunt the project of theatrical representation can become metaphors for the play's epic subject, calling in question the glory of the war and the methods and motives of the king. *Henry V*'s reflection on the inadequacy of the stage can be read, that is, not as the humble apology it pretends to be, but as a vehicle for the current of doubt and subversion so many recent critics have detected beneath the play's celebratory surface.[1]

Laurence Olivier's film version of the play, completed in 1944, aligns itself with the affirmative, heroic energies of *Henry V* and, in doing so, gives the metatheatrical reflections of the prologue a very different function from the disjunctive or critical one I have just described. For Olivier the disclaimers were to be taken literally ("In *Henry V* more than in any other play, Shakespeare bemoans the confines of his Globe Theatre"),[2] and provided a mandate for the representational amplification film could provide. Reading certain scenes as "frustrated cinema,"[3] Olivier's conception of his role as adaptor was shaped by patriotic fervor and sanctioned by what he describes as an almost mystic or dyadic identification with Shakespeare: "I had a mission. ... My country was at war; I felt Shakespeare within me, I felt the cinema within him. I knew what I wanted to do, what he would have done."[4]

Cinema subsumes and transcends the past, including its own theatrical past, effacing differences. Its power to do so is linked in this passage to a particularly intimate version of the fantasy of Shakespeare as mentor. The relation of adaptation to source thus parallels one pattern of male identification with fathers and elders. The paternal inheritance descends from King Henry V to Laurence Olivier as heroic spirit and from Shakespeare to Olivier as representational ambition. As in the play, coming into this inheritance will depend, in the film, on a kind of "claiming from the female," an outward appropriation of the female image that balances the director's internal possession of Shakespeare.

In Shakespeare's *Henry V* the historical action itself is framed partly in gendered terms. Henry's relation to his "mighty ancestors" depends on making a legal claim to France through the female line; in appealing to his troops he asks them to "dishonor not your mothers" and to show they are their fathers' sons through their bravery. The conquest of France is complete when, as "chief article" of the treaty, Princess Katherine is betrothed to King Henry. The play's meditation on its representational practices is also gendered: the limits of the stage are tested by the task of representing a legendary *male* warrior, and at the end the peace between England and France is made to depend on the success of a representational illusion, the "perspectival" substitution of the virgin princess for the "maiden walls" of French cities (5.2.301–23).[5] The representational plot moves from hyerbolic inflation (how can the actors or the soldiers "assume the port of Mars") to anamorphic compression, from war to peace, from male to female through figures that are incipiently sexual at the outset and more explicitly and violently so in the course of the action. The "swelling scene" imagined in the prologue anticipates the stretched bodies, bent up spirits, and stiffened sinews of Henry's advice to the troops at the seige of Harfleur; the "cramming" of the fields of France into the little "O" of the playhouse[6] prefigures the literal defloration with which the king threatens the virgins of the town, as well as the peaceful forcing of sexual acquiescence from Katherine in the last scene. These tropes themselves are forced and uncomfortable; their strain is a reminder of the potential violence that underlies the marital conclusion and the brief unstable peace.

But although the representational tropes of *Henry V* frequently invoke sexual difference, Shakespeare does not exploit the most distinctive gender convention of his theater, the playing of all female roles by boys. In this respect *Henry V* differs from the comedies, most notably *Twelfth Night* and *As You Like It*, in which the underlying male gender of the women in the play complicates the contrast between actor and role. Perhaps the greater decorum expected of history plays explains this difference, but the representational problem posed by the "boy actress" may have been awkward for Shakespeare for another reason: the Salic Law ("No woman shall succeed in Salic land") barring King Henry's claim to France was also the law of the English stage, where no woman could appear. The play ignores—perhaps suppresses—the analogy between the gendered basis of the historical action and the gender exclusions of its own medium. For Olivier the cross-dressing of the Elizabethan stage is emphasized, and its improvement by filmic means is central to his attempt to correct or complete Shakespearean practice. Like the king, who must pursue a matrilineal claim and secure his conquest through a dynastic marriage, the boy player can succeed only by "claiming from the female" (1.2.92), appropriating women's dress and manner, assimilating "feminine" traits to male performance. Film makes this possible in a unique way.

The film *Henry V* begins in the playhouse, with a historical recreation of late-sixteenth-century Bankside and the Globe Theater, where a performance of Shakespeare's *Henry V* begins, attended by a noisy Elizabethan audience. In the course of the "play" the camera moves closer to the stage, and we gradually lose awareness of the theatrical and historical ambience. Through a series of inward tracking movements, set changes, musical cues, and shifts in makeup and acting style (which becomes less gestural, oratorical, and inter-active), the bare stage of the playhouse gives way to in-

4

creasingly illusionist sets and finally to the unbounded outdoor spaces of cinematic epic, complete with the armies and horses whose absence Shakespeare's chorus laments. At the end this process is reversed, and the film ends, as it began, on the stage of the "Globe."[7]

Robert Weimann has described the interplay of levels of representation on the Elizabethan stage as a tension between the *platea*, or performative function, and the *locus*, or representational function, as these had been inherited from medieval practice and adapted to the public playhouse. The platea was, roughly, the downstage portion of the large platform stage; there performers could interact with the audience and move freely in and out of role. The platea was where most of the "low" and unscripted clowning Hamlet complains of took place, and where the actors could be seen for the lowly, even disreputable urban artisans they were. On the upstage, or locus portion of the stage, impersonation took precedence over performance, greater decorum prevailed, and the doubleness of actor and role was less emphasized. This was the narrative or historical "place," and it retained traces of the sanctity or high seriousness of the biblical locations of the medieval mystery plays from which it derived. The subversive potential of the stage is linked to this distinction: kings may be no better than the ragged players who represent them. Unruly and carnivalesque, the disreputable platea deflates and critiques official ideology.[8]

Olivier's presentation of the Elizabethan stage, which predates Weimann, observes in broad terms such a distinction between downstage and upstage, partly exploiting its antiauthoritarian potential: the undignified clowning of the Bishop of Ely and the Archbishop of Canterbury in setting forth the Salic Law takes place downstage,[9] as does the insulting gift of tennis balls to the king, while the rear is reserved for the throne and is treated with more dignity and a more complete identification of performer with historical role. More important, however, Olivier maps the difference between locus and platea onto the relation between the Elizabethan playhouse *as a whole* and the more realistically conceived historical and cinematic space that replaces it. Just as in the relation of platea to locus a movement *inward*, to the rear of the image, is used to announce that the historical subject matter is being presented with proper reverence, rather than as material for burlesque, and to signal the dropping away of the actors' personalities and the decisive emergence of the historical characters. Even more emphatically than the rear of the represented Globe stage, the cinematic locus is a decorous, almost santified space.

In the film, as in Elizabethan practice, the contrast between platea and locus is closely related to the presentation of gender. The shift from "playhouse" to cinematic space is prominently marked by the replacement of boys by women, and the return to the theater is effected by a complex filmic transition in which, by means of a hidden cut, the adult performer who plays Princess Katherine "becomes" the boy actor who is her counterpoint in the frame narrative, unsettling audience perceptions of gender and imparting to the final image of the "boy actress" an effect of the real beyond the range of the transvestite theater. Like "real" battles, "real" women serve to mark or index the superseding of the bare platform stage by the representational plenitude of epic filmmaking.

The boy actors are first introduced, briefly and incompletely, in the rapid survey of the tiring house in the film's opening minutes. Two boys are seen shaving, helping each other to dress and wig for their female roles. The presentation emphasizes their friendly professionalism. When one of the boys tries to stuff oranges in his bosom and then abandons the attempt, opting for a flat chest, we see what he does as a technical problem of the theater, perhaps suggesting a degree of improvisation and individual discretion in how boy actors approached the details of female impersonation (photos 1.1, 1.2). The camera moves away from the boys quickly, before they are fully dressed. This contrasts with the treatment of the king, who enters backstage, fully robed, rouged, and crowned at our first sight of him. In the case of the female roles, the moment at which the boy performers appear in character is deferred, so that the presentation *on stage* of this aspect of Elizabethan theater most different from modern practice will be a surprise. One of the boys returns fairly soon afterward as Mistress Quickly; the other appears as Princess Katherine only at the very end of the film.

The first appearance of a fully cross-dressed boy takes place in the Boar's Head tavern scene, in which Falstaff's illness is described to Pistol, Bardolph, and Nym by Mistress Quickly. These are the indecorous, "low" characters of the play, and their style—compounded of bragging, brawling, obscene humor, and cynicism toward the war—is contrasted with the relative decorum of the historical narrative. The scene opens with a quarrel between Pistol, now husband to Mistress Quickly, and Nym, his former rival for her affections. Pistol's phallic braggadoccio ("Pistol's cock is up, and flashing fire will follow") and easily offended honor serve as foil to the king's more restrained rhetoric and the measured power of his response to insult. Mistress Quickly, played by

Photo 1.1

Photo 1.2

Photo 1.3

Photo 1.4

a boy, shares in the bawdy punning and coarse humor of the scene (photo 1.3). At this point in the film the location is still "the Globe": high-angle long shots and fixed camera placement keep us aware that the action is taking place on a stage. The boy Quickly overacts, playing up the bawdy double entendres of the text with hammy giggles and knowing glances at the audience: her establishment is no brothel, but a respectable inn where "honest gentlewomen ... live by the prick of their needles." The scene presents a travesty of the chivalric premises of the war, with Pistol and Nym as burlesque knights offering to duel over a "lady" who is a lewd-tongued adolescent boy in drag.

With the mention of Falstaff's illness the tone of the sequence becomes serious, and a somber musical passage initiates the transition to "real" space, with a forward tracking movement toward and through an upper window into a room where Falstaff lies sick. He is attended by a woman dressed in a costume that bespeaks her serious function as nurse and comforter (photo 1.4). This performer looks nothing like the boy actor she replaces in the role of Mistress Quickly—casting and costume underscore the difference. The presence of the actress completes the shift toward seriousness, and as Falstaff cries out his poignant farewell to the absent king who has abandoned him, the tableau of the dying former friend and his grave, compassionate nurse may seem a reproach not only to the king but also to the stage, contrasting with the levity of the playhouse slapstick we have just witnessed.

Mistress Quickly's return to the courtyard of the inn signals a change in tone and a further shift from "theatrical" to "cinematic" representation. The men remain costumed as they were, played by the same male actors, but the space they occupy is now an outdoor location or realistic set, and the reentry of the Hostess, now played by a woman, converts their banter into quiet listening as they attend to her news. Her bawdy lines, which continue unabated in Shakespeare's text through the entire description of Falstaff's death, are now downplayed and lose their interactive quality as well as their sexual point. Cinematic representation, even in these tavern scenes, is more decorous and exhibits greater closure or self-containment than the stage: the film audience is never directly acknowledged, and language loses some of its unruly equivocation.

In the text the Hostess' celebrated speech on Falstaff's death is serious, but some of its pathos derives from the earthy, carnival qualities of Mistress Quickly's jokes and errors. Falstaff goes to "Arthur's bosom," not Abraham's, and echoes of lower-body humor may be heard in her description of feeling "upward and upward" along Falstaff's body for signs of life. With Quickly now played by a woman, the film version of the speech is more decorous. Quickly is seated on the ground, and as she describes the moment of death she runs a hand over her husband's knee and "upward" to his comforting arm (photo 1.5). The tactile perception of the death is replaced by contact with a loved one in shared grief. It is a moving gesture but one that dissociates the mature woman from the bawdy boy player and, in contrast to the text, desexualizes the encounter with death.[10]

In the diegetic or narrative sections of the film, then, in contrast with the playhouse scenes, "real" women are associated with an emotional depth, seriousness, and compassion beyond the range of boy players. But their presence also goes with a muting of the bawdiness and sexual punning of the text. This is true for the scenes involving Princess Katherine and her companion, too: the obscene joking on "foot" and "gown" in the English lesson is made maximally obscure; Katherine is played as ultrarefined; and the crudely witty exchanges between King Henry and her uncle concerning her excessive sexual modesty (5.2.281–300) are cut in Olivier's screenplay.

As the transition from playhouse to "real" world is marked and indexed by the replacement of the boy actor who played Quickly by a woman, so the transition from the French court back to the stage of the Globe is coupled with a return of the transvestite conventions of Shakespeare's theater.

This is handled in an extraordinary way. To seal their union, Olivier and Renee Asherson as Katherine don robes of state and walk hand in hand to the rear of the set (photo 1.6). The camera follows them, and when they have reached the far wall, there is a cut to a single shot of the king (photo

Photo 1.5   Photo 1.6

1.7). I continue with Harry Geduld's description of this sequence:

> Henry turns and is seen to be wearing the crude make-up in which he first appeared in the Globe Theater scenes. Then the camera pans to the right and shows a boy made up as Katherine. To the sound of applause, the camera next pulls back, revealing the stage of the Globe Theatre.[11]

Other indications of the transition back to the Globe, even before the backward-tracking movement, include the reprise of the Elizabethan music that introduced the play and the king's upward glance acknowledging the audience in the upper tiers. Olivier has hidden the transition so that, unlike the corresponding movement *into* filmic space, we are momentarily disoriented in regard to both the level of representation and the gender of "Katherine."

As in the comedies, one effect of this switch from actress to boy player may be to "unsettle gender distinctions."[12] The conventions of film narrative and continuity editing create the expectation that figures the camera follows in such a sequence will remain the same; however, the special stylistic markers Olivier has employed to distinguish diegetic space from "playhouse" space override that expectation. In making the adjustment, the customarily firm boundary between genders may be called into question. This may be one of the ways in which Olivier perfects Elizabethan practice, creating

10

a cinematic equivalent of the playful crossing of genders in the comedies.

In order to understand how this sequence completes Olivier's contrast between levels of representation and caps his development of the motif of "claiming from the female," it is necessary to provide a fuller description. Geduld's account overlooks a second transition that takes place *after* the royal couple turn and face the Globe audience. The pulling back of the camera is actually two separate shots, a close-up (photos 1.8, 1.9) followed by a track-back (photos 1.10, 1.11). Because the sets are matched, the close-up is brief and the backward movement rapid, it is hard to see the cut. We "read" the two shots thus joined as one, but when individual frames are examined, it is easy to see that the princess shown in the close-up is a female performer. Her appearance differs from that of the boy player in several respects: her nose and chin are smaller, the features are softer, the hair is looser, the gown is cut much lower, the robe is not gathered so tightly round the bust, and the performer is wearing a rich double string of pearls knotted below the neck.[13] Flushed and excited by applause, she moistens her lips, smiles, and acknowledges the look of the playhouse spectators.

Although it is clear that we are looking at a performer responding to applause, that response is conveyed through the conventional signifiers of female sexual attraction: loose hair, flushed cheeks, mobile glance, and pleasure in being looked at. The actress *may* be Renee Asherson, but if so, her makeup, dress, and demeanor are far different from those of the demure princess of earlier scenes (photo 1.12). The eros that is deferred or muted in the wooing scenes is present here, displaced from the decorous space of historical narrative into the milieu of the theater—the warm response Henry cannot quite get from Katherine as princess is given to the audience by Katherine as player. As the camera cuts and tracks back, the "king and queen" assume static, hierarchical positions reminiscent of Elizabethan formal portraiture: as we adjust to the fact that we are watching two males, the image, in its storybook tableau aspect, abruptly loses its interactive quality. This is no longer a woman offered to and

Photo 1.7

Photo 1.8

Photo 1.9

Photo 1.10

Photo 1.11

Photo 1.12

returning an appreciative gaze, but a boy—in fact, it is the boy we saw beginning to dress for the part in the opening minutes of the film—in a rigid pose, averting his eyes from the spectators.

If this sequence alludes to the homoerotic playfulness of

12

Shakespeare's stage, it also once again instances the film's prejudice in favor of actresses. The image of a "real" woman is covertly blended with that of a Shakespearean boy player, imparting to the latter a more convincing "feminine" appeal. As in the case of the other artificialities of the Elizabethan stage, the playing of women's parts by boys *is* a deficiency in Olivier's mind, one that can be made good by film.

There are other Shakespearean inadequacies, discontinuities, and ironies at the end of *Henry V* which this sequence replaces with images of harmony and completion. There is no marriage in the play, which jumps from the king's final speech in France ("prepare we for our marriage ..." 5.2.370–74) to the epilogue spoken on the English stage, which reminds the spectators of the brevity of Henry's reign, the civil turmoil that followed, the loss of France and insists (once again) that theatrical representation is a debasement, a "mangling" and "confining" of what it stages. Although the king had achieved "the world's best garden," its Edenic perfection—like that of the marriage that was its dynastic vehicle—is brief, unstable, and present in the play only by report.

Olivier's film softens some of the ironic quality by textual cuts, but the chief vehicle for its revision of the close is the staging of the last scene as a state wedding. At the end of 5.2 the couple don royal robes and crowns, and choral accompaniment expresses santification and holiness. The actual moment of exchanging vows is elided, but at the end of the transition from France to the playhouse they appear as king and queen, and the Archbishop of Canterbury pops between the pair from behind the inner stage curtain with a sign of blessing. The moment is thus not merely a wedding but a wedding in England. Henry has not only won the princess (a victory marred by her silence in the text) but brings her back to England, where she appears as his wife *on the stage of the Globe*.

The joining of Henry and Katherine is also the moment at which the medium of film and that of stagecraft join as seamlessly as possible, so that the several levels of the film—political (the union of France and England), personal (the marriage of Kate and Henry), historical (fifteenth century, late sixteenth century, midtwentieth century), and representational (film, stage)—are unified in a single, sanctified tableau.[14]

Shakespeare's Henry must "claim from the female" literally, basing his claim to France on a rejection of the Salic Law and securing his victory by a dynastic marriage. In the film male artistic achievement "claims from the female" as well, incorporating the depth, compassion, and sexual presence of "real" women into the all-male institution of the Shakespearean stage. The princess is not merely the prize of dynastic struggle and personal completion—she is also, in the complex representational allegory Olivier has constructed, the warrant of artistic closure, the mark of the completion and perfection of Shakespearean theater by the art of the film.

Olivier's *Henry V* also intimates an integration of the feminine within the king's personality. In the play there are strong indications that the king's outward successes mask an inner void, an emptiness analogous to the poverty of means the chorus associates with the stage itself. His winning of France and of the princess is made possible by a frightening and humanly costly self-suppression: "We are no tyrant, but a Christian king,/Unto whose grace our passion is as subject/As is our wretches fettered in our prisons" (1.2.241–43). The qualities curtailed or sacrificed—"mortified," as the Archbishop puts it—in Henry's pursuit of his goals are associated, in the play as in the wider culture, with women: undisguised expression of feeling, intimacy, compassion. Maleness, especially the kind of masculinity required of a king-conqueror, defines itself largely as a departure from the female realm and its stereotypic personal and emotional qualities.[15]

In the campfire scene when he visits the common soldiers, in the "band of brothers" speech, and in the wooing of Katherine Henry tries to achieve wholeness and connection to others, but the play offers powerful suggestions that his efforts fail because he has sacrificed too much of his humanity to his political and military role. His encounter with the common soldiers leaves him resentful and conscious of his guilt in enjoying a crown secured by the murder of a lawful king; the battlefield promises of brotherhood with his troops are undercut by his subsequent meeting with Williams, in which the king is cool and distant, and his condescending gift of money is mediated by Fluellen; his wooing of "Kate" is often played as charming, but the threat of renewed violence may be heard in the speeches he makes as plain and love-struck soldier. In contrast, Olivier opts for wholeness, "completing" Shakespeare's characterization of Henry as film completes the bare platform stage. For this Henry V outward success is matched by an inward integration of a "feminine" capacity for tenderness, nurturance, and intimacy.

The deep cuts Olivier made in the texts are relevant here: Geduld (understating) notes that "passages indicating Henry's ruthlessness have been omitted."[16] These excisions soften the presentation of specifically male forms of ruthlessness directed both literally and figuratively against women. *All* of the many references to rape are missing, including the horrific threats Henry speaks at the siege of Harfleur (3.3.1–43) and the significant echoes of those threats in the metaphors of the marriage negotiations (5.1.316–28). In addition, the actual violence employed or approved by the king is minimized: Olivier has cut the execution of Bardolph, Cambridge, Scroop, and Grey and completely omits the crucial presentation of the king's order for the murder of the French prisoners. In keeping with the reduction of violence and the suppression of the moral and psychological questions the text raises concerning its use, the impressive outdoor sequences portraying the Battle of Agincourt, though exciting, are euphemistic by design. For all the energy of the fight and for all the careful historical realism of the scene, we see very little of the *pain* of combat, very little of its terror—and no blood at all. "I showed no bloody gashes."[17]

One of the ways in which cinematic realism might have improved on stage practice is thus rejected. The violence of war and the manifestation of that violence in the king's character are softened and replaced by chivalry, humane reluctance to do injury, and warm and nurturant affection for the troops. In the play text two alternative motives (rage at prior French atrocities or strategic calculation: 4.6.35–37 and 4.7.8–10) are given for the king's most disturbing act, the order for the murder of the French prisoners. The film substitutes a scene of paternal concern and gallantry. Touched and angered at the sight of one of the English boys killed by the French, held toward us in the extreme foreground, his throat cut (the only gashes shown in the film are those in this brief sequence), Henry challenges the Constable of France to single combat: an honorable, bloodless duel replaces a counteratrocity.

The film offers a vision of war that is certainly masculine but aspires to an un- or antiphallic condition conveyed partly by Olivier's emotional range as an actor, which enables him to combine great confidence and power with gentleness.[18] The gentle side is most fully developed, perhaps, in the campfire scene, in which the disguised king goes among his soldiers.

This scene begins with a group long shot of two of the men seated on the ground and a third reclining and propped on one elbow, fighting off sleep. As they meditate on the coming day of battle, one of them becomes aware of an intruder, and, at his verbal challenge, there is a cut to Olivier alone, only his face visible under the hood of a borrowed cloak (photos 1.13, 1.14). His quiet reply, "A friend," is the private, personal counterpart of the king's powerful public oratory. As in the great speeches, Olivier is seen in long shot, centered in the image, speaking from the depths of the represented space. The discussion between Henry and the men concerning the moral issues of the war is filmed in crosscut close-ups, with commoners and king seen at equally intimate distance. Because the close-ups show us Henry at closer range than his men see him, the impression that we are the privileged observers of the king's inner or real self is enhanced. The king is vulnerable to the moral challenges the men voice, especially to these lines spoken by Court, the soldier who had been trying to sleep:

But if the cause be not good, the king himself hath a heavy reckoning to make when all those legs and arms and heads, chopped off in a battle, shall join together at the latter day and cry all, "We died at such a place," some swearing, some upon a surgeon, some upon their wives left poor behind them, some upon the debts they owe, some upon their children rawly left. I am afeared there are few die well that die in a battle; for how can they charitably dispose of anything when blood is their argument? Now if these men do not die well, it will be a black matter for the king that led them to it.

The king listens intently and respectfully to Court, now seen to be a boy in his teens (photo 1.15). In the play these lines are spoken by Williams, not Court, who has only one line. Olivier's amplification of Court's part has the effect of isolating the moral seriousness of these lines from the testy, almost cynical challenge to the king's motives Williams goes on to make ("Ay, he said that to make us fight cheerfully, but when our throats are cut ..."). After his speech Court lies down again, disappearing beneath the frame line, and the

Photo 1.13

Photo 1.14

Photo 1.15

Photo 1.16

angry discussion about the insincerity of the king's promise of equal risk in battle ensues. Then the common soldiers exit and the king remains and delivers his soliloquy on the vanity of royal pomp. This speech includes a bitter, resentful characterization of the common people of England as all too ready to "lay on the king" all their moral, financial, and family responsibilities. In the play text the king's meditation leads not to peace with himself but to the guilty memory of his father's theft of the crown and an unsuccessful attempt to pray. But in the film the scene works to restore the fellowship breached by Williams's challenge and to show the king in harmony with himself, pious and confident.

The first part of the speech is delivered with the king seated alone in the image. But as he thinks of the ungrateful commoners who benefit from his care, the camera pulls back to discover the boy, Court, asleep by the king's side. The king strokes his head while speaking of the burdensome responsibilities of office, balancing the distance between himself and the common people suggested by the words with a powerful though brief image of paternal care and contact (photo 1.16). There are potential ironies in the moment at which the king strokes Court's head: Court is asleep, so the king's affection is revealed only when response is impossible; there is a cultural paternalism in the choice of an Irish boy for the part; and, perhaps most important, the king's tender gesture runs counter not only to his words but to his hazard of his men's lives in an uneven battle. But these are not ironies the film knows or acknowledges. For Olivier the king is—in this the only fully private moment in the film—a gentle father, and it is out of his capacity to be one that his strength as a warrior and his charm as a lover flow. His own personality incorporates qualities of nurturance, warmth, compassion, and intimacy that are the opposites of Pistol's phallic bragging and posturing and which suggest a psychic integration, a "claiming from the female" on the level of the personality that is an analogue of the dynamics of gender at the level of plot and representational strategy.

The point, finally, of the various ways in which women, the images of women, or qualities thought to be proper to women are transposed into male forms is the restoration of bonds of love and solidarity among the men—the resuscitation, in an age of doubt and cynicism, of the mythology of the loving father-king. This resuscitation, so brilliantly achieved in the film, entails a thorough and idealizing but by no means trivializing reconception of the play. Yet the strategy of modifying definitions of manhood based on denial of feeling and defensive difference from women by an admixture of "feminine" traits is dubious in several ways. It does not question the cultural construction of these traits but takes them as given. It is based on appropriative strategies that suppress or misname the force and deception that make them possible. It "claims from the female" without negotiation or mutual recognition. Its intimations of psychic and political wholeness take place, despite their *use* of female images, within male and male-dominated institutions centered in a powerful, directing male will and consciousness. In this the fifteenth-century battlefield, the sixteenth-century stage, and the twentieth-century milieu of film production meet. These are real limitations of the film's utopian vision and, I think, important differences between the critical dissonances of Shakespearean theater and the totalizing aesthetic of realist filmmaking as Olivier practiced it. But to the extent that the film offers a vision of maleness that acknowledges its derivation from the female and presents the usually rigid boundaries between genders as permeable, its achievement is significant.

At the end of the film, as the stage curtain is drawn over Henry V and the boy actor who now stands behind him as Kate, the camera cranes up to reveal a boys' chorus singing on the upper stage conducted by the prissy Bishop of Ely, whom we saw in the opening sequences drinking too much ale backstage and fussily assisting the archbishop in the exposition of the Salic Law (photo 1.17). The ecclesiastical robes he wears link the "Elizabethan" boys' chorus to the church choirs and choir schools of twentieth-century England, in which the boys we hear sing were actually trained. Laurence Olivier attended such schools, which were early training grounds for actors as well as singers. His autobiographical writings emphasize their importance in his developing sense of theatrical vocation and, significantly,

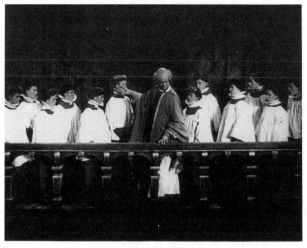

Photo 1.17

also their part in his early confusions about gender identity. I turn to that story in conclusion.

Olivier was the third and youngest child, and by all accounts he became the focus of parental quarrels.[19] His mother was devoted to him and his father was hostile, unpredictable, and punitive. From early childhood through late adolescence this pattern of conflict in the family was associated—again, not only by Olivier himself but by other witnesses as well—with *acting* and with *questions about gender identity*. Agnes Olivier had a small stage built for Larry at home when he was five, and he performed for the family, enjoying a privileged status that must have exacerbated whatever jealousy the father actually felt for his son. In addition, he was reportedly feminine in manner and slow to attempt activities conventionally appropriate for boys. According to Olivier's older brother, Richard, "by the time Larry was nine he began to get a sense of himself as a male."[20] Whatever such a designation meant, Larry was thought of as a "feminine" boy, and this designation or tag carried over to his school years, where it was reinforced by attitudes toward sex and gender in the all-male institutions Olivier attended. Here, as at home, for a boy to be "beautiful" and notably talented at singing or dramatics meant risking being considered effeminate, with the added expectation that he wanted or would accept the sexual attentions of older males.[21]

At All Saints choir school, where Laurence started at age nine as "solo boy," he was nearly raped by an older boy during his first days while wearing a Sunday kilt and experienced frequent beatings, which he thought of (perhaps rightly) as a response to his attractiveness: "I reportedly sang like an angel and was as pretty as was needed to bring out the worst in certain males."[22] At St. Edward's, his public school, much to his dismay he was again soloist in the choir and subject to the same sexual stereotyping and harassment: "I was ostracized. I was a flirt."[23] Olivier tells his readers that although on one occasion he was sexually attracted to another man, he never indulged in homosexual activity.[24] Nevertheless, these early experiences in school, and perhaps the family patterns that preceded them, left him with a sense of defensiveness in regard to this issue:

> It must be exceedingly difficult to believe that, in spite of my history as a pampered choirboy, and the attentions paid to me at the next school (which, no matter how unwelcome, unfairly labeled me as the school tart), I felt that the homosexual act would be a step darkly destructive to my soul. I was firm in my conviction that heterosexuality was romantically beautiful, immensely pleasurable, and rewarding in contentment.[25]

A central theme in Olivier's account of his school days concerns his attempts to be manly and free himself from the imputation of passivity and femininity. Yet his bid for acceptance by other boys involved dramatics, which he himself thought of as unmasculine. Many of his dramatic successes involved the playing of female roles in Shakespeare plays. If playing female roles helped to confirm the perception of Laurence Olivier as "school tart," his skill enforced respect. His transvestite roles also helped to establish his masculine identity in another, more circuitous but highly significant way: they made possible a nurturant connection to older men that had been lacking with his father, and they enabled him to make creative use of his powerful identification with his mother.

The key incident in this regard, and one of the founding moments of Olivier's vocation as an actor, was the production of *Taming of the Shrew* at All Saints in 1921. The beloved Father Heald, who directed the dramatic productions at All Saints, played Petrucchio, "and I was allowed to be his Kate." This was Olivier's greatest childhood success, and he attributes it to the influence of his mentor: "Father Heald's direction was brilliant, and he injected into my consciousness the conviction that I was, in fact, being a woman."[26] However, other accounts suggest that an equally important influence was Agnes Olivier, who provided the model for his characterization of Kate. Olivier does not connect the two events in his autobiography, but Agnes Olivier had died earlier that year, and according to a number of accounts of the performance that survive, he modeled himself so closely on his mother that those who knew her were astonished at the resemblance. Sybil Thorndike, who was a friend of the family, saw the performance and later commented on Olivier's resemblance to his mother.[27]

Olivier's sister Sybille reported that their father walked out and was so distressed that he forbade Laurence ever to act again.[28]

The death of Olivier's mother and his extraordinary early accomplishment in acting were also jointly effective in making possible a partial and guarded but very important rapprochement between father and son: Olivier's father had promised his wife on her deathbed to be kind to her "baby" (Olivier was then fourteen). Despite his initial anger at seeing his deceased wife impersonated by his son, Gerard Olivier decided to back his son's theatrical career, announcing his decision while the young Olivier was bathing, as was the family custom, in his father's dirty bathwater.

> Lowering myself into the water, which was, I noticed unhappily, a little cleaner than usual, I snatched the hot tap on for the allotted number of seconds, and after a minute or so I asked my father how soon I might reckon on being

allowed to follow Dickie to India. My father's answer was so astonishing that it gave me a deep shock: "Don't be such a fool; you're not going to India, you're going on the stage." "Am I?" I stuttered lamely. "Well, of course you are," he said; and as he went on I realized not only that he had been thinking of me quite deeply, which was something I had long before decided he never did, but that he had been following these thoughts through in pleasingly creative and caring ways.[29]

Olivier begins his autobiography with this story, for it marks the beginning of his professional life and the moment at which his adult male identity was confirmed by his father. The story may also be read as a symbolic recapitulation and resolution of temporally earlier stories about men. The sequence, arranged chronologically, would be fear of a threatening and rejecting father; sexual and physical abuse by older males because of supposed feminine attributes; artistic use of those attributes under the guidance of a male mentor (whose influence is described in penetrative terms that are a benign analogue to the abuse suffered or feared from other males); and a rapprochement with the father that ratifies the boy's "feminine" side (maternal identification; acting) and, perhaps, in a much diluted form, repeats the motif of male insemination suggested by both the stories of abuse and mentorship.

This sequence suggests a complex pattern of merger with the father while maintaining an important link with the mother.[30] I want to emphasize the importance of *acting* in Olivier's story of what, from his point of view, was a troubled and painful but successful growth toward an adult male heterosexual identity. The effeminacy he displayed in early childhood and feared as an unwanted fate during his school years becomes, when suitably bracketed and mastered as the content of his art, an important part of his connection to his father and the basis of an acceptable and appropriate career choice. The "feminine" aspects of Olivier's story of his early life, then, turn out to have a crucial role in his development as a man.

In a recent study of the transvestite conventions of Greek

23

drama, Froma Zeitlin has suggested that "theater uses the feminine for the purposes of imagining a fuller model for the masculine self, and 'playing the other' opens that self to those often banned emotions of fear and pity."[31] I suggest that a related dynamic is expressed in *Confessions of an Actor* and that what appears there as a feared *departure* from masculine norms is, by being worked through on the plane of culturally licensed impersonation, actually the means by which a connection between father and son is established and by which Olivier acquires a masculine identity appropriate to his social milieu.

It is worth insisting, too, that although Olivier presents his experience as unusual or deviant, the terms in which his early experience is described are deeply imbricated with preexisting social patterns. The fact that upper-class English boys are educated in gender-segregated facilities that duplicate within the all-male environment the hierarchical binary divisions (dominant/passive, male/female) of adult, mixed-gender society; the idea that boys should prefer sports, that being the favorite of their mothers may be effeminizing, that corporal punishment has a role to play in making a boy a man, and that, in playing that role, it can (must?) shade into sadism and/or sexual assault—all of these are part of the sex-gender system in place in early twentieth-century English society. Olivier's painful traversing of difficulty and paradox on the way to heterosexual adulthood is transacted in terms set down by society and inscribed in specific institutions and their practices and values. Indeed, the fear of the feminine and of effeminization, which Olivier feared as so potent a threat to his masculinity, functions—in his story as in the wider culture—to promote and enforce the norm of exclusive adult heterosexuality, either in the uncomplicated form represented by his brother, Dickie, and the boys he envied at school or in the more complex variant appropriate to the "English actor."

Choir schools like All Saints' were not acting schools—such did not exist at the primary or secondary school level; and, indeed, the two major professional academies, Central School and RADA had only recently been founded (1906 and 1904, respectively).[32] But choir schools could have an important place in the career of actors, for their schoolboy productions were attended by eminent professionals, who could provide encouragement and evaluation. Olivier's portrayal at age nine of Brutus had been praised by Sir Johnston Forbes-Robertson,[33] and Ellen Terry is said to have written in her diary that "the small boy who played Brutus is already a great actor."[34] In light of such encouragement, Gerard Olivier's support for his son's career appears less idiosyncratic than Olivier presents it. Father Heald's productions may be thought of as part of a loose educational system linking the choir schools of London, the new dramatic academies, and the English stage. In this system, as in the very different institution of theatrical apprenticeship in place in London in the late sixteenth century, the playing of female roles by boy actors had a central place.

In light of their overdetermined relation to Olivier's biography, the final sequences of *Henry V* may suggest both the supersession of the transvestite theater by the conventions of film and may also point to powerful institutional continuities that link Shakespeare to the construction of masculinity in early twentieth-century England. The final tableau, a marriage of male lead and boy actor, evokes the specific terms of Laurence Olivier's assumption of an adult male identity. In a cinematic rescension of the ancient male ritual of "playing the other," the final moments of the film offer an image of the triumphant, nurturant union of father and son.

Notes

1 See, among others, Roy Battenhouse, "The Relation of *Henry V* to *Tamburlaine*," *Shakespeare Survey* 27 (1974): 71–79; G. R. Smith, "Shakespeare's *Henry V*: Another Part of the Critical Forest," *Journal of the History of Ideas* 37 (1976): 3–26; Karl P. Wentersdorf, "The Conspiracy of Silence in *Henry V*," *Shakespeare Quarterly* 27 (1976): 264–87; Norman Rabkin, "Rabbits, Ducks, and *Henry V*," *Shakespeare Quarterly* 28 (1977): 279–99; Stephen Greenblatt, "Invisible Bullets: Renaissance Authority and Its Subversion, *Henry IV* and *Henry V*," *Glyph* 8 (1981): 40–60, reprinted in *Political Shakespeare: New Essays in Cultural Materialism*, ed. Jonathan Dollimore and Allen Sinfield (Ithaca, NY Cornell University Press, 1985) and reprinted and revised in Greenblatt, *Shakespearean Negotiations* (Berkeley:

University of California Press, 1988); Jonathan Dollimore and Allen Sinfield, "History and Ideology: The Instance of *Henry V*," in *Alternative Shakespeares*, ed. John Drakakis (London: Methuen, 1985), 206–27.

2 Laurence Olivier, *On Acting* (New York: Simon & Schuster, 1986), 269.

3 Ibid.

4 Ibid., 275.

5 Shakespeare is cited from *The Riverside Shakespeare*, ed. G. Blakemore Evans (Boston: Houghton Mifflin, 1974). When citing dialogue from Shakespeare films, I use my own transcription rather than published screenplays.

6 On the genital symbolism of this passage see David Willbern, "Shakespeare's Nothing," in *Representing Shakespeare*, ed. Coppélia Kahn and Murray M. Schwartz (Baltimore: Johns Hopkins University Press, 1980), 255–57.

7 See Dudley Andrew, *Film in the Aura of Art* (Princeton: Princeton Univeristy Press, 1984), chap. 8, "Realism, Rhetoric and the Painting of History in *Henry V*," for a sensitive and careful map of the representational levels of the film, which, according to Andrew, form a perfect chiastic pattern.

8 See Robert Weimann, *Shakespeare and the Popular Tradition in the Theater* (Baltimore: Johns Hopkins University Press, 1978), passim; idem, "Bifold Authority in Shakespeare's Theatre," *Shakespeare Quarterly* 39 (Winter 1988): 401–17.

9 This sequence in the film, even more than its counterpart in Shakespeare's play, has the potential for calling into question the very principle of female inheritance upon which the historical action is based and on the strength of which Elizabeth I occupied the throne. The lengthy exposition of the text of Pharamond's chronicle and the Salic Law by the Archbishop of Canterbury is answered, in Shakespeare's text, by the king's simple question: 'May I with right and conscience make this claim?" (1.2.96). In the film the sifting of textual authorities by the archbishop is literalized in the prop work in an undignified and comic shuffling of antique and bulky bound volumes and loose archival documents. This is platea work: a near burlesque of the dynastic questions involved by the indignity of their representation. The papers spill on the floor, the book comes apart, the actor playing the archbishop stumbles over lines and draws laughs from the audience, while the king patiently tries to interrupt, or condescends to kneel and select a document from those that have fallen for the clergyman's perusal. In this context even the Bible (here a large folio fetched to produce a text in favor of female inheritance from the Book of Numbers) is a prop for farce. In this sequence the archbishop's pedantry, his dependence on the letter of the Salic Law, intersects with the actor's dependence on his script—neither the prelate nor the

actor who plays him can speak without text; the recovery of voice and the location of a scrap of written text occur together (the devalued text is Shakespeare's as well as "Pharamond's") and together suggest that performance so slavishly under the sway of the dead letter is contemptible.

In contrast, the king needs no script, no prompting: his question, "May I with right and conscience make this claim," is here an assertion not merely of plain speech over legal obscurity but of the voice over the written word, of Olivier's resonant performance over the unenacted, idolatrously literalized printed text it speaks. The devaluation, even fragmentation of the book thus empowers and liberates performance: for the skilled actor as for the effective monarch, if there is a script that precedes performance, its traces are effaced in favor of an apparently spontaneous, even improvisatory performance. King Henry does not act because the chronicles and statute books authorize him to do so; rather, his performance, his voice *replaces* the tattered documents as a source of authority. According to the archbishop, Henry's title to the French crown, falsely impeded by the misapplication of the Salic Law, is a "claiming from the female." To assert that claim, as Olivier stages the sequence, means effacing it, substituting a virile logocentrism for the written law. An army of invasion commanded by the powerful royal voice must settle a claim shakily based in an oversubtle interpretation of the texts that support inheritance through the female.

10   The Hostess' inadvertent pun in recounting how Falstaff "handled" women is also played down.

11   Harry M. Geduld, *Filmguide to Henry V* (Bloomington: Indiana University Press, 1973), 9.

12   Catherine Belsey, "Disrupting Sexual Difference: Meaning and Gender in the Comedies," in *Alternative Shakespeares*, 166–190. Lisa Jardine has argued that such scenes were primarily homoerotic in effect: see *Still Harping on Daughters: Women and Drama in the Age of Shakespeare* (Brighton, England: Harvester, 1983), chap. 1, "'As boys and women are for the most part cattle of this colour': Female Roles and Elizabethan Eroticism," 9–36. See also Laura Levine, "Men in Women's Clothing: Antitheatricality and Effeminization from 1579 to 1642," *Criticism* 28 (Spring 1986): 121–43; Stephen Orgel, "Nobody's Perfect: Or Why Did the English Stage Take Boys for Women?" *South Atlantic Quarterly* 88 (Winter 1989): 7–29.

13   These faces are so obviously different when examined frame by frame that the reader may find it hard to credit my claim that they cause confusion, or that photos 1.4, 1.5, and 1.6 could ever have been intended to be understood as images of the same performer. Yet not only Geduld's but all other accounts of the film—including the recent, highly detailed analyses by Dale

Silviria, *Laurence Olivier and the Art of Film Making* (Cranbury, NJ: Fairleigh Dickinson University Press, 1985) 138; Dudley Andrew, *Film in the Aura of Art* (Princeton: Princeton University Press, 1984), chap. 8, "Realism, Rhetoric and the Painting of History in *Henry V*"; and Anthony Davies, *Filming Shakespeare's Plays* (Cambridge: Cambridge University Press, 1988)—miss the hidden cut and the *second* change of performers. My work relies on tape and disk replay and on the study of frame enlargements. The results shed light on a director's conscious and unconscious designs (I hope) but do not reproduce and, in fact, distort the normal experience of viewing, as do all aggressive interpretive interventions. I am asking the reader to see the change of performers and also to believe that it is almost invisible at normal projection speed.

14 This is perhaps the place to note that despite its unruly, carnivalesque character, to which Olivier pays tribute, by the twentieth century the Elizabethan stage *itself* had become part of a quasi-sacred national mythology. The strategies by which Olivier lends an aura of sanctity to the playhouse parallel the idealization of the Elizabethan era and the canonization of Shakespeare as its leading spirit. See Graham Holderness, ed., *The Shakespeare Myth* (Manchester: Manchester University Press, 1988).

15 My sense of the defensive, reactive aspects of male identity in Shakespeare has been influenced by Coppélia Kahn, *Man's Estate: Masculine Identity in Shakespeare* (Berkeley: University of California Press, 1981), and by the work of Edward A. Snow and Janet Adelman. For the reproduction of male difference in the context of the contemporary family see Nancy Chodorow, *The Reproduction of Mothering: Psychoanalysis and the Sociology of Gender* (Berkeley: University of California Press, 1979), and Jessica Benjamin, *The Bonds of Love: Psychoanalysis, Feminism and the Problem of Domination* (New York: Pantheon, 1988).

16 Geduld, *Filmguide*, 54.

17 Olivier, *On Acting*, 277.

18 It is commonplace in discussions of Olivier's acting to credit him with a "feminine" capability. The case is argued in greatest specificity by Michael Billington in *The Modern Actor* (London: Hamish Hamilton, 1973), 209–10. His analysis concludes:

> Olivier is a great actor because he shows us so much of himself in his performances, partly because he is unafraid to reveal those elements in his personality that most of us are trained to keep hidden. Men are taught from their childhood to be ashamed of their femininity: Olivier exploits his brilliantly, and therefore enables all of us to come to terms with a part of ourselves (p. 210).

"All of us" is male here, and Billington's "femininity" means "what is defined as feminine in Anglo-American culture." But the quality he sees has been frequently noted, most recently by Gielgud, who spoke of Olivier's "marvelous femininity" in a television interview aired January 1989 on PBS Boston.

19   See Thomas Kiernan, *Sir Larry: The Life of Laurence Olivier* (New York: Times Books, 1981), 3–11 and refs.

20   Ibid., 14, citing *The Sunday Times* (London), November 16, 1953.

21   Laurence Olivier, *Confessions of an Actor* (London: Weidenfeld and Nicolson, 1982; New York: Penguin Books, 1984), 17–35.

22   Ibid., 31–32.

23   Ibid., 32.

24   Ibid., 86.

25   Ibid.

26   Ibid., 24.

27   Logan Gourlay, ed., *Olivier* (London: Weidenfeld and Nicolson, 1973), 24.

28   Kiernan, *Sir Larry*, 22, citing *Saturday Review of Literature*, September 13, 1946.

29   Olivier, *Confessions*, 15.

30   The material from *Confessions*, like the interplay of paternal nurturance and female impersonation in *Henry V*, can be described in terms of the passive Oedipal dynamics set forth by Freud. See *The Standard Edition of the Complete Psychological Works of Sigmund Freud*, ed. and trans. James Strachey (London: Hogarth, 1953), 24 vols., 17: 6, 27–28, 35–36, 45–46, 19: 31–33; and Peter Donaldson, "Olivier, Hamlet, and Freud," *Cinema Journal* 26 (1987): 22–48. I am now inclined to see the motif of union with the father in Olivier's work, *even when it is sexualized* as related to the need for paternal identification in separation and the stabilization of male identity. See Margaret S. Mahler, Fred Pine, and Anni Bergman, *The Psychological Birth of the Human Infant* (New York: Basic Books, 1975), 91; Ernest Abelin, "The Role of the Father in the Separation-Individuation Process," in *Separation-Individuation: Essays in Honor of Margaret S. Mahler*, ed. J. B. McDevitt and C. F. Settlage (New York: International Universities Press, 1971), 229–53; and "Triangulation, the Role of the Father, and the Origins of Core Gender Identity during the Rapprochement Subphase," in *Rapprochement: The Critical Subphase of Separation-Individuation*, eds. R. F. Lax, S. Bach, and J. A. Burland (New York: Jason Aronson, 1980); Ralph Greenson, "Dis-identifying from Mother: Its Special Importance for the Boy," *International Journal of Psycho-analysis* 49 (1969): 370–74; Benjamin, *Bonds of Love*, 100–107. Peter Blos, in an important revision of his earlier accounts of "Oedipal replay" during male adolescence, has written extensively on the continued male need for the "dyadic father" during adolescence. See *Son and Father* (New York: Free Press, 1985). The term may occasion some confusion, as the

"dyadic" father's role is to foster separation, but it speaks to the way images of merger with the father simultaneously signal new achievements and a renewed sense of individuality in the son in Olivier's films and writings (Compare "I felt Shakespeare within me. I felt the cinema within him," cited above, n. 4). For Benjamin and Blos the homoerotic component of "identificatory love" (Benjamin, *Bonds of Love*, 106) expresses the intensity of the need for the father's support in separation and in the consolidation of male identity.

31 "Playing the Other: Theater, Theatricality and the Feminine in Greek Drama," *Representations* 11 (Summer 1985): 63–94. For a related, more wide-ranging argument about the appropriation of the female in classical Athens, see David M. Halperin's brilliant essay, "Why Is Diotima a Woman," in *One Hundred Years of Homosexuality and Other Essays on Greek Love* (London: Routledge, 1989).

32 See Michael Sanderson, *From Irving to Olivier: A Social History of the Acting Profession in England 1880–1983* (London: Athlone Press, 1984), on the status of actors and the institutional and social affiliations of the London stage at this period. In 1895 Henry Irving became the first English actor to be knighted, and an increasing number of actors at the top of the profession had attended public schools. Sanderson cites the *Henry V* film as an instance of the influence of the elite Actor's Club, another of the institutions linking the stage and the upper or upper middle class—eight members of the club appear in the film: Aylmer, Banks, Hannen, Genn, Robey, Shepley, Laurie, and Olivier (p. 138).

33 Olivier, *Confessions*, 24.

34 John Cottrell, *Laurence Olivier* (Englewood Cliffs, NJ: Prentice-Hall, 1975), 19.

2

Olivier, Hamlet, and Freud

Laurence Olivier's film of *Hamlet* (1947) announces itself as a psychoanalytic, Oedipal text. The phallic symbolism of rapier and dagger, the repeated dolly-in down the long corridor to the queen's immense, enigmatic, and vaginally hooded bed, the erotic treatment of the scenes between Olivier and Eileen Herlie as Gertrude all bespeak a robust and readily identifiable, if naive, Freudianism.[1]

Although Freud himself had written only briefly on *Hamlet*,[2] the play was central to his formulation of the Oedipus complex. Ernest Jones, a prominent British psychoanalyst, had expanded Freud's suggestions into a full-scale interpretation of the play in an article first published in 1910 which was to undergo numerous revisions and republication, finally appearing in 1949 as *Hamlet and Oedipus*.[3] It was through Jones that Olivier first learned of the Freudian approach to *Hamlet*. As part of their planning for the Old Vic production of 1937 director Tyrone Guthrie and Olivier, who played the lead, made a weekend visit to Jones.

> He had made an exhaustive study of Hamlet from his own professional point of view and was wonderfully enlightening. I have never ceased to think about Hamlet at odd moments, and ever since that meeting I have believed that Hamlet was a prime sufferer from the Oedipus complex— quite unconsciously, of course, as the professor was anxious to stress. He offered an impressive array of symptoms: spectacular mood-swings, cruel treatment of his love, and above all a hopeless inability to pursue the

course required of him. The Oedipus complex, therefore, can claim responsibility for a formidable share of all that is wrong with him. There is great pathos in his determined efforts to bring himself to the required boiling point, and in the excuses he finds to shed this responsibility.[4]

Olivier never mentions Freud here or elsewhere in his autobiography, though of course Jones's "own professional point of view" was that of Freudian psychoanalysis. Olivier's compassion for Hamlet as one suffering from an emotional disorder is succeeded by a more negative attitude when he remembers that Hamlet was an actor like himself:

Apart from Hamlet's involuntary pusillanimity, there is another factor in the character-drawing—his weakness for dramatics. This would be reasonable if the dramatics spurred him to action, but unfortunately they help to delay it. It is as if his shows of temperament not only exhaust him but give him relief from his absorption in his purpose, like an actor who, having spent all in rehearsal, feels it almost redundant to go through with the performance.[5]

The passage raises the question of whether acting for Olivier can ever be a form of "action," or preparation for action, or whether it must always be a sign of weakness. Does the career of a successful actor celebrate mastery of Oedipal conflict or merely give evidence of Oedipal evasion and repetition?

Olivier's account of the 1937 Old Vic *Hamlet* and the reviews suggest several ways in which Guthrie and Olivier tried to implement a Freudian approach to the play. According to Freud, Oedipal conflict is universal. Hamlet's particular problem lies in the fact that his uncle has acted precisely those desires that for Hamlet must remain repressed. Hamlet delays in his mission of revenge because Claudius's deeds confront Hamlet with his own unconscious wishes and fill him with self-hatred: "the loathing that should drive him on to revenge is replaced in him by self-reproaches, by scruples of conscience that remind him that he himself is literally no better than the sinner whom he is to punish."[6] An important consequence of this theory for the acting of the role is that it provides a rationale for playing Hamlet as a decisive, vigorous personal-

ity, *disturbed* by the intrusion of these special and psychologically distressing circumstances: "Hamlet is able to do
anything—except take vengeance on the man who did away
with his father and took that father's place with his mother,
the man who shows him the repressed wishes of his childhood realized."[7]

Although none of the critics of the Old Vic production
detected a psychoanalytic subtext, they did respond to Olivier's
decisive departure from the delicate-souled dreamers and
thinkers of nineteenth-century tradition. This was a daring
and agile Hamlet who could, as Freud said he could, "do
anything"—except kill the king.[8] The *Times* critic noticed a
"special tenderness of sympathy" in Hamlet's scenes with
Gertrude, without suspecting pathological excess. Developing
Freud's notion that Hamlet cannot kill Claudius because to do
so would be to punish himself, Ernest Jones had claimed that
Hamlet's turn to action at the end of the play was in fact suicidal:

> In reality his uncle incorporates the deepest and most buried
> part of his own personality, so that he cannot kill him
> without also killing himself. This solution, one closely akin to
> what Freud has shown to be the motive for suicide in
> melancholia, is actually the one that Hamlet finally adopts.
> The course of alternate action and inaction that he embarks
> on, and the provocations he gives to his suspicious uncle,
> can lead to no other end than to his own ruin and,
> incidentally, to that of his uncle. Only when he has made
> the final sacrifice and has brought himself to the door of
> death is he free to fulfil his duty, to avenge his father, and
> to slay his other self—his uncle.[9]

Olivier's acting was already notable for an athletic daring
near to folly,[10] and the hint of reckless physical risk in the
reviews may indicate that he used this aspect of his style to
convey Jones's sense of Hamlet's self-destructiveness.

In regard to the film we can be more certain: the actor believed
that he had actually risked his own life in the fourteen-foot leap
onto the stuntman standing in for King Claudius:

> The dangers involved for what I had conceived for this
> moment presented themselves to me in the light of the

following five possibilities: I could kill myself; I could damage myself for life; I could hurt myself badly enough to make recovery a lengthy business; I could hurt myself only slightly; or I could get away with it without harm. The odds seemed to me to be quite evenly disposed among these five alternatives.[11]

Thus at least in his version of these events, Olivier came close to enacting the "final sacrifice" Jones had spoken of as the enabling condition of Hamlet's heroism in the last scene. Such a leap could not have been a regular part of the 1937 production.[12] Even the stuntmen for the film were willing to demonstrate the move only once before Olivier's attempt, and the stand-in for Claudius was knocked out.[13] In other ways as well, what was merely a Freudian intention in the stage production is salient in the film: the royal bed, always looking just slept in, is a repeated motif (photo 2.1); weapons evoke phallic assertion and competition and also (when dropped or taken away) the castration anxiety, which, in Freud's view, gave rise to Oedipal dynamics; Hamlet and Gertrude kiss like lovers (photo 2), wrestle on the bed as anger shades into sexual assault.

But the film's psychological explorations are also informed by autobiographical pressures and do not wholly conform to the orthodox Freudian interpretation Olivier learned from Jones. In the reading of the film I propose here, the Freud/Jones interpretation of *Hamlet* is a central, structuring presence the contours of which may be clearly discerned. At the same time, the Oedipus complex, so evident and even intentional in Olivier's

Photo 2.1

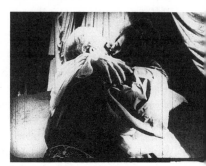

Photo 2.2

Hamlet, serves partly as a mask or screen for other, perhaps even deeper issues. First, Oedipal conflict, especially as it is manifested in Hamlet's interactions with the ghost of his father, often has a passive or submissive character in the film. Although Freud had elaborated a theory of the negative Oedipus complex, in which conflict is resolved through a "feminine" or passive attitude toward the father,[14] neither Freud nor Jones applied this theory to *Hamlet*. In addition, Olivier's film portrays, beneath the drama of Oedipal guilt and self-punishment, the narcissistic injury of Oedipal *success*.[15] This Hamlet's relationship with his mother is too stimulating, and his interactions with his father are too tenuous and violent for him to have internalized a realistic and stable sense of self-worth, so that he oscillates between grandiose aloofness and empty depression, plagued by persistent doubts about the worth and coherence of the self.

In the previous chapter I discussed in some detail the complex way in which, in negotiating the stresses of his family situation, the young Olivier suffered from doubts and questions about his sexual orientation and "effeminacy,"[16] and how acting seemed to offer a way of maintaining an identification with his nurturant mother while establishing connection to mentors and earning the respect of his peers at school and of his father. In his teenage portrayal of Katherine in *Shrew*, for example, family friends noted the astonishing resemblance between the young actor and his recently deceased mother, while Olivier's own account stressed Father Heald's impregnating and feminizing influence. Acting is consistently associated in these stories with a passive, or "feminizing,"[17] resolution of Oedipal tension, as well as with a narcissistic merging with the mother. I have also suggested that the violent, sexualized attention Olivier received in school and the more benign stories of mentorship and nurturance are linked, in Olivier's text, by language that presents nurturance received from men as a kind of penetration of the self. One story—Olivier's account of being raped, or nearly raped, on a staircase at All Saints School at age nine—needs to be given in full here because in the particular way it associates paternal gifts and sexual abuse, it echoes powerfully in the visual design of *Hamlet*.

Describing his adolescent experience at St. Edward's school, where he "very soon caught the attention, rapidly followed by the attentions, of a few of the older boys," Olivier explains that unwelcome sexual advances had plagued him since his first day at his previous school:

> I did not in any way welcome such attentions; I knew well enough what they spelt. My first experience of that had been a somewhat frightening one. Calling at the All Saints church house one day before I joined the choir, I was stopped by a large boy, an old choirboy, who offered to show me the stage upstairs where the choir school plays were performed. I was dressed in my kilt, Kerr tartan (my second name, as was my father's, is Kerr; no one has ever found the Scottish connection), with the velvet jacket and silver buttons, a customary Sunday outfit inherited from my brother. This boy flung me down on an upper landing, threw himself on top of me and made me repeat again and again, "No, no, let me go, I don't want it." This I did willingly enough, but it only increased his ardor. His "exercises" were getting more powerful when to my relief he thought he heard someone coming up the stone stairs. He pushed me down these steps and himself disappeared farther up towards the top of the building. I rushed down, tearful and trembling, in search of my mother, into whose arms I gratefully flung myself. On the way home she asked me the lad's name, which she recognized; a year or two back he had come to a birthday party for me to which Mummy had invited all fourteen boys. She made me promise to tell her if anything of the kind should ever happen again.[18]

The kilt here is a dangerous inheritance: supposedly conferring a masculine tribal identity and offering connection to brother, father, and distant Scottish kinfolk, it looks much like a skirt, feminizing its wearer and exposing him to rape. Interest in acting, Olivier's childhood sphere of grandiosity, sponsored to this point principally by his mother, also exposed him to deflation and assault.

Olivier began work on the film of *Hamlet* a year after his remarkable, even glorious success in that other great Freudian part, Sophocles' Oedipus. His love affair with Vivien Leigh had been regularized by marriage in 1940. His father had died in

1939. He was a successful film actor, and his *Henry V* had gained the first ungrudging critical success accorded any Shakespeare film. He was at a plateau of success and respect. Yet the *Hamlet* film was in some ways the boldest of his enterprises, for in addition to playing the lead and directing the film, he drastically cut Shakespeare's text and imposed on it a powerful interpretation, partly Jonesian and partly his own. His daring was not without its doubts, hesitations, and denials of the significance of the enterprise. Apologizing for the extent to which the text had been reworked, Olivier preferred to call the film "an essay in *Hamlet*."[19] He describes his playing the lead in terms that are simultaneously self-effacing and grandiose: he would have preferred another actor "of sufficient standing to carry the role, or one upon whom I could have imposed my interpretation without resenting it"; his own gifts were for "the stronger character roles." In the end he found it "simpler" to play Hamlet himself.

> But one reason why I dyed my hair was so as to avoid the possibility of Hamlet later being identified with me. I wanted audiences seeing the film to say, not, "There is Laurence Olivier dressed as," but "that is Hamlet."[20]

The wish to distance himself from the role may have been partly a result of the Freudian interpretation he intended to give it. Another instance of such distancing may be the choice of Eileen Herlie (who was twenty-seven) as Gertrude. Although her youth helps to bring out the sexuality of the part *for the audience*, it might also work to undo or reverse the generational direction of the incestuous subtext for the forty-year-old actor who played her son (like Olivier's flight from Thebes to Corinth the year before). In addition, Olivier was concerned about too close an indentification with Hamlet's irresolution, passivity, and failure:

> Perhaps he was the first pacifist, perhaps Dr. Jones is sound in his diagnosis of the Oedipus complex, perhaps there is justification in the many complexes that have been foisted on to him—perhaps he just thought too much, that is, if a man can think too much.... I prefer to think of him as a nearly

great man—damned by lack of resolution, as all but one in a hundred are.[21]

Such a description, while conveying the author's wish to be resolute where Hamlet had wavered, inscribes irresolution in its own interpretation, backing away from the Freudian theory while proposing alternatives that on examination are merely restatements of the question. The film itself pursues a similarly self-canceling strategy, offering an undeniably Freudian reading while proclaiming that "this is the tragedy of a man who could not make up his mind"—as if such a pronouncement were itself an interpretation rather than that which for centuries has seemed to require interpretation. Oedipal interpretation, like the Oedipal fantasies it explains, tends to generate itself as one of its own consequences, proposing polysemy and ambiguity as meaning; disguising decisions as evasions; blurring distinctions between fathers and sons, texts and their interpretations.

It is interesting that although Olivier could be somewhat evasive in what he said about interpretation and character in the film, he was much more direct about the genesis of its visual structure: "Quite suddenly, one day, I visualized the final shot of 'Hamlet.' And from this glimpse, I saw how the whole conception of the film could be built up."[22] This shot is a long shot of Hamlet's funeral procession ascending a steep staircase to the top of a bare tower (photo 2.3). The film begins with a closely related shot, a high-angle view of this tower, the bearers having reached the top (photo 2.4). The human figures then dissolve out of the image as the action of the film begins in flashback. The narrative is thus framed by this ascent, by the elevation of Hamlet in death to the highest place in the castle, a place from which there is nowhere to go, even to complete the funeral. The procession vanishes from the screen at the end as it had in the opening sequence. One of the ways this complex symbol functions in the film, therefore, is to intimate the futility of Hamlet's "success" in his grandiose mission: he accomplishes the revenge his father's ghost had charged him with, reestablishes an intense connection to his mother, and even momentarily takes possession of the throne. With this solemn funeral Hamlet's completion of his task is acknowledged in a

Photo 2.3   Photo 2.4

way that reminds us that it is achieved at the cost of annihilation.

The final shot of the film does more than give this frame to the story. As Olivier said, it is the generating image for the film as a whole, the last of a long series of staircase shots and sequences that occur throughout. These are consistently associated with Hamlet's meeting with his father and his attempts to fulfill his father's commandment to revenge. Staircases are often the setting for violence, the locus of a repeated pattern in which someone is thrown down on the steps and the attacker flees upward, leaving the victim in an ambivalent state in which elements of reproach and pain are mingled with feelings of loss. Thematically this motif points to the well-studied problematics of revenge in *Hamlet*, whereby the revenger takes on the moral taint of his victim in a compulsive and cyclical pattern. Psychologically it is used to explore Hamlet's passivity, his oscillation between grandiosity and depression, and the blurring of his own identity in a partial fusion with the ghost. As I discuss its use, it will be seen that various aspects of the staircase motif as it is used in the film evoke, with surprising literalness, the traumatic incident the director suffered at All Saints in 1916 and first made public in 1982.

The towers and external staircases of Elsinore are introduced at the start of the film. The castle first appears directly after the credits, which are shown on a background of crashing surf. It has two towers, one in the middle of the castle and one, at the near corner, overlooking the sea. As in the opening shots of *Henry V*, there is some confusion

39

between these two architectural features.[23] The camera moves in on the corner tower from a high angle and stops. There is a fade to mist as Olivier in voice-over recites, "So oft it chances in particular men ..." while the text of this speech is displayed on the screen. After Olivier's somewhat reductive addition, pointing the moral ("This is the tragedy of a man who could not make up his mind"), the central tower reappears, filling most of the image, and the camera moves in, as if continuing the movement begun before the speech, on four soldiers carrying Hamlet's body, his sword laid on his chest and face invisible as his unsupported head droops back, the body appearing almost headless from the spectator's point of view. The procession then dissolves from the image while the tower remains, and in a rapid series of cuts we are shown parts of the exterior of the castle, emphasizing the steep external staircases that give access to the ramparts and the towers (photo 2.5).

It is on these staircases that the sentries challenge one another as the guard changes and on which Hamlet is soon to ascend for his colloquy with the ghost. The ghost appears on the ramparts as Bernardo narrates to Horatio the story of its prior visit, and his first appearance establishes him as a numinous and intimately invasive presence. The camera

Photo 2.5

moves in from a high angle to the terrified face of Marcellus (Anthony Quayle) in a disturbing stop-start rhythm, losing focus and regaining it as we hear an exaggeratedly loud pounding heartbeat in accompaniment. Because we cannot assign with certainty the beating of the heart and the loss of focus either to the ghost or to Marcellus, this treatment effects a blurring of the boundaries between the apparition and the human self to whom it appears. When the camera securely assumes Marcellus's point of view again, we see the ghost as a helmeted figure, his hollow-eyed face half shrouded in mist. It will not speak to the guards and disappears with a cut to the roaring surf.

The ghost is ponderously slow, dignified, sorrowful, and stately, but his effect on others is violent. The heartbeat, the blur of focus, and the insistent, pulsing downward move-ment of the camera are repeated when the ghost makes his second appearance, this time to Hamlet, whose response is to fling himself violently backward into his companions' arms. A low-angle shot follows from behind the human group, looking up several low steps to the ghost. As Hamlet ques-tions it, the ghost begins to ascend, and Hamlet, reaching out his hand to it, begins to follow in a long, slow climb lasting nearly two minutes of screen time, punctuated by dissolves as we pass from one landing to the next. At the top of the central tower Hamlet, his sword hilt held before him, stops and declares he'll "go no further," but this limit-setting gesture is ironic here because there is nowhere further to go.

Hamlet kneels as the ghost speaks, and the revelation of the murder, partly spoken by the ghost and partly rendered visually in a flashback to the murder scene, is shot from behind him looking toward his father. As the queen's infidelity is revealed the ghost fades out and, in the ambient mist, the royal couch fades in briefly, so that Hamlet's gesture (hand outstretched to the apparition) becomes am-biguous, as his longing for his father becomes confused with the question of his relation to the incestuous bed his father's discourse evokes (photos 2.6, 2.7). Such a treatment derives from Jones, but the connection between the poignant absence of the father and the Oedipal impulse is Olivier's own.[24]

His charge to his son complete, the ghost fades in the

Photo 2.6

Photo 2.7

morning air as Hamlet reaches forward to touch him. The camera pulls high above him as he stands and falls full length backward, overcome with what he has seen and heard. As he revives, his rage against his uncle and vows to revenge his father are delivered in a manic tone: the depressed and affectless mourner of the opening sequences becomes the precipitate revenger his father wants him to be—yet even in his assertions of murderous anger there are elements of passivity. Shakespeare's text suggests at this point that becoming a revenger entails a kind of self-obliteration for Hamlet: he offers to wipe clean the tables of his memory, leaving a blank page for the word of the father to be written upon. Olivier develops this, making his commitment to revenge with his eyes blazing and sword brandished, while still on his knees. At the climax of the vow "Yes, *by Heaven*," he throws his rapier down upon the stones, a gesture that registers his anger but also, like similar actions later in the film, leaves him without a weapon at the very moment when the idea of using one is strongest.

In a way what the reappearance of the father visits on Hamlet in both film and text is a kind of abuse. Hamlet's potential for independent life is compromised and he becomes a mere agent of paternal aims, important himself only insofar as he is able to "do what is required of him." Even though Hamlet loves his father and accepts his "commandment" to the point of self-obliteration, he is flung back, hurled down, and invaded while the ghost, inaccessible to Hamlet's longing reach for contact, ascends higher up the steps and finally disappears. The abusive character of the interaction becomes even clearer when one notices how closely the main features of the imagery in which Olivier renders the visit of the ghost resemble the incident of sexual assault the director had suffered as a nine-year-old on the staircase of All Saints. Not only the actual assault on the stairs but also the curious detail about the attacker fleeing further up are reprised in the film. Like the childhood memory, this sequence is presented as a kind of feminization: the ghost does to Hamlet what he has just done to a woman; the symbolic casting down of the sword replaces the kilt as the emblem of castration; the suggestion that Hamlet has been invaded by the ghost replaces the near-rape; the father replaces the older boy as the abuser.

This pattern—assault on a staircase followed by flight upward—is repeated in the scene in which Ophelia is rejected by Hamlet. Ophelia has been set by the king and her father as "bait" to discover whether or not Hamlet's madness is a result of love. Polonius and Claudius observe from behind an arras while Ophelia returns Hamlet's love tokens. Following Dover Wilson's *What Happens in Hamlet*,[25] Olivier has Hamlet overhear the plan to spy on him and feels betrayed by Ophelia's complicity in it. But there is also an earlier sequence, purely visual and invented for the film, that establishes a background for the rejection. In the Council chamber Hamlet customarily sits in a chair at the foot of the table, a special chair marked by distinctive decoration, pulled back from the others in distance and distaste. It is the chair in which he sits in sullen rejection of the court and its endorsement of his mother's marriage, and in which he remembers and mourns for his father. But it is also strategically placed in relation to Ophelia's chamber: by looking over his shoulder he commands a view of a long corridor leading to her room. After Polonius warns Ophelia not to accept Hamlet's love, Olivier, using the resources of deep-focus photography to the full, staged what he was to call, somewhat inappropriately, the "longest distance love-scene on record."[26] Ophelia, in distress, looks down the corridor to see Hamlet seated in his chair some one hundred feet away. Hamlet cannot see Polonius and registers Ophelia's refusal to

Photo 2.8   Photo 2.9

come to him as a rejection (photos 2.8, 2.9). Thus even before he learns of the plot, he has begun to feel that Ophelia has turned away from him. This sequence links the failure of trust between the lovers to something already present in Hamlet's character. He is paralyzed not only by grief but by the opportunity the empty chamber affords for imaginary sovereignty. His inability to rise and approach Ophelia manifests the power of his Oedipal resentments and grandiose fantasies. Because he cannot leave the empty chamber, he mistakes Ophelia's reluctant giving in to paternal command for rejection.

This Hamlet comes to the scene in which Ophelia returns his tokens with realistic suspicions as well as fettered emotions. He is moody, wary, and in distress; yet he also tries to establish a basis for trust by speaking to Ophelia about his low opinion of himself:

> I am myself indifferent honest; but yet I could accuse me of such things that it were better my mother had not borne me: I am very proud, revengeful, ambitious, with more offenses at my beck than I have thoughts to put them in, imagination to give them shape, or time to act them in. What should such fellows as I do crawling between earth and heaven?

This is spoken in a quiet, reflective tone, partly to preserve the possibility of an intimate exchange despite the spying of the king and Polonius behind the arras, and partly because he recognizes that his own low self-esteem and guilt feelings constitute a barrier to intimacy. He glances frequently at the arras and back to Ophelia, as if to see whether she will lie to him or accept his offered confidence. She does lie, and the tone and pace of the scene shift:

> ... crawling between earth and heaven. We are arrant knaves all; believe none of us. Go thy ways to a nunnery. Where's your father? [still in a quiet tone] *Ophelia:* At home, my lord. *Hamlet:* [now loudly and in anger] Let the doors be shut upon him, that he may play the fool no where but in's own house.

Here he shoves her away violently and his discourse shifts from disesteem of himself to condemnation of women. When she attempts to embrace him, he throws her down on the steps to sob and then flees up them. The camera, in a series of backtrackings and vertical cranes approximating the point of view Hamlet would have if he were looking back down the stairs, pulls back and up from the prostrate figure of Ophelia, her hand still extended after Hamlet, as his own hand was after the fading apparition of his father (photo 2.10). As the camera cranes upward with Hamlet, Ophelia disappears

Photo 2.10

45

then briefly reappears in longer shot as the backward and upward ascent of the camera reaches another landing.

The circling ascent of the camera continues as if following Hamlet to the top of the castle until, suddenly, there is a cut to a shot of the cloudy sky above the castle which fills the screen, and then a rapid crane down so that Hamlet's form rises abruptly into the image. He is seated on the parapet of the tower that overlooks the sea, his back to us. The camera moves in to an extreme close-up of the whorl at the top of his head, and, as if entering his skull, the inward movement continues with a dissolve to the rocks and crashing surf he is contemplating.

This is Olivier's introduction to the "To be or not to be" soliloquy, which he has repositioned to follow the encounter with Ophelia, making it a reaction to the failure of that meeting to reestablish trust. In the text the scene comes earlier, just before Ophelia enters to him (3.1.90), and is a more diffusely motivated meditation. Olivier's delivery of the speech offers a sharp contrast to his fury at Ophelia's betrayal that immediately precedes it; in fact the moment at which the camera movement reverses its upward ascent marks a transition from rage to depression, from a grandiose and "noble" anger to deflation. Here he is at his most languid and limp, dangling his "bodkin" above his breast with a weak, three-fingered grasp while half reclining. At the end he proves too enervated or distracted to hold on to it and watches bemusedly as the tiny dagger falls into the sea far below. In this interpretation the meditation on suicide has no heroic quality but is played as an escapist revery, marking Hamlet's return to impotence and passivity.

In some sense Hamlet takes the place of the ghost in this sequence: it is he who casts down and ascends and is finally inaccessible, reached after in fear and longing. Yet at the top of the stairs, when the cut to the heavens likens him most closely to his father's ascending spirit, there is a sudden reversal to passivity and depression. The summit of the tower marks his mortal limits. Beyond is the air into which the ghost had vanished and the rocky surf is below. Retracing his father's path brings him to the prospect of self-annihilation.

The analogy between the ghost's treatment of Hamlet earlier and Hamlet's treatment of Ophelia here also suggests a reason, different from that of Freud and Jones, for Hamlet's condemnation of sex. For this Hamlet erotic response and abuse are closely linked. One is either abuser or abused, with little room for erotic shadings of activity and passivity that do not tend to extremes. One is either the mad figure who attacks and runs away or the figure left alone and hurt on the stairs. What the ghost does to Hamlet, which is in part a reenactment of a key incident of abuse the director suffered as a child, is the cause of what he does to Ophelia. He cannot break the cycle of abuse the ghost's visit initiated.

The staircase motif is again used in a thematically significant way after the "mousetrap" scene, when Hamlet makes a long ascent to his mother's chamber. Midway he comes upon the king in prayer and raises his sword for revenge ("now might I do it") but hesitates as the thought of sending his father's murderer to heaven detains him. Here the visual treatment of the scene again intimates a close relationship between the victims of violence and its perpetrators. As Claudius meditates on his guilty hand, he turns it over slowly, palm up, in extreme close-up, just as in the flashback to the murder, old Hamlet's hand slowly turned over and opened at the moment of his death. When his prayer fails, Claudius slumps from the altar, sliding to the floor in the posture in which King Hamlet had fallen from his bench in the orchard. Hamlet continues upward to his mother's bedroom in a slow, menacing ascent, his dark figure outlined against the jagged shadow of the overhanging steps, while his mother makes plans with Polonius to spy on him.

The bedchamber scene takes place after a climb, not during one, but is in other ways related to the scenes of abuse we have been examining. The scene is markedly violent and erotic, with the ghost's appearance dividing it into two sections, converting Hamlet's murderous threats into incestuous tenderness. In the opening exchange the play text calls for an unfilial degree of roughness: "Come, come and sit you down; you shall not budge/You go not till I set you up a glass/Where you may see the inmost part of you." Modern audiences may miss the insistent impropriety of the repeated

47

plural pronoun, but the verbal affront is otherwise clear and is intensified in the film as Olivier flings the queen backward on her bed and, in close-up, presses his dagger to her throat across her ample bosom (photo 2.11). As she cries for help and Polonius answers, Hamlet looks up with a maniacally rigid smile, runs to the arras, stabs through it, and delivers his next lines with the point stuck in the still standing body of his victim behind the curtain. He lets the body and his dagger fall, returns to his mother, and resumes his reproaches and attempts to force his mother to terms with her complicity in the murder of the king. As he compares Claudius with his father, he works up to a rage again and throws her down upon the bed, as simultaneously he hears the heartbeat that signals the approach of the ghost.

Eileen Herlie's performance during the threats and revelations of this scene is important to its meaning. Early in the film she had established Gertrude as a seductive mother willing to use a passionate, lover's kiss as part of her plea that Hamlet remain in Elsinore. This creates a triangle that Claudius registers by angrily pulling her away and dissolving the council. Here, as she struggles with the mix of emotions Hamlet's wild discourse evokes (fear, remorse, confusion), her expression returns repeatedly to erotic appeal. We see how she could have remained ignorant of the murder and the moral implications of her remarriage: her response to ethical difficulty is to seek the comfort of a sexual response, even from her son.

As Hamlet casts her down and looks up to find the ghost,

Photo 2.11

Photo 2.12

the camera repeats a movement from the ramparts scene, moving to a high-angle close-up of Hamlet as he half swoons and falls to the ground. He hears the admonition of the ghost from the floor, propped on one arm while reaching toward the vision with the other, a posture precisely that of Ophelia as she looks after the fleeing Hamlet, who has cast her down on the stairs (photo 2.12; compare photo 2.10). This shot, with its evocation of that parallel, is repeated four times, intercut with Gertrude's wonder and incomprehension as she sees her son gazing upon a presence she cannot perceive. It is the ghost who asks Hamlet to return to Gertrude:

> But look—amazement on thy mother sits:
> O step between her and her fighting soul;
> Speak to her, Hamlet.

At this point Hamlet's violence toward Gertrude, symbolically phallic all the while, becomes openly erotic as his appeal to her to abstain from intercourse with Claudius succeeds, and mother and son seal their union against the usurper with a fiercely passionate embrace and kiss accompanied by a romantic, circling movement of the camera in keeping with a cinematic convention reserved for lovers.

The influence of Jones is strongest here, for we see Gertrude trying to evoke an erotic response, which she ultimately gets, and we see how closely intertwined are the violence expected of Hamlet and the desire for his mother from which he cannot dissociate that violence. For him, to approach his revenge is also somehow to approach his mother's bed; being loyal to his father somehow entails flinging her down upon it. But also central to Olivier's conception of the scene are elements that derive not from Jones but from his own engagement with the issue of passivity and the compulsively cyclical character of abuse. As he had taken the place of the ghost in certain ways in the rejection of Ophelia, so here, at the point of a violent assault on his mother upon her own bed, he is himself cast down by the apparition of his father, on whom he gazes with a mixture of dread and longing evocative of Ophelia's response to his abuse earlier. In addition, the ghost's intervention does not put an end to the

Oedipal energy of the scene but, rather, is the signal for its conversion from violence to tenderness. In fact the ghost seems actually to sponsor the merger of mother and son enacted here. "But look—amazement on thy mother sits:/O step between her and her fighting soul" effectively annuls the earlier commandment to "leave her to heaven," and permits Hamlet to recover the quasi-romantic, spiritual union with his mother that had been breached by her remarriage. From this point she rejects Claudius's offers of intimacy and acts as Hamlet's ally, even to the point of knowingly joining him in death by drinking from the poisoned cup.

Hamlet's climb to his meeting with the ghost, his flight from Ophelia to the tower, his ascent to his mother's chamber, and the framing device of the funeral procession at the highest point of the castle are the principal uses of the elaborate, narrow, winding staircases Olivier and Roger Furse, the set designer, planned for the film. These stairways to the upper reaches of the castle are contrasted with the ceremonial double staircase that dominates the council chamber, winding down from each end of the balcony that overlooks the chamber to the floor below. This staircase figures prominently in the mousetrap scene, the fencing scene, and the final scene. In each case their use marks a stage in Hamlet's struggle with Claudius for mastery of the public space of the council chamber. At the beginning of the mousetrap scene the king comes down these stairs, holding Gertrude's hand and followed by his court, to William Walton's processional music. Hamlet, master of the revels, waits at the bottom and, with an air of triumph, takes his mother's hand and leads her to her seat. The staging is almost exactly repeated to the same music at the start of the fencing match, when Claudius leads Laertes, not Gertrude, down to the floor while Hamlet, the camera moving with him, descends an analogous staircase in the foreground. The overall effect is of a double spiral downward as Hamlet goes to meet his fate: "Here, Hamlet, take *this* hand from me." The hand now is not that of the mother but of Laertes, his opponent and executioner. The final conflict between Hamlet and Claudius also involves this staircase, which Hamlet climbs for his daring leap in the last moments of the film. The

ceremonial stairs are associated with Hamlet's public struggle with the king; the steeper and darker stairs are reserved
for his encounters with the ghost of his father.[27]

If the staircases of the set are important to Olivier's
complex approach to the Oedipal dynamics of *Hamlet*, so is
another central feature of the set design: the persistent use of
vacant chairs and empty rooms. This aspect of the film's
style, the frequent absence of human figures from the image,
is related to Olivier's interest in Hamlet's self-absorption and
in the special way in which, for him, Oedipal confusion
manifests itself in an irresolution of roles and meanings.
As early as our first introduction to its interior, Elsinore
is presented as a series of spaces empty of people and yet
pregnant with significances we cannot yet fully grasp. After
the first visit of the ghost, who is himself an absence and a
silence that portends significance but does not yet announce
it, Marcellus speculates that his appearance is linked to
"something rotten" in the state of Denmark. He glances
offscreen and the camera begins to move slowly, following
his glance, as if in response to the enigma he has proposed.
In a series of invisible cuts intended to be read as a single
long take, the camera explores Elsinore for the source of
corruption, descending the winding staircases of the castle
and pausing at several locations to dolly in for a closer look.
The royal bedchamber, a room later identified as Ophelia's,
and the empty council chamber are visited in turn. In this
last location the camera lingers on an ornate empty chair,
perhaps left vacant by the death of old King Hamlet. This
sequence, with its slowly moving and tentatively inquiring
camera, ends abruptly and definitively with a tight close-up
of the new king intemperately swilling wine from a large
goblet. He tosses the emptied cup to an obsequious attendant, and a close-up of the smoking cannon's mouth "re-
speaking earthly thunder" suggests that the rottenness in
Denmark centers in the king, his appetites, and his sancti-
monious court.

The sites visited on the way—each a possible, though
cryptic indication of the kind of corruption Marcellus had in
mind—are not definitive; they provoke us to interpret or
guess. At each site we hear a musical motif that will later

have meaning in the narrative. As yet we do not know that the smaller chamber is Ophelia's, the sunny musical passage her theme, or that the chair is Hamlet's. Most viewers guess that it is the empty chair of the murdered king; and though it is later identified as the chair Hamlet uses, it retains a fluidity of association and is often shown empty.

We know whose the bed is; and this symbol, in proximity to the phallic cannonade, is a kind of declaration of the film's Freudian intentions. The large chamber seems almost certainly the set for the scene to come. The chair, the bed, and the chamber are presented as if they pointed to some further significance: their literal vacancy suggests an as yet unspecified symbolic function. In the course of the film we come to understand them more fully, but they remain, at least partly, private symbols charged with meaning for Hamlet and not always for others. The queen's bed, with its "incestuous sheets," is on Hamlet's mind during the first soliloquy, even before the ghost has appeared, and it never becomes an object of special attention for anyone except Hamlet and the film audience. The symbols one learns to interpret are Hamlet's symbols, and therefore through much of the narrative the spectator shares with him not only a dramatic point of view but an orientation toward the significances of the world of Elsinore that is privileged and private.

After the close shot of the king, the vacancy discovered by the traveling camera gives way to busy plenitude. Now cutting and camera movement function more conventionally to support narrative, following the dynamics of the king's interaction with the court. In a series of shots of increasing distance, the council chamber is reintroduced as the sphere of Claudius's power. The brooding, solitary, and symbolic mode of Hamlet associated with the long take, the vertical movement of the camera, and the empty room is contrasted with the political, interpersonal mode of the king, whose central importance in the busy court is emphasized by horizontal camera movement and cross-cutting.

Most of the scene is shot from the foot of the long council table looking toward the raised thrones of the king and queen at its head. Hamlet's armchair, distinguished from the others by ball-and-point ornamentation, is at the right foot,

Photo 2.13

pushed some distance away from the council table and at right angles to the thrones and to the screen. This is the empty chair of the earlier sequence (photo 2.13), but it does not appear in the image until the council scene is well under way. In contrast to theatrical productions, in which Hamlet must be present from the start, the film stresses his absence: he is the reason for the king's anxious manipulations, but he is not present in the image until Claudius expresses his affection for Laertes: "Take thy fair hour, Laertes; time be thine,/And thy best graces spend it at thy will!" (photo 2.14).

"Time be thine" is the cue for the discovery of Hamlet, sitting in his distinctive chair in a passive and sullen mourning posture as, with a cut, the camera pulls back to a shot of the full room (photo 2.15). Claudius is on the throne with Polonius at his right hand and Laertes standing stage left in the foreground. Hamlet is excluded from the complex father-son-king affiliations implied by the mise-en-scène, yet he dominates the scene by his foregrounded position, clothes, posture, and striking blond hair. In some sense time will belong to Laertes, and never to Hamlet, in the film. The contrast between them as sons is one of the film's most successful exploitations of the implications of the Oedipal theme. Time (and timing) can only be mastered by a young man who finds his place in a temporal succession from father to son.

Space, on the other hand, seems to belong to Hamlet. If Old Hamlet haunts the ramparts, Young Hamlet is the ghost of Elsinore's interior. The freedom of the camera to explore at will is often associated with him. He stalks Elsinore's corridors overhearing, as Dover Wilson thought he should, the plan to use Ophelia to unravel the cause of his madness. And whereas the spying of others if always prepared for by elaborate and explicit conspirings, Hamlet seems to be there precisely when something is to be overheard. In fact even when he is not there we expect him, as when, during the plotting of the death of Hamlet by Claudius and Laertes, three times the camera cranes far above the speakers to privileged nooks above the chamber, where we have learned to expect the prince. But on this fatal occasion the camera's access to the secret is *not* matched by Hamlet's, and he enters

Photo 2.14

Photo 2.15

Photo 2.16

Photo 2.17

54

in the background after Claudius and Laertes depart, unaware of his fate. In the council scene he remains nearly
motionless and passive until the court departs and then
reveals in voice-over soliloquy how much the empty room is
his domain (photo 2.16) and how much its emptiness is the
condition for his access to his feelings and inner life. Vacant,
the thrones can evoke the imagined happy union of his
parents, as they do when he stands between and links them
with his hands, leaning on them for support against his
sorrow (photo 2.17); or they can stand for the present,
detested union of his mother and uncle; or they can intimate
his hopes for succession, and his fantasy of a closeness to his
mother impeded by Claudius's intrusion.

One function of the film's emphasis on emptiness, then, is
to suggest the narcissistic dimension of Hamlet's Oedipal
difficulties. He is often the sole inhabitant of a large, un-
peopled space, isolated and grandiose but unable to sustain
the conflicts that might lead to his finding a place in the
sequence of generations. The empty furniture so prominent
in the film also intimates that there is a way, though one
closed to Hamlet, by which Oedipal tensions can be and
normally are resolved. Because the roles in the Oedipal
situation are shifting, with sons becoming fathers in their
turn, the Oedipus complex is normally terminated by identification with the father and deferral of the wish for primacy
until it can be satisfied in adulthood by a substitute love
object of one's own generation. Such a resolution requires,
however, that empty chairs be occupied, vacant rooms pos-
sessed, ambiguous meanings clarified. The vacancy of space
in Elsinore, like the ambiguity of its symbols, is congenial to
Hamlet, but it prevents his succession to his father's rights.
A symbolism that invests its signs with a meaning that is
private, numinous, and unique may be the expression of a
sensibility that cannot relinquish claims of uniqueness and
transcendent value in the family.

A consideration of the player scene and its failure to
resolve Hamlet's dilemma may make this relation between
Olivier's stylistic choices and his Oedipal theme clearer, for
it too offers us a vacancy or emptiness that seems pregnant
with significance and yet proves impotent and self-enclosed.

The sequence begins after the "To be or not to be" soliloquy, Hamlet in his chair in a medium shot, his back to us, in a depressive, hand-in-chin posture. As Polonius announces to him the arrival of the players, he takes on his most joyous and elated mood, held until after his "mousetrap" plot is fully laid, when he pirouettes wildly in the empty chamber—the council chamber which will now become the theater for the "Murder of Gonzago," in the confidence that "the play's the thing." In his joyous, animated, and highly professional direction of the players, Hamlet's special chair shifts significance once again, becoming a metacinematic figure standing for the director's chair, which it resembles in its bare, cross-legged wooden outline. Hamlet coaches the players on dramatic theory and technique from this chair, leaving it to impart specific instructions and retiring back to it to address the whole company as its temporary leader. Hamlet has been an actor; now he is also a director, and in being one he doubles for Olivier himself, directing and starring in his own *Hamlet*.

Other metatheatrical possibilities of the set are developed during the player sequence. One end of the immense council room is taken over as a theatrical space even before the play is staged: as Hamlet completes his instructions, the props and costumes are moved behind the arras—now not the place behind which Hamlet is spied on but a tiring-house curtain or even, anachronistically, a theatrical curtain before which Hamlet stands in confident mastery, as if ready to deliver a prologue to the play that will unkennel his uncle's guilt. This composition is the climax of the sequence between Hamlet and the players, and significantly this moment of mastery is presented with Hamlet alone in the empty chamber. During the preceding sequence, as Hamlet gains confidence that his theatrical ploy contains the solution to his real-life difficulties, the camera has almost ignored the double thrones that symbolize Claudius's status in the family and in the state. Hamlet's chair dominates the set. But at the moment of his greatest poise, when he seems to have subsumed the powers of the stage in his own person and confidently awaits the arrival of the court, there is a dramatic cut to a reverse, low-angle shot from behind him. The juxtaposition of the two shots shows us that if from one point of view he is master of the revels, from the other he is still the hieratic son standing humbly below the looming empty thrones that dominate the room even in Claudius's absence.

As in Olivier's life, the theatrical solution to the Oedipal dilemma is a dubious one in which real mastery and narcissistic refuge are hard to distinguish. The visual treatment shows us that despite its energy and liveliness, Hamlet's theatrical experiment is another attempt to people the empty spaces of Elsinore with a cast of his own devising.

In contrast, the use of the empty room by King Claudius represents, even though it is wholly rooted in evil intentions, a mature and powerful appreciation of the relativity and contingency of power and its dependence on the establishing of bonds of trust and alliance between fathers and sons. Basil Sydney's Claudius, an uneasy yet powerful monarch in the early scenes and an affecting failed penitent after the mousetrap, comes into his own as a character in the scenes with Laertes in the last half of the film, converting Laertes's rebellion into loyal alliance. The groundwork of this alliance is laid before Hamlet returns from his sea voyage, when Claudius is able, solely by the force of his personal authority, to deflect Laertes's rebellious threats. This encounter is filmed in extreme long-shot so that Laertes's murderous rage seems little more than a minor personal quarrel taking place in one corner of the castle, while the mad Ophelia—the real focus of our concern at this point—wanders poignantly distracted in another. By the time Laertes sees her his anger against the king has already been defused. The opportunity for Claudius not merely to placate but to use Laertes comes in the graveyard scene, when he assists Laertes in converting grief for a dead father into a commitment to revenge, succeeding where the ghost had so far failed.

As in the council scene in the beginning of the film, so here the figure of Hamlet dominates the foreground (photo 2.18); meanwhile, the real nexus of power occupies a more modest part of the screen. As Hamlet realizes that Ophelia is to be buried in the fresh grave, he challenges Laertes: "What is he whose grief bears such an emphasis?/It is I, Hamlet the Dane." Here Hamlet, his back to us, immense in our foreground perspective, with arms spread looks sharply down from a hillock on the tiny figures of Laertes and the king grouped around a stone cross at the grave. After the tumult of Hamlet's mad challenge and his leap into the grave have subsided, the significance of the king's quiet placement of himself in relation to the cross and in relation to Laertes becomes clear. Left alone on screen, Laertes kneels in mourning while the king stands before the cross so that he insinuates himself in the place from which mourning is sanctified—an assertion of paternal power by mise-en-scène far more effective than his verbal attempts to occupy the same place for Hamlet in the first scene (photo 2.19). Laertes's submission to his grief becomes, through this placement, an implicit submission to the king, to whom he also seems to kneel, so that when Claudius places a comforting hand on his shoulder and gestures him to rise, grief for the dead is replaced by acceptance of the law as embodied in the king (photo 2.20). "Laertes, was your father dear to you, or are you like the painting of a sorrow, a face without a heart?" The funeral, of course, is that of Ophelia, not Polonius, but it is the death of the father that is the motive for a revenge directed against Hamlet, and the basis for the symbolic bond of sonship to Claudius. It is this bond which, despite the many ironic parallels between Laertes and Hamlet, distinguishes Laertes, who can "do what is required of him," and Hamlet, who cannot.

Claudius, with fatherly concern, leads Laertes into the council chamber, on the way revealing candidly his own weaknesses and limitations; his dependence on the queen, his fear of an uprising in favor of the more popular Hamlet. The king acknowledges, in short, his need for Laertes's assistance in a project he cannot accomplish alone. In the council chamber, exploring the possibilities of an attempt on Hamlet, he seats Laertes in Polonius's chair, while he himself takes one of the armless benches farther down the table. In the symbolic tableau Olivier has provided the potential double meanings in the king's speech reveal not merely an ironic relation to Hamlet but a complex and troubled self-understanding on the part of Claudius: "That we would do we should do when we would, for this 'would' changes, and

Photo 2.18

Photo 2.19

Photo 2.20

Photo 2.21

hath abatements and delays" is delivered with the king in medium shot, his hand knowingly laid upon Hamlet's empty chair (photo 2.21). This advice to Laertes not only brings to mind Hamlet's temperamental incapacity for action but also invokes (for us, though not Laertes) the king's own decisive but guilty act in pursuing his desires, an act to whose consequences he is still unhappily bound. In this context for a moment Hamlet's chair becomes again the empty chair of the murdered king, from which the tragic action took its rise.

The special function of the Laertes-Claudius subplot in the film, then, is to offer an alternative to the way Hamlet conceives of the father-son relationship. Instead of abuse, there is comfort; instead of distance and idealization, there is human contact and admission of paternal weakness; instead of being consigned to empty spaces and imaginary relationships, the son is seated in his father's place by an authority that symbolically takes precedence over his father. For Laertes the conflict between generations is stabilized, the death of the father provides the key to the resolution of Oedipal conflict. For Hamlet, however, the deceased father has become a ghost, compromising his autonomy and contributing, finally, to the tragic Oedipal resolution of refusion with the mother. The value of this normative succession from father to son as an alternative to Hamlet's malaise is negated, however, by its origins in murder and its resort to treachery in the use of the poisoned foil. In a sense the film's exploration of the father-son bond between Claudius and Laertes remains limited by Hamlet's perspective. The film offers an instance of psychological health, but one so morally compromised as to invite us to prefer Hamlet's deeply brooding Oedipal perfectionism.

Hamlet's "reconciliation" with Laertes before the fencing match is played so as to emphasize the unbridgeable distance between the two, Hamlet's exaggerated deference ("I'll be your foil, Laertes") masking contempt, as does his patronizing apology for Polonius's death ("Did Hamlet wrong Laertes? Never Hamlet. Hamlet *denies* it."). The mockery here is partly motivated by Hamlet's awareness that the positive relation to the father implied by the king's sponsorship of Laertes is closed to him. His challenge of the pretentious term "carriages" which Osric uses for the thongs attaching the sword to the belt likewise displays a rejection of manhood conceived as phallic competition. Hamlet understands the phallic symbolism of the rewards the king offers him for victory in the fencing match: "The word would be more germane to the matter if we might carry a *cannon* by our side: I would it might be 'hangers' till then—but on," the last two words spoken with a mocking lilt.

The contrast between Hamlet and Laertes is pressed home in Olivier's interpretation of the fatal touch. Laertes's weapon is, as we know, unbated and poisoned, and he is considered the better fencer; the king, in order to make the wager credible, has bet on Hamlet, but only with a substantial handicap as security. Nevertheless, Laertes cannot score a touch in fair combat, and it is only when trapped between the scornful disappointment in his manhood of Osric on one side and Claudius on the other that he strikes out in violation of the rules during a time out—"Have at you *now*." The shame Laertes feels when confronted with paternal disappointment is not unlike that which Hamlet has internalized, but it is momentary and calls forth instantaneous action.

There is a note of victory in the death scene that follows: in Olivier's version (though not in Shakespeare) the queen drinks the poison knowingly and almost joyfully, defying the king and seizing on this opportunity for suicide as a kind of triumph whereby she extricates herself from the king and affirms her union with Hamlet. But Oedipal victories are defeats for the self.

The pattern of being cast down and reaching after the attacker with reproach and longing recurs here: Hamlet and Laertes, both dying, reach out for each other, and the motif of the extended hand now signals mutual forgiveness and recognition that "the king's to blame." The king himself, fatally wounded by Hamlet, repeats the gesture, but his reach is toward the crown he has lost and the lifeless queen. Olivier's fourteen-foot leap is the climax of the action and a summative use of the staircase as a symbol of violence visited from above—a violence with which Hamlet now identifies himself (photo 2.22). The leap exemplifies a pattern

Photo 2.22

in Olivier's life and art in which the fear of passivity and indecision is allayed by a masculine daring that offers only an equivocal solution because of its association with self-destruction. It seems appropriate that for the final act of this character, whose uniqueness is so much a part of both his pathology and his greatness, Olivier should have chosen an acrobatic move impossible to repeat.[28]

The film ends with an extended reference to the opening sequence: Hamlet's body is carried up the narrow, winding steps to the top of the central tower. On the way the camera trails the procession behind the bearers as if it were a mourner, and as they ascend it breaks off from their upward course several times to revisit for the last time the symbolic locales: Hamlet's chair seen close-up in an upwardly spiraling camera movement, Ophelia's chamber, the chapel, the queen's bed. But there is no one left for whom these scenes will have the same importance and the endless play of possibility that they had for Hamlet. Elsinore has been presented from a point of view so close to that of Hamlet that his death drains meaning from the setting. In this context the final shot of the staircase to nowhere takes on its full value as an emblem of narcissistic self-enclosure: the tragedy of a man who could not make up his mind is the tragedy of a self that, for reasons we are meant to feel as valid and powerful, cannot give up the illusion of its own centrality and uniqueness, cannot invest itself in a symbolic order based on filial succession and the substitution of objects, and for whom, therefore, death is the destruction not only of the physical self but of the world of significances the self has sustained.

Olivier's film is thus firmly grounded in the Freud/Jones reading of *Hamlet* and incorporates the central insights of that reading: the erotic treatment of the mother-son relationship, the attribution of Hamlet's delay to an implicit equation between usurper and would-be revenger, and the understanding of Hamlet's final "success" as a kind of self-destruction. But the tragic quality of the film and its value as an interpretation of Shakespeare derives at least as much from the director's exploration of aspects of the play's Oedipal theme that had special relevance to his own early life. The tragedy here is located in the failure of Hamlet's relation to his father, which leaves him with a sense of fundamental defect, uncertain boundaries, and a powerful impulse toward merger, evident in his identification with the invasive ghost early in the film and in his mystical bond with his mother later. Olivier's Hamlet displays both the greatness of spirit and the tragic waste of his gifts that Shakespeare's text calls for. He is vigorous, courageous, intellectually powerful, and ethically sensitive. But neither his mission nor his factitious Oedipal victory can supply a firm sense of worth or provide a stable connection between this brilliant but isolated character and the human world around him. Olivier's *Hamlet*, unlike Freud's, is a tragedy not of guilt but of the grandiose self and its unmet need for context and validation, of a son unable to find a nonabusive relation to his father.

Notes

1 Noticed, for example, by John Ashworth in "Olivier, Freud and Hamlet," *Atlantic Monthly* 183 (May 1949): 30; Jay Halio, "Three Filmed Hamlets," *Literature/Film Quarterly* 1 (Fall, 1973): 317; Bernice W. Kliman, "The Spiral of Influence: 'One Defect' in *Hamlet*," *Literature/Film Quarterly* 11, no. 3 (1983): 159–66.

2 *The Standard Edition of the Complete Psychological Works of Sigmund Freud*, ed. and trans. James Strachey (London: Hogarth, 1953), 24 vols., 4: 264–66. Hereafter cited as *S.E.*

3 Ernest Jones, "The Oedipus Complex as an Explanation of Hamlet's Mystery," *American Journal of Psychology* 21 (January 1910); *Das Problem des Hamlet und der Oedipus-Komplex* (Leipzig and Vienna: F. Deuticke, 1911); *Essays in Applied Psychoanalysis* (London: Hogarth, 1923, reprint New York: International Universities Press, 1964), vol. 1, chap. 1; *Hamlet by William Shakespeare with a Psycho-analytical Study by Ernest Jones, M.D.* (London: Vision Press, 1947), 5–42 ("The Problem of Hamlet and the Oedipus Complex"); *Hamlet and Oedipus* (London: V. Gollancz, 1949, reprint New York: W. W. Norton, 1976).

4 Laurence Olivier, *Confessions of an Actor* (London: Weidenfeld and Nicolson, 1982), 102.

5 Ibid.

6 *S.E.*, 4: 265.

7 Ibid.

8 "*Hamlet* at the Old Vic: Mr. Tyrone Guthrie's Production," *The Times* (London), January 6, 1937. See also Ivor Brown, "Old Vic *Hamlet* (in Full) by William Shakespeare," *The Observer*, Janu-

ary 10, 1937; "*Hamlet* in Full by William Shakespeare," *The Manchester Guardian*, January 6, 1937.

9   Jones, *Hamlet and Oedipus*, 88.

10   See John Cottrell, *Laurence Olivier* (Englewood Cliffs, NJ: Prentice-Hall, 1975), 89–90, 110, 113, 134–5, 308.

11   Olivier, *Confessions*, 152.

12   The most daring move in the theater came earlier, during the play scene, when, at the line, "Let the stricken deer go weep," Olivier leaped from the raised throne platform, a much lower height than the balcony in the film, to the stage, and rolled forward three times to the footlights (Cottrell, *Laurence Olivier*, 120). This more moderately acrobatic moment was one that could be repeated each night.

13   Olivier, *Confessions*, 153.

14   *S.E.* 17: 6, 27–28, 35–36, 45–46; 19: 31–33.

15   The current literature on narcissism and related issues is voluminous, but see especially Bela Grunberger, *Le narcissisme* (Paris: Payot, 1975); Otto Kernberg, *Borderline Conditions and Pathological Narcissism* (New York: Jason Aronson, 1975); idem, *Internal World and External Reality* (New York: Jason Aronson, 1980); Heinz Kohut, *The Restoration of the Self* (New York: International Universities Press, 1977); Lynne Layton and Barbara Schapiro, eds., *Narcissism and the Text: Studies in Literature and the Psychology of Self* (New York, 1986), introduction. See also my "Conflict and Coherence: Narcissism and Tragic Structure in Marlowe," in Layton and Shapiro, *Narcissism and the Text*, 36–63.

16   These doubts, though partly resolved in late adolescence, continued into adult life. Although Olivier's adult adjustment was heterosexual, his account of his one homosexual temptation is a confusing amalgam of moral rectitude ("I felt that the homosexual act would be a step darkly destructive to my soul," *Confessions*, 86) and liberal toleration ("It would be dreadfully wrong if any of this should be taken to imply that I ever found anything in the remotest unrespectable about homosexuality," ibid.). The story of Olivier's attempt (again, on Ernest Jones's advice) to play a homoerotic Iago (105) is also interesting in this connection.

17   The association of passivity and femininity is central to Freud's account of the "negative" or homosexual resolution of the Oedipus complex, and *equally* pervades Olivier's account of his early life, as my extracts here and in the last chapter may suggest. I stress again my own view that there is no biologically given or essential connection between the terms so consistently associated in the discourse Olivier shares with Freud. Fear of effeminacy, fear of homosexuality, the belief that effeminacy and homosexuality are equivalent and consequent upon accepting a passive or submissive relation to another male are

the defining anxieties of prescriptive heterosexuality, which is the dominant mode of constructing sexual difference in the West. Although his own work proceeds from precisely such assumptions, Lionel Ovesey's analysis of "pseudohomosexuality" has been particularly helpful for understanding Olivier (see *Homosexuality and Pseudohomosexuality*, New York: Science House, 1969). See also Peter Blos, *Son and Father* (New York: Free Press, 1985), passim. For Blos in the adolescent replay of the Oedipal dynamics, the rebelliousness, aggressiveness, and hypersexuality of adolescent males, which superficially suggests Oedipal rivalry, actually mask and defend against a deeper need in late adolescence for boys to revive their connection to the "dyadic" father, the father in his role as ally in individuation: the boy turns to the father to resist the reengulfing mother (Blos, *Son and Father*, 19).

18   Olivier, *Confessions*, 31–32.
19   Brenda Cross, ed., *The Film Hamlet, A Record of Its Production* (London: Saturn Press, 1948), 12.
20   Ibid., 15.
21   Ibid.
22   Ibid., 11.
23   The corner tower is the one from which Hamlet will deliver the "To be or not to be" speech: its location gives point to the possibility of his suicide and to his inability to perform it as he drops his dagger into the sea; the surf crashing on the rocks manifests, metaphorically, the "sea of troubles" he cannot face as well as the annihilation that might "end them." The middle tower is similar in dimensions but has no decorative crenellation: it is the perfectly flat top of a cylinder. It too comes to stand for annihilation, though of a different kind: the nothingness from which the ghost comes and into which he vanishes, the absence from which the film arises and the emptiness with which it ends.

In the first sequences of *Henry V* the camera moves in on a model of sixteenth-century London, coming in close to one of two similar structures and then, as if correcting an error, moving to the second, which is the Globe Theater. The purpose of this device is to establish the camera as a fallible instrument, much as the theater itself is described in Shakespeare's text as a fallible and "unable" instrument in the prologue that is about to be spoken. In *Hamlet* the similar hesitation between the sea tower and the central tower may inscribe a Hamlet-like indecision in the narrative point of view—the story of a man who could not make up his mind will be one in which, visually, we cannot always locate ourselves quickly or unambiguously: furniture changes position, chairs are shifted, and we are not always sure which way the camera is facing in the immense council hall in which much of the action takes place. Some of the visual difficulties thus created were criticized in early reviews, but their relevance to the themes of the play was a matter of conscious strategy. Designer Roger Furse addressed the question directly in an interview for *The Film Hamlet*:

> In "Hamlet" I have taken liberties with the sets and am sure the audience will allow these liberties without quibbling about details of background. Art departments these days can imitate anything and produce real-life sets; but this seems to me missing an opportunity to create atmosphere. Distortions of actual scenery will not be resented mentally by an audience, but they will be sensed psychologically and will add to the dramatic effect of the film. Thus, in the Council Chamber scenes of "Hamlet," we have put our massive pillars on wheels and, for certain shots, have moved the pillars up or down the room. (pp. 36–37).

Apart from creating an appropriate sense of disorientation, wholly in accord with Shakespeare's Elsinore—in which sentries are challenged rather than challenge and in which Sundays and weekdays, funerals and weddings have become difficult to distinguish—the confusion between the towers contributes powerfully to the effect of the final shot. Hamlet's body will not be cast into the sea, as it might have been from the corner tower, in fulfillment of the suicide meditation spoken there. In fact there is nothing imaginable that can be done with it—the film simply ends at the highest and central point of the castle that has come to seem a mirror of Hamlet's troubled psyche.

24 It is significant too that the ghost, as well as the main character, was played by the director, with his voice played back at slower-than-normal speed. Olivier as director could find no Hamlet other than himself on whom to impress his strong interpretation, and in some sense his Hamlet can find no father but himself. There is thus a self-generative, narcissistic cast to Olivier's treatment of the Oedipal material the text offers at this point.

25 J. Dover Wilson, *What Happens in Hamlet* (Cambridge: Cambridge University Press, 1935), 106; Compare Olivier, *Confessions*, 101.

26 Cross, *The Film Hamlet*, 12.

27 The council chamber staircase occupies a space that is basically theatrical, whereas the winding staircases that lead to the towers are treated in a more distinctively cinematic way (the proscenium stage offers limited access to the vertical dimension as compared with film). The layout of the council chamber in the film is very similar to the set of the 1937 Old Vic production (see photographs in the Harvard University Theater Collection, Angus McBean File, *Hamlet, Old Vic, 1937*): a double staircase

with a half turn gives access to a walkway some eight or ten feet above the floor. Details of the film's staging such as the use of this staircase may well have derived from the Guthrie-Olivier collaboration on that earlier production. But the stage production cannot have invoked the flight-upon-flight repetition of narrow steps that is the film's dominant visual motif, through which the director makes his distinctive contribution to the interpretation of the play.

28   See above, p. 33.

3

Surface and Depth: Throne of Blood *as Cinematic Allegory*

Something Like an Introduction

Akira Kurosawa begins his partial autobiography by recalling a miraculous curative salve still peddled in prewar Japan by itinerant medicine men:

> A toad with four legs in front and six behind would be placed in a box with mirrors lining the four walls. The toad, amazed at its appearance from every angle, would break into an oily sweat. This sweat would be collected and simmered for 3,721 days while being stirred with a willow branch. The result was the marvellous potion.
>
> Writing about myself, I feel something like that toad in the box. I have to look at myself from many angles, over many years, whether I like what I see or not. I may not be a ten-legged toad, but what confronts me in the mirror does bring on something like the toad's oily sweat.[1]

This is the first of many fine moments of poised self-deprecation in *Something Like an Autobiography*, an incomplete memoir which, though published in 1982, breaks off in 1950 with the director's entry into international prominence with the release of *Rashomon*. When Kurosawa revised material that had originally appeared in the Japanese periodical *Shukan Yomiuri* for publication in English, he added the preface from which I have quoted the story of the ten-legged toad.

Like the abrupt conclusion of the book, just at the point when Kurosawa became famous *in the West*, the English preface negotiates a cultural border, positioning its author between Japanese folk wisdom on one side and the autobiographies of famous European and American film directors on the other. Kurosawa cites a specific Western text—Jean Renoir's *My Life and My Films*—as his inspiration and expresses regret that John Ford left no comparable work for his admirers. "Compared to these two illustrious masters ... I am no more than a little chick."[2] To balance the self-praise implied by comparison with these *auteurs*, Kurosawa presents himself as modest, awkward, and, like the toad, uncomfortable in the presence of his own reflected image. The "something like" of the title works, along with the story of the toad and repeated disclaimers of self-importance,[3] to differentiate Kurosawa's work from the Western texts, literary and cinematic, which he invokes as models.

But if, in moving from the lying peddlar's tale to the autobiography of Jean Renoir, Kurosawa sets in play a contrast between cultures, he also modifies that contrast by citing a European text that is uncharacteristic in its self-negation. Included in Kurosawa's quotation from *My Life and My Films* are these important, self-displacing sentences:

> The truth is that this individual of whom we are so proud is composed of such diverse elements as the boy he made friends with at nursery school, the hero of the first tale he ever read, even the dog belonging to his cousin Eugene. We do not exist through ourselves alone, but through the environment that shaped us.[4]

It was this passage, in which the authorial self is dispersed in the web of its influences and associations, that influenced Kurosawa's decision to publish his own memoirs.

In this chapter I read *Throne of Blood*, Kurosawa's adaptation of *Macbeth*, as a meditation on cultural difference. As in Kurosawa's autobiography, a Western model provides inspiration, raises the question of self-assertion in an acute form, and also, perhaps, provides the antidote to its own excess. In *Throne of Blood* Shakespeare's *Macbeth* is made to yield something like the sweat of the ten-legged toad.

Surface and Depth

Noel Burch has proposed that the history of Japanese film may be understood in terms of two widely divergent attitudes toward the cinematic image. In one the screen is regarded as a flat surface and image is treated as a sign, its status as inscribed and artificial medium frankly granted, and narrative style retains links with the ancient arts of scroll painting and Noh drama. In the other (Westernized) style, the perspectival depth of the image is more important and the screen is treated as a window offering, or apparently offering, an unmediated view of a "real," three-dimensional space.[5] This model contrasts "traditional"[6] Japanese cinema, with its manifold links to other Japanese arts and postwar, Westernized practice, which more fully emulates the realism of the Hollywood or Griffith codes for the representation of space, action, and continuity. Burch prefers the traditional or uncorrupted practice and is especially critical of many of the late works of Mizoguchi and other directors which have been most critically acclaimed in the West. Kurosawa falls largely in the camp of the traditionalists for Burch,[7] who especially praises *Throne of Blood* for its geometrical rigor.

In this chapter, using Burch's distinction between a cinema of surface and a cimema of depth, I argue that *Throne of Blood* displays both of these styles—"traditional" and "Westernized"—and dramatizes the relation between them. It is a self-reflexive work that examines its own seduction by Western practice, a representational allegory in which the power of the cinematic image to offer the illusion of depth and plenitude parallels the ambition, revolt, and parricide of its main character, Washizu, Kurosawa's Macbeth.[8]

Inverness/Wilderness

Shakespeare's Birnam Wood is not a labyrinth, Dunsinane is not named after it, nor does Shakespeare identify the weird sisters as *forest* spirits. In a sense the forest is all there is in Kurosawa's *Throne of Blood*, more properly translated "Spiderweb Castle." The forest is Spiderweb Forest. The lord, who corresponds to Duncan, is Lord of Spiderweb Castle. Washizu (Macbeth) is tempted by a spirit who sits in the middle of the forest spinning thread in a gossamer hut. Visual analogies between the labyrinthine forest and the castle constructed of its wood, between the branches of the trees and the arrows made of them, intimate the vanity not only of Washizu's ambition but of human order that does not sufficiently recognize its rootedness in natural process. In an early interview Kurosawa explicitly linked the set design to the reigning metaphor of labyrinth or trap.

> Interviewer: Did you design the sets with the Noh specially in mind? I think the room in which Macbeth murders the king resembles the Noh stage closely. Yet as the Noh drama originated in the age of civil wars which formed the background to this film the Noh might have provided the common style for the sets.

> Kurosawa: That's so. Historically, the castles of those days were in this style. When I went into the way castles were constructed in those days, some of them made use of the wood which was grown as if it had been a maze. Therefore the wood was named "the wood of spider's hair," meaning the wood that catches up the invaders as if in a spider's web. The title *The Castle of the Spider's Web* (Kumonosu-Djo) came to me in this way.[9]

Because the castle is made of the wood of the forest and is further related to the forest by its presentation as a (moral) labyrinth, the approach of the moving forest, Kurosawa's coming of Birnam Wood to Dunsinane, may be read as a return of nature to itself, an extrusion of the temporary reign of ambition—or even of human culture itself—when that culture sets itself in opposition to the order of the forest. However, as if to complicate such an interpretation, the interview tells us that the spiderweb forest was itself, and before its use by Washizu's enemies, a cultural artifact planted as a weapon of defense. The return of the forest to itself is therefore not a simple triumph of nature over culture but the obliteration of a temporary and unstable distinction.

As the film unfolds, this convergence of wood and castle, of "nature" and "culture," is conveyed on the narrative or diegetic level by the incursion of the soldiers carrying camouflaging branches into Washizu's domain and on the metacinematic level by the collapse of the illusion of depth of the cinematic image.

Feudal Geometry

Macbeth may be read in ethical terms, as the story of an individual's transgression and punishment. But there is also a sense in which Macbeth's moral choices exemplify the values of a social order. He is at least partly a victim in whom the contradictions of feudal violence play themselves out. The idea that the play can sustain a transpersonal, historical reading along such lines is a commonplace of contemporary criticism, but it represents a fairly recent tendency, dating perhaps to Harry Berger's influential article in *ELH* in 1980.[10] Anticipating this critical tradition, Kurosawa stresses the mutual entailment of the deeds of Washizu and the values and needs of the feudal order.[11]

That social order is embodied throughout *Throne of Blood* in strict and uncluttered rectilinear compositions that offer a vivid contrast to the tangled and impenetrable forest outside the castle gates. The principal motifs of this design are presented in the opening sequences of the film: the lord and his council sit rigidly before, a taut, horizontal war screen staring straight ahead (photo 3.1). The messengers, in great agitation, beat at the great gates (photo 3.2), filmed at stark right angles, then fall prostrate before the lord, who hardly lowers his eyes to receive their news (photo 3.3). The worldly power Washizu will be tempted by is typically exercised from high to low and, frontally, in the dimension of implied depth. The posture of these messengers will later be assumed by those bringing news to Washizu, who will, like the lord here, be shot from directly in front, his supplicants directly before and below him. Such a design is in one sense merely a replication of the geometry of feudalism, a faithful representation of the social decorum of feudal Japan. But the

Photo 3.1   Photo 3.2

Photo 3.3

camera placement underscores the rigidity of the hierarchy and offers an apparent contrast to the twisted and unfathomable forest. And as the fantasy of human ambition projects outward from itself (from the powerful, seated figure of the lord) to the prostrate messengers, beyond them to the castle gates, then to and through the "lord's" forest beyond, so the cinematic image can, as critics like Baudry and Burch have argued, assert a parallel and related claim to depth, power, and plenitude.

The Screen on Screen: Metacinematic Figures in *Throne of Blood*

The film's opening credits appear over a shot of tangled branches—the spider's web wood of the title—and these are the first of a variety of means, insistently deployed throughout, by which the movie screen is doubled, so that we see the action through a screen or curtain, natural or man-made, or at times cannot see the action at all because it is screened from us. These devices include the branches of the forest, the "walls" of the forest spirit's hut of sticks, the *shoji* partitions of the castle, balustrades and railings, interior room screens, moving human figures in the foreground, barred windows, and—perhaps most importantly—arrows, either stationary in their rack or as a fusillade hemming in the protagonist during the final sequence while partly screening him from our sight.

The narrative function of the branch-screen does not become immediately apparent, for the film presents two important sequences before we return to the forest in which Washizu (Macbeth) and Miki (Banquo) are lost after their victory over the rebels. The first is a framing sequence in which a mist-swept barren landscape is presented, the site of Washizu's tomb, to the accompaniment of a voice-over choral chant condemning ambition. This is substantially re-peated at the close: there is no line of kings, as in Shakespeare, pointing forward to a present to which the tragic action will have contributed. The second is the scene I have just discussed in which the war council of the lord is introduced.

The forest is first mentioned during the messenger scene by one of the lords, who suggests that men be stationed there to ambush the rebels because "it is a natural labyrinth"; yet when it is introduced visually, it has caught up not the rebels but the so-far loyal defenders, Washizu and Miki. The forest is a place of contradiction and illusion: sunlight streams down through rain, strange laughter arises from an offscreen source, and the protagonists declare that they have been lost for hours. They enact a *hubristic* defiance of the forest's power. Washizu shoots an arrow at the sun, yet their defiance circles oddly back into entrapment: "I will break through with my spear," Miki declares. "And I with my bow," Washizu adds. But we see them using these weapons *only in the direction of the path* as they ride at right angles to the camera, which tracks with them at an uneven and jerky pace, observing them through a screen of branches. What they believe is a head-on assault on the forest and the spirit whose presence they suspect is therefore merely a more furious tracing of the labyrinth. The effect of the screen of branches through which we glimpse them is multiple: the branches are a double for the movie screen and a reminder of its interposition between the spectators and the action. Because they are always parallel to the screen and the riders, they also reveal that the characters are *on the path*, not breaking through the brush as they somehow suppose. Our relation to the characters is therefore distanced (barred) and privileged. In addition, the uneven pace of the following camera makes us aware of its motion in a special way, as if we were looking through the eyes of a living and moving observer for whom the labyrinth presented no barrier. The point of view, that is, is close to that of the kind of being they fear and whom they are about to meet.

The scene at the forest spirit's hut has been studied in detail in a sensitive article by Jack Jorgens.[12] Jorgens suggests that the spinning wheel, with its double spools, is a metaphor for the film projector or editing table, a glance at Kurosawa's own act of creation (photo 3.4).[13] There are other metacinematic references here too: the flickering light source, the insubstantiality of the spirit and her hut, and, above all, the insistent screening effects which Kurosawa deploys not only in this sequence but throughout the film. The witch is first seen through a double screen; Miki and Washizu peer through a canopy of branches into the hut, whose cagelike walls of branches present another kind of screen between them and the spirit. Like the weird sisters in the source play, the spirit prophesies success to each of the men and, like Lady Macbeth, taunts Washizu with his failure to admit his deepest desires and enact them.

The scene is shot in a reverse field setup, so that we sometimes see her from Washizu's point of view or from a position behind him, and sometimes see Miki and Washizu from a low angle with the camera placed behind the spirit (photo 3.5). Her discourse finished, she vanishes from the image, and the warriors enter the hut, the camera tracking with them, and knock down the flimsy far wall of the hut with their spears (photo 3.6). The most crucial shot of the sequence follows as the men turn and look toward the camera in surprise. As they walk toward what had been the near wall of the hut, contiguous through much of the sequence with the plane of the movie screen, the camera tracks back, so that we see them cross what had been the boundary of the wall, and realize that the source of their surprise is that it is no longer there (photo 3.7). The effect of the shot is to suggest that they have crossed a critical but now invisible boundary. Unlike their ride through the maze, which took place almost entirely parallel to the screen and distanced from us by the foreground branches, they now move in an unbounded dimension of depth, in an unmediated space that had seemed to belong to us.

Yet in a way this is but a more complex instance of the spirit's power. Instead of destroying the remnants of the witch, they have entered fully into her world, and their crossing over into evil is confirmed by the appearance, in

Photo 3.4

Photo 3.5

Photo 3.6

Photo 3.7

77

this apparently freer and less restricted space, of icons of death—piles of bones topped by skulls in armor.

In addition, they are still lost. After the disappearance of the witch and her hut, Miki and Washizu, in a celebrated sequence, ride away from and toward the camera twelve times in a pattern Burch has praised for its inventive variation upon simple geometrical elements: camera distance and angle, arc of the turn the riders make, and so on.[14] The meaning of the sequence is that they are in a new kind of maze: they appear to ride freely; there are no trees, only thick mist; and they now have the freedom to move at a variety of angles to the screen, not only parallel to it as before. But they still can't get out of the "forest": the physical constraints of the tangled wood have been succeeded by more ethereal ones, and they seem under enchantment. This sequence also develops one more analogy between the "world" represented on the screen and the means of its representation, for the mist, which has accompanied nearly every shot since the opening sequence at Washizu's tomb, now becomes thick enough to perform the function of a fade-out or dissolve. As the riders recede from our sight and return to view, the obscuring haze that conceals them becomes difficult to distinguish from the cinematic convention of fade-out and fade-in marking the passage of time. At the end of the sequence we learn they have been riding for hours, but while it is unfolding we may think that they simply ride into thick mist, turn, and ride out of it.

Significantly, the mist, like the optical effects it doubles for, serves the viewer's needs, ensuring that the riders never leave the image more than momentarily. Whenever it becomes thick enough to obscure them, they ride out of it again toward us. In this way the viewer is again privileged, for the riders' movements are limited by our vision. This effect develops the association of the audience with the spirit, who not only knows and sees more than the protagonists but partly controls their actions.

Movement in the Screen Plane, Movement in Depth: The Geometry of Murder

Thus far the film is structured around a contrast between the futile ride through the trees, parallel to the screen plane and distanced by screening effects, and movement in depth. The former images the helplessness of the warriors in the face of nature; the latter seems—*but only seems*—to be associated with freedom and power: it is the dimension to which the witch gives access, the dimension in which the coveted power of the feudal lord is exercised vis-à-vis his subordinates. Both kinds of movement recur in the scenes that concern the murder and its aftermath.

The barred horizontal tracking of the first forest ride is echoed in the next section of the film by shots in which balustrades replace branches and in which weapons, particularly pikes, are foregrounded as powerful horizontal barriers sometimes filling the width of the screen. In the first of these sequences the lord, in confirmation of the prophecy, confers authority over North Castle and First Fort on Washizu and Miki. The long pikes used in this ceremony are centered in the image and perfectly horizontal. Their movement from high to low, from background to foreground, symbolizes the transfer of power from lord to retainer, and, in the context of the prophecy, evokes the possibility of regicide at the same time.

The pike is the murder weapon and the central prop in the long sequence in which Asaji (Lady Macbeth) succeeds (with many fewer words than in Shakespeare) in propelling her spouse toward the murder. Before the murder weapon appears, several kinds of preparation for our reading of its significance are made. One of these is the very strong visual identification between Asaji and the forest spirit. She is connected to the witch by her seated posture, her position in the image, and the strong direct lighting that nearly washes out her features. In addition, Asaji wears stark whiteface makeup, suggesting a Noh mask, and is the only character in the film so treated (photo 3.8).[15]

Another sequence that precedes the murder and prepares us for it is the purification of the chamber in which the

Photo 3.8

previous lord of North Castle, the rebel defeated by Washizu, committed suicide. Servants bear purifying tapers instead of weapons, but their slow progress toward the chamber anticipates the path Washizu will take in carrying out the murder of the lord. It also repeats some of the emphatic horizontal motifs of the sequence in which Washizu received the ceremonial pike, thus linking that occasion with the murder to come.

This sequence begins with the entry into the frame of two servants sent to prepare the "forbidden room" for Washizu and Asaji, who have been displaced by the arrival of the lord. They are challenged by the lord's bodyguard, whose pike offers a contrast to their tapers. Their mission explained, they pass slowly behind a balustrade and the sliding walls of the castle, the camera tracking with them left to right. This movement in a confined path at right angles to the camera echoes the movements of Miki and Washizu in the "natural labyrinth": perhaps, despite the stark contrast of the forest and castle in other ways, the intrigues of feudal social organization also constitute a (man-made) labyrinth. In addition, below the balustrade a succession of armed guards sit in the extreme foreground facing the camera, and as the servants make their journey to the forbidden chamber, each guard in succession rotates his pike and holds it horizontally in his lap as they pass, forming yet another kind of barrier. As the servants enter the chamber, Kurosawa emphasizes the candle in closer shots until only one outstretched hand and a candle are seen against the wall of the chamber. This room, with its blood-stained walls, is the setting for Washizu's almost wordless decision to go through with the murder, and it has been symbolically probed, illuminated, and revealed as the place of treason and bloodshed in advance, becoming almost a third character in the dancelike interaction between Washizu and Asaji.

They have already discussed the possibility of killing the lord, and, more directly than in *Macbeth*, Asaji has argued (laconically) from a demystified view of feudal power relations. Washizu speaks of his loyalty in tones of awe and respect, but Asaji points out that the lord had killed his own predecessor. The cue for the first action in furtherance of the murder—Asaji's drugging of the guards—is the flickering lights of the candles, shimmering hauntingly on the other side of the *shoji* screen, showing that the guards are settling down for the night. But as we perceive it from behind the couple, the illuminated screen is another instance of the equation, in this work, between the temptations of ambition and the medium of film. This association is perhaps deepened when, for Asaji's departure and return with the wine jars, she does not merely walk into the darkness and return but (subtly though distinctly) fades out of the image and then back into it after the drugging. Next, she confers the pike upon a trembling Washizu. The actual moment of transfer, an echo with significant variation of the hierarchical transfer of the lordship over North Castle earlier, has the husband and wife facing each other in full shot with the pike now foreshortened at right angles to the plane of the screen. As they both grasp it, Washizu's face appears contorted with suffering and a sense of entrapment. Yet he takes it, and his reversal of the weapon, so that it is again parallel to the screen plane, like the candles and pikes of the guards, marks his decision.

The actual murder takes place offscreen, an example of the decentering of action that Burch sees in the film: we see

Washizu move toward "the deed" and back, walking backward into the image, returning to the same tightly confined space in which the servants had moved to prepare the rebel's room for him (photo 3.9). Left alone in the empty room, Asaji occupies our attention while the murder is taking place: there is a bloodstain on the wall, and perhaps some of its ironic significance catches her eye. She runs to the corner where the rebel slew himself and performs a dance derived from Noh traditions which seems to express anxiety and apprehension as well as celebration while also conveying, as does her makeup, a bizarre sensation that she is not quite in the right artistic medium. This oddness, at any rate, as well as the camera distance (long shot), alienates or distances the dance; as most often in the film, we do not share in her feelings but observe them as best we can and are not drawn in. This distancing is enhanced by the fact that we see her through the vertical lines of a rack of arrows that screens her movements from the waist down, creating perhaps the most remarkable of the many screening effects in the film (photo 3.10). A dance, seen through an arrow rack, takes place in a tiny space bounded by a bloodied wall while the dancer awaits the completion of a murder. Although the murder of the lord takes place offscreen, we do see Washizu kill one of the sleepy guards, and the visual treatment is in accord with the style of the other sequences shot at "North Castle." We see one of the guards wake up and stagger to his feet, then there is a cut to Washizu, some fifty feet away, reacting to him. Washizu, filmed against a wall, draws his sword and runs to the guard, the camera tracking with him, so that we see only the victim again only at the moment of assault (photo 3.11). Rather than seeming a clever act of cold calculation (compare Macbeth's "yet I repent me of my rage that I did kill them"), the action seems a blind and futile repetition of the angry forest ride, with its insane and useless "attack" on the unseen spirit.

Because this is so, one's reaction to the exciting shots that follow (the lord's battle screen is torn off its posts by horses) is more muted than it would otherwise have been, and a similar muting or pall falls over the very lengthy progress of Washizu with the lord's coffin through the gates of Forest

Photo 3.9

Photo 3.10

Photo 3.11

Castle.[16] The latter in particular carries little sense of even temporary triumph, for Washizu's procession is greeted by the lamentations of the castle women, who are mourning the suicide of their lady but whose mourning ironically coincides with Washizu's entry. The scene is pervaded by a sense of the presence of death, and Washizu cannot even begin to make something more celebratory of it.

The murder of Miki (also offscreen, symbolized by the return of his riderless horse to the castle) takes place while we see Washizu for the first time presiding over a banquet as lord of Spiderweb Castle. The arrangement of figures in the banquet room is dictated by feudal custom: the lord and lady at the head of the room on tatami mats, the guests in two rows facing each other across the width of the room. But the ghost of Miki appears at the feast. His posture, his spatial relation to Washizu, and the lighting of the scene all evoke Asaji's typical "subservient" position and, beyond her, the forest spirit. Washizu's first assumption of his new dignity is ruined, as in *Macbeth*, by the ghost. The failure of ceremony is here conveyed by Washizu's mad rushing toward the camera, whose placement approximates the point of view of Miki's ghost for part of this sequence, and his undignified assault on the empty air. In the aftermath of the banquet his position is symbolized several times by an ironic use of the geometry of lord/servant relations, filmed directly from the front, as the reception of the messengers had been in the opening minutes. In the first of these the murderer appears suddenly in the background of a long shot, kneeling and holding a wrapped object that surely must be Miki's head. Lady Washizu leaves the two men alone in the now empty banquet room, and Washizu, on hearing news of Miki's son's escape, draws his sword and kills the prostrate subordinate without a word. We see this in long shot, emphasizing not the anger or passion or even the fear of the moment but its symbolic geometry. Washizu's back is to the wall and the murderer, in the center of the image, on the floor directly before him (photo 3.12). After he has received his death stroke, however, his death agony becomes a terrifying apparition to Washizu, forcing him back against the wall (photo 3.13) and finally into flight from the room. This effect of reversal is heightened by the mise-en-scène: the murderer, seen from the back in his black armor as he struggles for life and tries to rise and reach toward Washizu, resembles a monstrous dying insect or, more precisely, the black scorpion that is Washizu's own emblem.

A second instance in which the posture of feudal subservi-

 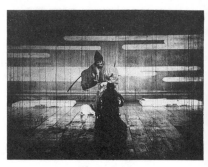

| Photo 3.12 | Photo 3.13 |

ence becomes charged with terror of the supernatural occurs shortly after this when Washizu is told of his wife's miscarriage. Altering the source, Kurosawa had made Asaji pregnant, her pregnancy a further incitement to the murder of Miki because if Washizu has an heir of his own, he will not be content to keep his bargain that Miki's son succeed him. But only shortly after the murder, its futility is announced by means of the stillbirth of Asaji's child. The sequence begins with a closed *shoji* filling the screen and a hand that comes into the image to draw it back, revealing Washizu. As the servant tells her story, she repeatedly takes up the posture of full obeisance on the floor in the foreground, with Washizu in a standing pose directly behind her, facing the camera. As in the sequence with Miki's murderer, which it closely resembles, Washizu experiences his own "dominance" not as the access of power the murder was to have brought but as an excruciating attack by an inhuman nemesis: death and birth are not within his control but beyond him and, in their independence of his will, mock the attempt at self-realization to which the spirit, his own nature, and his wife had provoked him. Because this sequence so closely parallels that of the death of the armored murderer shortly before, even Washizu's control of his anger here, his refraining from violence against the servant, is made to convey his growing perception of the futility of his position.

Birnam Wood and Dunsinane: The Triumph of the Forest Spirit

Like Macbeth, Washizu's position is hopeless, and the last third of the film chronicles his desperate resistance to the obvious truth. As his enemies unite and approach, his war council have no strategies to offer. As lightning flickers outside Washizu abandons the council, as though summoned by the bad weather, and seeks the forest spirit again. Though powerful, dominating, and more derisive in her manner, she seems to offer words of comfort, very close to those of the source, declaring Washizu invulnerable until the forest moves against him. As the final battle nears,

Washizu is called to Asaji by a servant and, removing a curtain, finds her at her mad compulsive handwashing ritual. There is no contact between the two: even with the curtain down the curtain frame remains, a double horizontal barrier between husband and wife, and they never speak.

Washizu's address to his troops in which he brags of his invincibility and at the same time gives his troops the information they need to recognize the doom represented by the movement of the forest when they shortly thereafter see it for themselves, is filmed at a mockingly low angle, often raked, with Washizu strutting on a walkway high above the troops. The balustrade here serves the function of the almost ever-present screen or barrier (photo 3.14).

Kurosawa's moving forest is significant in ways that go beyond the use of the symbol in *Macbeth*. Not only does its movement break down the forest/castle opposition on which so much of the visual structure of the film is built, but it also, in its motion, squeezes out the dimension of depth. This movement alludes to and reverses the visual design of the film's opening minutes. There a great lord, seated above his servants and vassals, looks out from his throne to the gates and beyond them, surveying the space he controls, a space that continues with the line of his gaze through the "lord's

Photo 3.14

forest." Here feudal power, expressed in cinematic terms as controlling gaze, is mocked as the "wood" of the forest moves closer to the "wood" of the castle and the depth of the portrayed space diminishes almost to the two dimensions of the actual screen.

The final battle takes place between Washizu and his own troops. When they see the forest move, they seem almost to turn to wood themselves, greeting Washizu's plea for action with absolute stillness. Finally a voice cries out the question, "who killed his lordship?" and an arrow speeds past Washizu and sticks in the wall behind him. In this long and celebrated sequence Washizu survives dozens of wounds, finally bristling all over with arrows that have pierced him. His movements, which the camera follows closely, are furious in the lateral direction, and even in the vertical, as he climbs up and down external staircases fleeing the arrows. But he cannot or will not enter the castle, his back is to the wall, and his face is to the troops and to the railing. At points the camera takes an oblique position, momentarily relieving the stark right-angle style. But no sooner do we briefly share with the protagonist the feeling that there may be somewhere to run to than a hail of arrows strikes the wall, re-creating the screen effect, and we see Washizu through them as if in a cage (photo 3.15).

Few viewers of the film fail to remember the coup de grace. Washizu, like Macbeth, comes closest to his vaunted invulnerability when he has given up hope of its literal truth. He survives more bowshots than humanly possible, almost as though his sheer rage has given him extra life. But the troops are moving closer and now have begun to climb the stairs at the left of the screen. The death stroke, which shocks audiences, does so partly because it comes from a place we do not expect. Most of the arrows have come from directly in front, but Washizu is killed by a single arrow that transfixes his neck, a perfectly horizontal shot parallel to the screen plane, shot from a place to which we have seen no archers ascend: offscreen right (photo 3.16). The shot is not merely unexpected, then, but hints at a supernatural retribution, and completes the collapse of the illusory geometry of human violence that has been Kurosawa's subject. With this shot

Photo 3.15   Photo 3.16

Kurosawa's reduction of screen depth to surface is completed. "Birnam Wood" has returned: the branches of the Wood of the Spider's Web have entered the gates of the castle constructed of that wood, and the camera work supports the collapse of distinctions, the squeezing out of depth this implies. In addition, the startling shot in which Washizu is shot through the neck stops the action, so that an effect similar to that of a freeze frame is created within the narrative. The strange climax of this often exciting film is a flat, almost still picture. The theme of the humbling of ambition and the symbolic implications of the depth/surface contrast both conclude in a brilliant image in which the stylistic preoccupations of the film fuse with its moral and political concerns.

Washizu, stricken by the final arrow, continues his course, walks down and out looking directly at the troops who have killed him, and even attempts to draw his sword for combat before yielding to death. It is hard to say exactly what Mifune's striking facial expression at this moment conveys. The Noh mask of rage is gone and has been replaced by an expression in which shock and pain yield to an odd serenity.[17]

His final fall in clouds of dust before his troops is filmed in reverse angle. The shot echoes the messengers' prostration before the lord in the opening minutes, and that of Miki's murderer before Washizu later. But now the dying Washizu assumes the posture of feudal submission, with the soldiers massed in stony and indifferent rows above him facing the camera. Our final view of him is thus an ironic reversal of normal feudal relationships, with the lord humbled before his retainers.

Perhaps this image also intimates a reversal in the relation between film spectacle and audience in which the silent and massed spectators—the soldiers, our counterparts—become actors in the drama of state and the protagonist, in whose struggles and contradictions the director himself is so heavily invested, loses his preeminence.

In treating *Throne of Blood* as an allegory of cinematic practice, I have tried to suggest that Macbeth's temptation by visions of power and self-realization is paralleled in the film by the lure of Western perspectival cinema and its calm to representational plenitude and depth. In a series of contrasts between vision (or action) in depth and the treatment of the screen as a flat or iconic surface, Kurosawa dramatizes his own temptation by Western modes of representation and Western values, his departure from and return to a more characteristically Japanese cinematic practice and the values embodied in that practice.

Notes

1 Akira Kurosawa, *Something Like an Autobiography* (New York: Knopf, 1982), xi.
2 Ibid., xii.
3 E.g., "Take 'myself,' subtract 'movies' and the result is 'zero'" (p. xi).
4 Kurosawa's translator, Audie Bock, cites the English translation by Norman Denny (New York: Atheneum, 1974), 12, which I use here, and also refers to the Japanese translation published in Tokyo by Misuza Shobu. Many moments in Kurosawa's book pay tribute to this passage, and a particularly telling instance might be the story of how a man Kurosawa had listened to for an evening in a bar and then forgotten dominated the director's "creation" of a fictional character in the film *Scandal*: "The character of Hiruta was written by that man I met in the Komagata-ya bar. He was not written by me" (p. 180).
5 Noel Burch, *To the Distant Observer: Form and Meaning in the Japanese Cinema* (Berkeley and Los Angeles: University of California Press, 1979).

6 I use quotation marks because, though cinema began in Japan very early, like other aspects of Japan's modernization, it is ultimately Western in origin. Whatever links with traditional Japanese art forms and habits of mind early Japanese cinema may have, it is always at least partly Western in its associations, and its European origins can be emphasized by particular directors.

7 On Kurosawa's "traditionalism" see also Ana Laura Zambrano, "*Throne of Blood*: Kurosawa's *Macbeth*," *Literature/Film Quarterly* 2, no. 3 (Summer 1974). Zambrano relates *Throne of Blood* to a number of Japanese art forms, including Noh, Kabuki, and, most extensively, picture scroll. Kohei Esaki, a contemporary practitioner of this ancient form, served as art consultant on *Throne of Blood*.

8 This metacinematic dimension of *Throne of Blood* has its parallel in Shakespeare in the theatrical metaphors and similes that relate stage practice to the tragic action. Macbeth, as bad actor or "poor player," comes to instance both the great ambition of Renaissance drama and the emptiness of its illusions. For Kurosawa the figures are metacinematic rather than meta-theatrical, but they also, and in parallel ways, connect the pretensions of the medium—and particularly its Western practice—to the story of the main character.

9 Roger Manvell, *Shakespeare and the Film* (South Brunswick and New York: A. S. Barnes, 1979), 104.

10 Harry Berger, Jr., "The Early Scenes of *Macbeth*: Preface to a New Interpretation," *English Literary History* 47 (1980): 1–31.

11 In fact, as Graham Holderness has noted, *Throne of Blood* has often been criticized for departing from Shakespeare in its emphasis on the historical context in which Washizu's parricide is embedded. See "Radical Potentiality and Institutional Closure," in *Political Shakespeare*, ed. Jonathan Dollimore and Alan Sinfield (Ithaca, NY: Cornell University Press, 1985), 190–91.

12 Jack J. Jorgens, "Kurosawa's *Throne of Blood*: Washizu and Miki Meet the Forest Spirit," *Literature/Film Quarterly* 11 (1983): 167–73.

13 Ibid., 172 and compare Jorgens, *Shakespeare on Film* (Bloomington: Indiana University Press, 1977), 153–59.

14 Burch, *Observer*, 313: "one of the most sustained variation structures in narrative cinema."

15 Some of the other characters' facial expressions were consciously modeled after Noh masks, especially the grimace Mifune repeatedly adopts to express rage, but these allusions to Noh are less startling than the effect created by Asaji's painted and immobile face.

16 This is Washizu's ruse to get Miki, who is acting as temporary lord of the castle, to open the gates despite his suspicions.

17 This expression may also be an attempt to convey something of the tragic knowledge or self-acceptance of Shakespeare's Macbeth. Shakespeare's tragedies often bring an assertive, self-realizing protagonist to a point at which his singularity is reflected back as monstrosity, and his self-knowledge, useless to himself, is part of a process whereby the community is benefited or healed. Like Macbeth peering into the witches' mirroring displays, Washizu is forced to confront various images of himself as monster. Although Kurosawa did not apply to Shakespeare his story of the peddlar's etiology of the healing salve derived from the sweat of the ten-legged toad in his mirrored box, it seems an apt image not only for Kurosawa's autobiographical artistry but for his approach to Shakespearean tragic vision.

4

Mirrors and M/Others: *The Welles* Othello

The Grandiose Subject of Cinema

In his widely influential article on the "cinematographic apparatus," Jean-Louis Baudry argued for a connection between the experience of the spectator at a conventional film and the Western idea or myth of the "transcendental subject."[1] Baudry begins with Renaissance painting and linear perspective as precursors of the cinema's ambition to present a "total vision" that corresponds to the conception of "the fullness and homogeneity of being."[2] The representation of plenitude not only depicts a world but constructs a "subject": the viewer of a great Renaissance painting is in some sense a master of what is displayed, a self constituted by the totalizing work of art and sharing in its claim to plenitude. The cinema immeasurably increases this claim:

> If the eye which moves is no longer fettered by a body, by the laws of matter and time, if there are no more assignable limits to its displacement—conditions fulfilled by the possiblity of shooting and of film—the world will not only be constituted by this eye, but for it. The movability of the camera seems to fulfill the most favorable conditions for the manifestation of the transcendental subject.[3]

In this view the spectator identifies "less with what is represented, the spectacle itself, than with what stages the spectacle"[4]; identifies, that is, with the projector. The movie screen thus functions as Jacques Lacan thought the mirror did for the human infant, reflecting back to the viewer a factitious unity of self:

> Just as the mirror assembles the fragmented body in a sort of imaginary integration of the self, the transcendental self unites the discontinuous fragments of phenomena, of lived experience, into unifying meaning.[5]

Baudry's theory at first seems to include all cinematic experience in the orbit of the transcendental subject and therefore to implicate the medium as a whole in the false consciousness of Western, bourgeois culture. But he also allows for an oppositional cinema in which the illusions of bourgeois subjectivity are unmasked:

> Both specular tranquillity and the assurance of one's own identity collapse simultaneously with the revealing of the mechanism, that is, of the inscription of the film work.[6]

The classic instance of such revelation, the text from which Baudry draws his title, is Dziga Vertov's *Man with a Moviecamera* (Russian: *Chelovek s kinapparatom*), in which the filming *camera* itself frequently appears in the image, but any foregrounding of the medium—any self-reflexive or metacinematic representation—can be used to call into question the grandiose presumptions of the cinematic "eye," and to create a text that is critical of rather than complicit in the ideology of domination.

Baudry's formulation seems especially relevant to Welles, for not only does his work often draw attention to itself and its "inscription," but from the start of his career Welles was also interested in grandiose, arrogant, totalizing protagonists whose excesses reveal contradictions in the social values they instance and whose claim to personal greatness masks an inner void. The following study of Orson Welles's *Othello* explores the film's ambivalent treatment of the grandiose subject, attending to the psychological patterns that inform Welles's interpretation and to the metacinematic figures—

particularly the use of mirrors and barred images—that disturb or complicate our relation to the screen image, implicating the spectator with the spectacle, and locating the question of spectatorship at the center of the tragedy of *Othello*.

Mirrors

Welles's *Othello* is notable in its frequent use of mirror reflection. There are at least four actual mirrors, and there are several shots in which a reflected image appears in water. In addition to literal reflection, the motif of mirroring is extended metaphorically by reverse angle shots, which offer something like mirror images of one another, and by the film's insistent equation between the mirror gaze and the gaze of the anxious husband.

Several later *Othello* films use mirrors too, perhaps influenced by Welles, and I will begin by discussing these briefly before turning back to Welles in order to suggest how a single visual motif, not required by the text but perhaps suggested by it, can serve widely divergent interpretations.[7] Because visual style does not contest the text, does not or need not emend the text, it often provides a privileged access to unconscious or partly conscious interpretive patterns. This is particularly true for Welles.

In Liz White's *Othello* (USA, 1980) and in the Sergei Yutkevich film (USSR, 1955) mirror imagery is used, very differently in each case, primarily to explore the protagonist's ethnic *identity* and Iago's assault on that identity. In the Yutkevich film the mirror is the reflecting surface of a public well or rain pool, a central feature of the architecture of the plaza of the temple of Poseidon at Cyprus. We see this location first when Iago stares into it meditating on "the web that will enmesh them all." A low-angle close-up here suggests a camera placement below the surface of the water. As his plot takes shape, he reaches into the well and disrupts the surface, effacing his own features (photos 4.1, 4.2). He attacks his own image but is thinking of Othello, of fragmenting Othello's self-image as he does his own. Othello's reaction to the lengthy temptation scene (3.3) is a reprise of this scene at the well. Disturbed that Desdemona may have betrayed him because of his color, he rushes to the well (now seen in extreme long shot, revealing its place in the design of the temple and its relation to the beautiful Cyprus coast and examines his face in the water. Yet though the image wavers, it does not fragment (photos 4.3 and 4.4). His blackness is *not* cause for self-doubt here. Such a treatment is in keeping with Yutkevich's interpretation of the character: he is the "noble Moor" throughout and is never shaken inwardly. This scene conveys Iago's failure to evoke an inner disintegration equal to the evil he is able to accomplish in the action.

In Liz White's *Othello*,[8] an independent, all-black production completed in 1966 (released 1980), a mirror scene stands at the center of the design and is again used to explore the question of Othello's ethnic identity, though in a very different way. In this production Othello is played as an

Photo 4.1

Photo 4.2

Photo 4.3

Photo 4.4

African, whereas the "Venetians" are American blacks of lighter skin color. The complex historical and psychological relationship between black Americans and their African heritage is sensitively used in the film as a vehicle for conveying Shakespeare's play of radical alterity and kinship. In White's interpretation black-white contrasts are softened but are perhaps all the more painful because Othello at first feels himself to be a full member of an ethnic community he only partly understands. As in the Yutkevich film, the mirror scene comes after the temptation scene.[9] White uses the "haply for I am black" speech only to dismiss its implication, at least initially—in fact altering the text, so that Othello pridefully says "happily, I am black."

Yet the issue of color is not so easily disposed of. Unsure what to make of Iago's insinuations, Yaphet Kotto as Othello goes into his bedroom, dresses in African robes, and examines his reflection. He sees his own regal image but also remembers the details of the wooing of Desdemona, whose image appears in the mirror as he thinks of her. Her image is in turn replaced by that of her father. Othello muses, "her father loved me," but a light-skinned urbane Brabantio speaks words of contempt from the mirror, questioning how his daughter could ever have chosen "the sooty bosom of such a thing as thou." For Liz White color prejudice, whose origins lie in the white culture not directly represented in the film, manifests itself in black self-deprecation, and especially in the social hierarchy of skin color within the black community. Her Othello is relatively unaware of these tensions in the community he has joined, but they are powerful enough to destroy him. White's use of the mirror stresses paternal aspects of Othello's self-image: it is ultimately the rejection by Brabantio, not Desdemona, that proves decisive in his undoing; an uncertain and misunderstood relation to the father is central to the tragic action.

In contrast to Yutkevich and White, the mirror scenes in Welles's film do not emphasize ethnic identity. Welles plays a light-complexioned Moor and consistently underplays any sense of racial difference. Like White, he uses the mirror to explore the psychological dimension of the play, but for Welles the psychological issues involve disturbance in the maternal rather than the paternal sphere, and it is Desdemona, not Brabantio, who appears in the mirror at the climax of the temptation scene.

The mirror imagery begins early in the film and undergoes several transmutations before we get to that moment. The first instance occurs in the brawl Iago provokes to rouse Othello from his nuptial bed and disgrace Cassio. The celebration of the victory over the Turks takes place in a vaulted subterranean crypt open at one point to the sky by means of an oval opening or skylight. As the brawl develops, the soldiers fight in a flooded area beneath this opening, sometimes ankle deep in water. The first mirror reflection occurs in a shot of this flooded floor, where the tiny image of the guard, reversed and bounded by the reflected outline of the skylight, appears in the water, contrasting the anarchy of the brawl with the order and calm that would prevail in Cyprus if the soldiery did not "outsport discretion." The image is clear and still but very tiny. We may not be able to interpret it alone, but it is glossed by the next shot, a closer shot of the guards peering down into the crypt, this time not reflected but photographed directly (photos 4.5, 4.6). Immediately after this we see the tiny image again, and then its fragmentation by the feet of a pair of struggling combatants (photos 4.7 and 4.8). The precariousness of civil order and the debasement of this value so precious to Othello are conveyed by the contrast between the unseemly low parts of the fortress and the dignified and ordered upper reaches, and by the fragility of a reflected and reduced image.

The climax of the scene is the rousing of Othello from his bed in a chamber high in the tower. At this point in the film the interplay between the wedding chamber and the crypt is established by intercutting, though later—and especially in the murder scene and its aftermath—the bedchamber and the crypt will be more closely linked by emphasis on nearly identical architectural details. For now the lovers and the brawlers inhabit visually distinct realms, though we may sense the potential for a sullying of the marriage bed that their juxtaposition implies. In the play text the decorum of marital sexual relations and the decorum of the citadel town are associated. When Othello says "silence that dreadful bell:

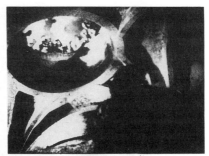

Photo 4.5   Photo 4.6

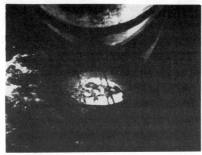

Photo 4.7

it frights the isle from her propriety," he mentions only the public aspect of the disturbance, but the festivities for the victory over the Turks celebrate "Othello's nuptials" as well and take place during the withdrawal of the couple to their bedroom. Iago makes the link between the two "scenes" clear when he compares the mood of the combatants before the brawl with "bride and groom divesting them for bed."

The analogy between the marriage and the brawl is developed in a variety of ways, of which two may be noted. First, when Othello is first shaken in his confidence in Desdemona and is briefly restored to trust, Desdemona wipes his brow with a handkerchief, which is then accidentally dropped. In the film there is a close shot of Othello's foot unwittingly trampling the handkerchief, and this echoes the shot in which the mirror image of the onlookers is fragmented by a brawler's boot in the crypt (photo 4.9; compare photo 4.8). Second, in the final moments of the film, as Othello is dying alone in his bedchamber with Desdemona's body, we get a dizzy, rotating point-of-view

Photo 4.8

shot of what appears to be an oval window or casement. As the camera movement stabilizes and the barred oval opens to reveal Cassio and others looking down, we realize that what we have been seeing is the skylight of the bedroom, now linked decisively to the crypt as a place of violent and unseemly disorder witnessed from above (photo 4.10). In the last shot before the dissolve to the credits (photo 4.11), Cassio closes the barred skylight hatch, an action that substitutes for Shakespeare's "Look on the tragic loading of this bed ... the object poisons sight./Let it be hid." This final shot is a summing up of several other visual metonymies: oval windows or mirrors and barred images of many kinds prepare us for the complex, summative effect of the closing of the hatch on the marriage/murder bed, but full discussion of these images must be deferred. For now it is important that the final sequence invokes the brawl, relating the murder to the careless effacement of the tiny human image mirrored briefly in the dirty water of the crypt.

At this point it may be helpful to remember places in the text where the dirtying of sexuality is presented in terms that may have suggested this symbolic use of the crypt.

I had rather be a toad
And live upon the vapor of a dungeon

Than keep a corner in the thing I love
For others' uses. (3.3.270–73)

But there, where I have garnered up my heart,
Where either I must live or bear no life;
The fountain from the which my current runs
Or else dries up: to be discarded thence!
Or keep it as a cestern for foul toads
To knot and gender in! (4.2.57–62)

The next and principal mirror sequence is the temptation
scene (3.3.) where, as in the films of Liz White and Sergei
Yutkevich, Othello, partly shaken by Iago's intimations,
consults his mirror to see if his reflected image can rebut or
confirm Iago's insinuation that Desdemona sees him as a
gross and unhandsome alien. For Welles, Othello's anxious
self-examination is inconclusive, its irresolution figured for
us in Othello's movement from a wall mirror to a table mirror
of similar design and in the variety of perspectival problems

Photo 4.9

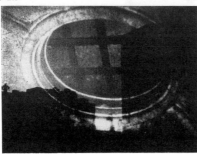

Photo 4.10

Photo 4.11

101

Photo 4.12

Photo 4.13

Photo 4.14

Photo 4.15

that characterize the sequence. We have trouble seeing what Othello sees—sometimes the angle is wrong, showing us a mirror but not the image in it; sometimes Othello's face or his shadow fall over the image (photos 4.12, 4.13). When we do see the whole image, it is juxtaposed with Iago's face, or Othello, unsatisfied by the evidence he sees, turns away from it to the other mirror in the room (photos 4.14, 4.15).

As Iago advances his theory that Desdemona's choice of Othello indicates the perversity of her sexual desires ("One may smell in this foul disproportions, thoughts unnatural ..."), Othello suddenly leaves the frame and the chamber and finds Desdemona in another room in the fortress. The brief scene between them, in which Desdemona attempts to wipe Othello's brow with the fatal handkerchief and he rejects her comforting gesture, letting the handkerchief fall, is wordless. The effect of the elimination of dialogue (about the "pain" on Othello's forehead and the insuffiency of Desdemona's "little napkin" as a bandage) is to continue the emphasis on Othello's anxious gaze. When contemplation of his own image cannot help him to respond to Iago's poisonous insinuations, he turns to Desdemona and looks at her. But this is no answer either, and he returns to the mirrored chamber as precipitously as he had left it, and looks again.

Again, both the face and his mirror image are presented to us obliquely and incompletely. As he gazes, a long shot of Desdemona is intercut, and then we see him turn from the mirror toward her. At this point the frame includes Othello's face, the mirror image of the back of his head, and, most important, the tiny image of Desdemona in the center of the mirror, an image so small that we need the previous full shot of her, which functions almost as an insert, to know how to read it (photo 4.16). (As in the crypt scene, what is shown in miniaturized reflection is also shown full size; what is seen in a mirror within the frame is also seen in the larger mirror of the screen.[10]) Othello leaves the chamber again, returns to her, and stares into her eyes, holding her face in his hands (photo 4.17). Thus twice her eyes replace the looking glass where he seeks an answer. He forsakes the mirror finally only when she appears there, reduced to a minuscule reflection. His own image cannot be seen clearly or steadily, and a tiny image of the other replaces it. The eyes of the beloved cannot be interpreted either, though he gazes into them twice: perhaps because they reflect the tiny image of the self. From this troubling interrogation of self and other, of face and mirror, Othello flees to the bedchamber, parting its curtains

Photo 4.16

Photo 4.17

as a forward tracking movement from the bed meets his matching and opposite movement into this intimate space. (The curtain parting was seen earlier, just before the married pair consummate their nuptials, and will be repeated just before the murder.) The sequence of the inquiring gaze is threefold: the mirror, the eyes of the beloved, the marriage bed that may have been betrayed. That the questioning gaze is finally directed at the bed is important, for, as in Edward Snow's brilliant critique of the play, Welles's Othello comes to confuse Desdemona's imagined adultery with his own sexual possession of her—this is "the bed she hath contaminated," "lust-stained" by his own knowledge of her as much as by Cassio's.[11]

Now follows a sequence in which Desdemona searches for Othello in the arched colonnades of the fortress. Crosscut tracking two-shots in deep focus convey unbridgeable emotional distance and create an extreme disproportion in scale between the two figures (photo 4.18; compare photo 4.16). Emotional distance is reciprocal: though it is only Othello whose mistrust has caused the breach, he appears as tiny and far away to her as she does to him.

The sequence of the gaze as it moves from the mirror to the eyes and then to the far-away figure of the beloved intimates an analogy between emotional mirroring and the perspectival principles that govern the representation of space. Desdemona enters the mirror at its vanishing point when Othello can find no solace there; because their mutual gaze cannot reassure him of her love, the sequence ends with her failure

Photo 4.18

to reestablish contact with him, as he recedes to the vanishing point of the screen image. The perspectival reduction of the visual image manifests the power of the gaze to order space and bridge distance, but it also indicates the limits of that power. Here the interplay of large and reduced images enacts the subtle reciprocities of marital intimacy, but it also points to their fragility and loss.

The eye is literally as well as figuratively a mirror. Welles seems to know this; his use of mirrors resembles the lover's game of finding one's image reflected in another's eyes. In contrast to Yutkevich and White, Welles is primarily concerned not with identity (who am I? whom do I see when I see my image in the mirror?) but with intimacy and with reciprocity of intersubjective experience. But for Welles's protagonists (Kane and "Black Irish" in *Lady from Shanghai* as well as Othello) the very things that make intersubjectivity possible—the relativity, symmetry, and mutuality of our views of each other—seem to demonstrate that there can be no love. In the eyes of another, even a lover, one's image nearly vanishes, reduced to a point. Space itself vanishes in linear perspective. If we are transcendent subjects in relation to projected space, as Baudry holds, so are other people, even that far-off other person who stands in our vanishing point and to whom we appear diminished. For Welles fantasies of omnipotence and transcendence are often associated with the power of the film medium. But he is also aware of the capacity of the medium to degrade and diminish and associates it, as here in *Othello*, with the failure of love.

There is a scene in Olivier's *Hamlet* that is superficially similar to the reverse-angle sequence in which Desdemona stalks Othello in the Welles film. The differences may help to bring out clearly the way Welles thematizes the cinematic medium. At one point in the Olivier film Ophelia looks down a long corridor to Hamlet, seated in a chair a hundred feet away.[12] A reverse-angle shot shows Hamlet looking back at her as she leaves the image to go into her chamber (photos 4.19, 4.20). Hamlet does not see that her departure is a response to her father's command and cannot rise to question what appears to be a rejection for he is psychologically bound to his lonely chair in the empty throne room, brood-

Photo 4.19   Photo 4.20

ing over his father's death and his mother's remarriage. This sequence was nicknamed "the longest-distance love scene on record" by Olivier and his associates. Although this sequence marks the failure of Hamlet's relationship with Ophelia, it is really a love scene in one sense because it conveys the love that was and could be if the lovers were not constrained, she by her father and he by his complex psychological and moral involvement with Claudius, Gertrude, and the memory of his father.

Camera distance and reverse-angle shots convey a painful sense of emotional distance, as in Welles's *Othello*. But in comparable scenes in Welles's work the alienation between lovers is felt as a property of space, as if emotional distance were a consequence of the geometric principles governing the diegesis. There are some stylistic differences: Welles tracks with the foreground figure rather than alternating between fixed camera positions, which lends a greater effect of instability and relativity. But the main differences between the two directors is that with Welles these reversals of point of view are seen in relation to a sequence in which connection is sought but not found: the inspection of the mirror, the appearance of the tiny image of the beloved in the mirror, the closing of the physical distance between the pair, the failure of the gaze into the beloved's eyes, the angry visit to the conjugal bed, and then the return of the tiny, distanced image of the other in the unreflected or "actual" space outside the mirror. The failure of connection thus moves outward from the mirror Othello looks into to the mirror (the film screen) we, as audience, see. The utter hopelessness of establishing connection to another expressed by these sequences is not uncommon in contemporary life, but fortunately it is not universal. Where such alienation is normative and indeed inevitable, however, is in watching a film. It *is* the case that we can have no response from the screen and that the properties of scale, projection, and linear perspective constitute that world as unreachable.

For both the protagonist and the viewer, then, the lesson of the mirrored gaze, as it is explored in Welles's *Othello*, is one of alienation and lovelessness:[13] Desdemona's beauty, which seemed to hold the promise of a rich and reliable satisfaction, is experienced as cold and denying. For this film Brabantio and Cassio, the father and the rival, do not figure prominently, nor do the Oedipal dynamics Othello's position between them implies. The problem is not jealousy or infidelity but the failure of trust the possibility of infidelity has given rise to. In many interpretations of *Othello* both on stage and in films, Othello is so blinded by jealousy that he cannot really look at Desdemona, and we sometimes have the feeling that if he could put his anger aside for a moment, he could see that his wife loves him. In this film Othello looks into Desdemona's eyes, but he has lost the hope or the faith that could animate their mutual gaze. His mistrust has made their interaction empty and unsatisfying, quite apart from the truth or falsehood of the charge of adultery.

Mothers

Another way of putting this is to say that the psychological issues that determine the tragic outcome here are maternal ones. It is not conflict with rivals or with internalized Oedipal guilt that plagues Welles's character; it is the failure of the maternal object to mirror and to satisfy. The terms in which such an emotional pattern might be described are various: Erikson might speak of a failure of basic trust; Klein, of envy of the withholding breast; Lacan, Winnicott, or Kohut, different as they are in other ways, might speak of maternal mirroring; Mahler and her followers, of incomplete separation from the mother. Whatever the terms, the issues are maternal and center not on guilt or conflict but on a basic insecurity in the unmirrored self.[14]

Because this is so, scenes from the play in which Oedipal conflict is most prominent, like the council scene, in which Othello makes his case against Desdemona's father are muted for Welles. In fact this scene is remarkably dull and empty in the film. Instead of the busy, complex, and exciting play of generational, racial, and gender conflicts that the scene offers and which are put into play in most productions, we find a serenely confident Othello, who appears not to notice the presence of anyone else in the chamber, filmed mostly in isolating medium shot or close-up. This is a grandiose Othello who does not so much come into conflict with others as fail to take note of them, especially to take note of them as separate, autonomous persons. He has invested himself solely in his wife, who plays the role of a self-object reflecting his grandiosity. When this function fails, when it is even called into question by the possibility of her infidelity, the character faces a terrible isolation and emptiness, which he reacts to with depression or rage.

The quasi-maternal treatment of Desdemona in the film is developed perhaps most strikingly in the brilliant interpretation of the encounter between Othello and Desdemona in 4.2. This comes after Othello's recall to Venice and his replacement as governor by Cassio (4.1), a scene in which he strikes Desdemona. Welles cuts Emilia's role in the confrontation between man and wife that follows, and with it much of the paranoid suspiciousness ("You have seen nothing then?" "This is a subtle whore, a closet lock and key of villainous secrets; And yet she'll kneel and pray; I have seen her do't" 4.1.121–23) and all of the histrionic pretense that Emilia is actually a procurer ("Some of your function, mistress," 4.1.27). The role Desdemona plays in Othello's need stands out more clearly: "Let me see your eyes; Look in my face" (25–26) here takes on the urgency of the earlier mirror/face sequence, though now Othello's placement in the foreground obscures Desdemona's face from us just at the moment when he looks into her eyes. Disappointed, he slumps into a seated depressive posture in a vast hall, alone until Desdemona, as in the earlier sequences, seeks him out again. The speech that begins "Had it pleased heaven to try me with affliction" (48–64) is spoken from the defeated, passive posture Othello has assumed and is intercut with shots of Desdemona standing near him. The lines she speaks in self-defense are cut, as is her assurance that if her father is the cause of Othello's dismissal, she is on her husband's side ("if you have lost him, I have lost him too," 46–47). She simply stands silent.

> alas, to make me
> The fixed figure for the time of scorn
> To point his slow, unmoving finger at!
> Yet I could bear that too, well, very well;
> But there, where I have garnered up my heart,
> Where either I must live or bear no life;
> The fountain from the which my current runs
> Or else dries up: to be discarded thence!

The maternal associations of these lines have often been noted.[15] The wife has replaced the mother in this image as the source of life itself, and a source that remains so intimately connected to the life of which she is the source that independent existence is compromised—this language evokes not merely the mother but the symbiotic mother of early childhood. Desdemona is alone in the image during this part of the speech. As it starts she is seen in medium shot from face to waist in a gown that falls loosely below the bodice. At the words "the fountain," Othello's hand comes into the image as he touches her just below the bust (photo 4.21). As his hand moves downward in the folds of the gown along her belly, the camera moves downward with his hand, so that her face disappears from the shot (photo 4.22). "The fountain from the which my current runs/Or else dries up": the gesture or caress begins below the breast and ends just below the genitals. At "dries up," the hand clutches the folds of the dress momentarily in a gesture of infantile dependence: Welles presents the failure of sexual connection as if it were a withholding of the breast, a failure of maternal nurture. And not of nurture only, but of a connection so close that he can trace the broken path of his defeat on her body.

Photo 4.21   Photo 4.22

The current of *his* life runs from the breast to the vagina of a woman.[16] The final lines of the speech suggest that his interpretation is right, that the "there" of the text is rightly thought of as *both* the site of maternal nurture and sexual property:

> But there, where I have garnered up my heart ...
> The fountain, from the which my current runs
> Or else dries up; to be discarded thence!
> Or keep it as a cestern for foul toads
> To knot and gender in!

"There," "thence," and "it" imply a stable, single referent that the speech does not actually provide: the heart or breast that is a fountain becomes a foul site of sexual coupling in the course of the passage. The speech intimates that sexual union is debasing and possessive and that it constitutes revenge for the failure of nurture. One can "keep" the polluted cistern (compare "or keep a corner in the thing I love for others' uses") of marital sexual property even when "discarded" from the maternal source of life and selfhood.[17]

The "cestern" of the speech has appeared earlier as a visual image, as we have seen, and the marriage bed, sullied with the sexual consummation of the marriage, with the imagined adultery and the actual murder, will be seen as its double in the film's powerful conclusion. At this point both Shakespeare's text and Welles's images suggest that sexual experience can evoke the trauma of maternal rejection and

110

that the anger of sexual "jealousy" has as its deepest object not the rival or the wife but the mother. The nuptial bed, which seems to offer the hope of restoring the mother-child dyad in all its magical perfection, thus becomes the place where the failure of that perfection is reexperienced and then revenged.

This sequence ends with the last attempt Othello makes to reestablish connection to Desdemona through his gaze, and gives us the closest shot (brow to lips) of her face as he looks at her (photo 4.23). But as before, beautiful as she is, how she looks back is determined by what she hears from him ("O thou weed!/That art so lovely fair and smells so sweet/That the sense aches at thee, wouldst thou had never been born!") and she is sad and distant even in extreme close-up[18]

The character Welles develops, supported by this complex visual design, is grandiose and enormously demanding; passive and enraged by turns. The violence that erupts at the close is not that of jealousy but of narcissistic rage, which knows no limits when the object in whom the protagonist's sense of self is uniquely invested fails him.[19]

Photo 4.23

The Barred Subject

The many barred or crossed images in the film are closely related to the mirror motif, in that they are often seen from both sides and, like mirror scenes, raise the question of whether what is on one side of a screen or barrier replicates or differs from what is on the other. Even more than mirrors, bars have the potential for blocking the flattering relationship Baudry posited between the screen image and the "transcendent subject" constituted by that image. Bars reveal the work of inscription, marking the screen as the barrier it is, dispelling the illusion that it is a window. And in their special relevance to the themes of social constraint, imprisonment, and slavery in *Othello*, they can be used to explore the political dimension of the play.

But not all barred images are used as Welles uses them. The Yutkevich *Othello* is in part a powerful historical allegory in which barred windows, grates, gates, and cages suggest that there are two sides of the Venetian mercantile order Othello serves: it can express itself in crude restraint or more subtly in architectural features that combine beauty and force. We see this in the stunning and beautiful shots of Desdemona looking out through the ornate wrought iron half-bars across her window (photo 4.24), in the cage Othello is placed in when he is "captured by the insolent foe" (photo 4.25), and in the contrasting images of scope and freedom held out by the treatment of Venetian mercantile adventure in the film—the spinning globe, the sea, the vast reaches of

Photo 4.24   Photo 4.25

Photo 4.26

shore at Cyprus controlled by Venetian power. But in Yutke-vich's heroic tragedy iron bars do not imprison lovers situated on the progressive side of the historical dialectic, and barriers, though real, are not dispiriting. Bondarchuk as Othello is actually at his most dashing and handsome best when caged, or when under the whip of the galley overseer.

For Liz White bars appear during Othello's epileptic fit. The chain that Othello wraps around his jaw to prevent injury during the fit, and the bars of the staircase he struggles up and through which we view his suffering, function as reminders of African-American oppression (photo 4.26).

In both these films the bars, though they often have a metonymic use extending beyond their function in the narrative, are essentially diegetic, part of the represented world, in contrast to Welles's insistent use of this motif to problematize of the relation of viewer to spectacle.

Several technical aspects of Welles's handling of this figure may help to distinguish what he does from Yutkevich and White:

1. Welles frequently moves the camera, tracking parallel to bars, sometimes at a raked angle, or tracking in. Examples: Othello's search for Desdemona, Roderigo's death (photos 4.27, 4.28).

2. He often gives the reverse angle so that, as with the mirror shots, the relation between outside and inside becomes problematic.

3. Low-key lighting often renders bars in silhouette, so that any interest they might have as aesthetic objects is denied. Silhouetting also contributes to the association between barriers (especially the cruelly spiked window grate of the bedchamber [photo 4.29] and the rows of pikes and other weapons shown frequently in the film, which are also often reduced to silhouette, so that their points or edges are emphasized [photo 4.30]).

4. Our view of characters is often partially occluded, our power to see all compromised by bars, gates, and even the slats of flooring under which Roderigo hides in the bathhouse.

All of these techniques help to "reveal the inscription of the filmwork." Further, they work to extend the metaphor of

Photo 4.27

Photo 4.28

Photo 4.29

Photo 4.30

Photo 4.31   Photo 4.32

imprisonment to that part of the world of the film that is nominally "outside" the bars, and beyond that to imply that we who see the tragic action are in some way implicated in and imprisoned by it.

An example from the crypt scene may be useful: as the brawl goes out of control there is one point at which the camera dollies rapidly past bars at a tilted angle, with fleeing soldiers seen as a blur on the far side of the bars (photo 4.31). This is followed by a shot with the camera placement and tilt angle reversed, so that we are given a fleeting glimpse *into* the bars, which we now understand is a dungeon. Our point of view had been that of the half-dressed, emaciated wretches who are momentarily revealed clutching the bars (photo 4.32). The point-of-view shot *followed* by a shot that reveals whose point of view we have been seeing from is frequent in the film. In one notable instance we see birds in a sky and tiny figures upside down on the tower parapets before we learn that we are looking through Othello's eyes as he regains consciousness after an epileptic seizure. In the scene in the crypt we discover simultaneously that the fortress in which Othello is attempting to enjoy the "fruits" of newly married bliss contains a loathsome prison, and that we have been sharing a view of the chaos below with its prisoners.[20]

In the opening minutes of the film the bodies of Othello and Desdemona are carried in solemn funeral procession while Iago is locked in a cage and hoisted up the tower wall to hang, presumably until dead, near the window of the fatal bedchamber (photo 4.33). These haunting images of Iago in

115

his cage linger over the rest of the film and announce the motif of caging and imprisonment. They also provide the film's first reversals of the expected relation between spectator and character. The sequence is rich and complex, and several examples must suffice:

1. The moment at which Iago is locked into the cage is rendered in two shots that appear continuous, with a crucial reversal of angle in the middle. First we see the cage from Iago's point of view, and the camera tracks almost into it with him, until all we see are a few of its bars in close-up. The bars appear to draw nearer to us rapidly in the same direction, but as details of the funeral procession that was formerly behind Iago can be seen through the bars, we realize we are still seeing the bars from Iago's view point but now from the inside as he pulls himself to them and looks out (photos 4.34, 4.35). The apparently continuous forward tracking that conceals or elides a 180-degree reversal is closely related to reverse-angle shots elsewhere in the film, especially the matching reverse-angle long shots that conclude the presentation of the emotional breach between Othello and Desdemona. Here the effect is not only to equate or compare the inside of the cage with the world outside but also, because the viewer shares Iago's point of view through a full but momentarily confusing reversal, to equate one side of the screen with the other.

2. Once Iago is in the cage, the viewer's relation to the spectacle is associated with his in yet another way. With him we watch the funeral procession through the crossed bars of the cage, rising and rotating slightly with him as his cage is hoisted up. Then we see the procession from another angle, another high angle but independent of Iago's point of view, and watch the funeral approach with a large cross borne in front of the mourners (photo 4.36). As this cross approaches, it repeats almost exactly the framing effect of the cage bars (photo 4.37; compare photo 4.35). This links the cross and the cage. The rituals of sanctification (including marriage) and the rituals of torture mirror each other.

There is no indication, as there is in Yutkevich, that the repression the film evokes is the expression of a particular society at a particular historical moment. Welles's concern is

Photo 4.33

Photo 4.34

Photo 4.35

Photo 4.36

Photo 4.37

not with Venetian mercantile power and its relation to the Renaissance Church but with a more general and unchallengeable pattern. The world of the film is cruelly repressive, cold, and violent, but the insistent implication of the barrier imagery—that we are inside this prison house world too—is that it cannot be changed. Othello, who seems to stand apart from it in his virtue and courage, is drawn in by the surfacing of a chilling mistrust within himself that echoes the cruelty of Iago and Iago's tormenters. In its political dimension the Welles *Othello* offers no way out. Othello's murder of Desdemona manifests a violence already present in the social world of the film from the opening shots, and neither he nor any other character is given a place in which to stand apart from the pattern of repression and oppose it.

This sense of helplessness extends to the film spectator, who, like Othello, is implicated in the evil world he observes. We have examined many of the visual strategies by which this implication is suggested. The final and perhaps most impressive instance of the inscription of the audience's gaze in the image on the screen occurs, I think, in the last shot, where Cassio closes the barred skylight. That moment can now be seen as the completion of the visual analogy between the marriage bed and the prison. It is also, I suggest, a concluding restatement of the mirror/eye motif. The shape of the oval, the placement of figures within it, and the low angle from which we see it all repeat elements of the scene in which the guards look down into the crypt and are mirrored in the water below. In addition, previous reversals throughout the film have prepared us to see the resemblance of the skylight to an eye, with miniature human figures reflected in its dark surface. It stands, in one sense, for the eye of Othello as it closes in death. In another sense, it is a mirror of the spectator's gaze, and the closing of the barred hatch is the final and most powerful example of the film's denial of the freedom of that gaze.[21]

Reflections on American Slavery: The Suppression of the Other

Othello's blackness does not count for much in Welles— at least not on the surface. He is played as very light-complexioned, not at all rude or exotic in speech or manner, and little emphasis is given to lines that evoke his strangeness or cultural alterity. Welles introduces the film with voice-over narration that presents the marriage with Desdemona as natural ("... it happened that he fell in love with a young and noble lady called Desdemona, who, drawn by his virtue, became equally enamored of him."). The complex process by which readers of Shakespeare come to know, in the course of the first act, how they are to receive this marriage is foreclosed by a liberal American presumption of nondifference that is followed through in text editing, characterization, and visual style. Yet such a position can be thought of as a suppression of racial difference, as we find it in Shakespeare and as we know it in the painful history of black oppression after the Renaissance. I want to suggest that the film's refusal of the text's racial contrasts (which are often stark and vicious), though well-intentioned, is disabling, a failure of recognition akin to Othello's own failure to recognize Desdemona as separate from and other than himself.

In the film's displacement of race, the caging of Iago is central. Welles's invention has several sources in the text: Iago will be punished and made to speak ("torments will ope your lips"); though Othello had been a slave in his youth, in the last scene of the play it is Iago who is referred to several times as a "slave," a "damned slave." In putting a white rather than a black man in a cage Welles may have been responding to these cues and making use of the accident that the Moroccan castle where much of the film was shot was equipped with such a device. But whatever the origin of the idea, it offers an image that is deeply resonant for Americans because of the history of black slavery and oppression. The reserve with which this "torment" is presented works with the racial reversal to create the sense of something left out—we see Iago hoisted up but nothing of the pain such a punishment entails; the torture is in the future.

Caging was a frequent punishment for rebellious slaves and was first described in American literature in a well-known passage in de Crevecoeur's eighteenth-century *Letters from an American Farmer*. Walking before dinner at the home of a slaveowner, de Crevecoeur was startled by a flock of birds surrounding a cage hung in a tree. Looking up, he "perceived a negro, suspended in the cage, and left there to expire."

I shudder when I recollect that the birds had already picked out his eyes, his cheekbones were bare; his arms had been attacked in several places, and his body seemed covered with a multitude of wounds. From the edges of the hollow sockets and from the lacerations with which he was disfigured, the blood slowly dropped and tinged the ground beneath ... I sought, though trembling, to relieve him as well as I could. A shell ready fixed to a pole, which had been used by some negroes, presented itself to me; filled it with water and with trembling hands I guided it to the quivering lips of the wretched sufferer. Urged by the irresistible power of thirst, he endeavoured to meet it as he instinctively guessed its approach by the noise it made in passing through the bars of the cage. "Tanké you whité man, tanké you, puté some poison and givé me." "How long have you been hanging there?" I asked him. "Two days, and me no die; the birds, the birds; aaah me!" Oppressed with the reflections which this shocking spectacle afforded me, I mustered strength enough to walk away, and soon reached the house at which I intended to dine.[22]

This letter, "Reflections on Negro Slavery," is a well-known text in the literature of protest against racial injustice, and it is possible that Welles read it. The point, however, is not to establish a specific source but to suggest what Welles leaves out, the kinds of expectations Welles's caging of Iago plays against, resists, and reverses. Being hung in a cage is, as de Crevecouer reminds us, an unspeakable torture. Welles ends the scene before any physical pain might occur, displacing the horror thus elided into images of effort, work, and solemn spectacle. Further, for Americans, torture this monstrous has special associations with the oppression of blacks.[23] This is so whether we think of de Crevecoeur, of the many echoes and repetitions of his story in later literature, or of the descriptions of lynchings and mutilations so prevalent in the accounts of black oppression in America. (A recent example is the treatment of the murder of Emmet Till in the television documentary, *Eyes on the Prize*.) Liz White's film uses this history in her treatment of Othello's epilepsy, where Yaphet Kotto's sightless, bulging eyes and horribly distorted features, though the result of illness, allude to the horrors of slavery.

Welles elides the pain; the scene is followed by the opening credits and the beginning of the story which Iago's punishment concludes. During the narrative the empty cage reappears at strategic moments, and its position outside the window of the fatal bedroom means that we never see that place without remembering the funeral and execution that will end the action. At the end of the film the motif of mirror reflection and that of the cage combine: as the final credits begin, we see an inverted image of the tower with the cage tiny in long shot reflected in the water of a Venetian canal. The image of the cage thus haunts the refined civilization that employs it. But this final shot of the cage brings us no closer to the suffering that will take place there.[24]

In contrast to de Crevecoeur, Welles's use of the image of the cage omits something else as well: the human contact between the horribly suffering victim and the chance witness to his fate. Despite "recoil" and "horror" de Crevecoeur is able to make a small gesture of relief.

And of course Iago is white and unspeakably vicious. The question is not whether Iago deserves relief but rather of the ways in which the film's reversals and displacements make such a gesture impossible. The substitution of the white villain for the caged slave is meant as an indictment of racism and parallels the verbal reversals of Welles's radio polemics of the period.[25] But an indictment so thorough, so wish-fulfilling in its revenge, perhaps carries with it confusion and denial: confusion between oppressors and oppressed, and denial of the experience and pain of others.

Concluding

Orson Welles's *Othello* offers a powerful and coherent interpretation of the play informed by a remarkably complex structure of visual imagery. This *Othello* is far more consistently bleak and despairing than is generally recognized, perhaps a good deal more than the play justifies, though

121

Welles's interpretation resonates with a number of contemporary readings, especially those of Edward Snow and Stanley Cavell. The psychological affinities of the film are with theories that stress the importance of maternal "mirroring" and the disastrous consequences of its failure.

Welles's art strives consistently to foreground the work of inscription, to disturb the mirror function of the screen as Baudry understands it, and to deflate the omnipotent position of the film spectator. In this sense his *Othello* is a critical text, one that makes us aware of its own methods and of the psychological and social contradictions that inform them. Welles's practice embodies, before the fact, Baudry's program for an adversarial cinema:

> Both specular tranquillity and the assurance of one's own identity collapse simultaneously with the revealing of the mechanism.[26]

This *Othello*, however, cannot go beyond its own revelations, its own collapses; it remains psychologically and politically caught in its own evocation of entrapment. Its politics are the liberal politics of equality. But equality is so complete here that, like the tragic narcissism of the protagonist, it is a denial of pain, of history, and of otherness. Society is a prison in Welles's film because social life—like marriage—cannot be imagined except as a mirror of the self.

Notes

1 Jean-Louis Baudry, "Ideological Effects of the Basic Cinematographic Apparatus," *Film Quarterly* 28, no. 2 (Winter 1974–75): 39–47.
2 Ibid., 42
3 Ibid., 43.
4 Ibid., 45.
5 Ibid., 45–46.
6 Ibid., 46.
7 The Stuart Burge film starring Laurence Olivier (U.K., 1966) will be omitted from discussion here. Although its interpretation of the play is relevant at a number of points to the issues discussed in this chapter, it is a work that was only lightly reconceived for the film medium and aimed to recreate the

magisterial National Theater production of 1964. Thus it does not offer as much material for visual analysis as the other films.

8   For a fuller account of this interesting film, see chapter 5.

9   See below, pp. 136–37 and photos 5.10–5.13.

10 There is a suggestion here that Desdemona's presence is evoked by Othello's gaze. This aspect of the shot will be important to recall when we discuss the similarity between this sequence and the process of maternal "mirroring" in psychoanalytic theory. In the murder scene Desdemona also appears to evoke Othello: she whispers his name and his face suddenly appears from the darkness, unexpectedly close to hers.

11 Edward A. Snow, "Sexual Anxiety and the Male Order of Things," *English Literary Renaissance* 10 (1980): 391.

12 See above, p. 44.

13 This is perhaps the place to note that Roderigo, whose passion for Desdemona is in many other ways a burlesque of Othello's, also has a mirror in the film. It is steamed over with mist from the Turkish bath that is the setting for his death scene; he fingers it absurdly and forlornly as he muses about Desdemona's "rejection" of him.

14 The literature on maternal mirroring is vast. I confine myself to several particularly resonant authorities: a psychoanalyst and a film theorist. See D. W. Winnicott, *Playing and Reality* (New York: Basic Books, 1971), chap. 9, "Mirror-Role of Mother and Family in Child Development," 111–18. "In individual emotional development the *precursor of the mirror is the mother's face* (p. 111); "What does the baby see when he or she looks at the mother's face? I am suggesting that, ordinarily, what the baby sees is himself or herself. In other words the mother is looking at the baby and *what she looks like is related to what she sees there*" (p. 112). "When the average girl studies her face in the mirror she is reassuring herself that the mother-image is there and that the mother can see her and that the mother is *en rapport* with her" (p. 113). Christian Metz, *The Imaginary Signifier: Psychoanalysis and the Cinema*, trans. Celia Britton et al. (Bloomington: University of Indiana Press, 1982) speak of how the "*other mirror*, the cinema screen" activates the Lacanian mirror stage, which "alienates man in his own reflection" and extends the "subterranean persistence of the exclusive relation to the mother" (p. 4). In cinema "the perceived is not really the object, it is its shade, its phantom, its double, its replica in a new kind of mirror" (p. 45). For Metz film is like a mirror except that the spectator's own body is never reflected in it (p. 45). Metz is drawing on Jacques Lacan, *Ecrits. A Selection*, ed. A. Sheridan (London: Tavistock, 1977), "The Mirror Stage," pp. 1–7.

15 As by Snow, "Sexual Anxiety," 404–5; Marianne Novy, *Love's Argument: Gender Relations in Shakespeare* (Chapel Hill: Uni-

versity of North Carolina Press, 1984), 132. Snow speaks of "maternal betrayal" here, whereas Novy's interpretation, like my own, sees the lines as expressive of a fantasy of symbiotic fusion with the mother. Stanley Cavell does not use the language of fusion, but in his interpretation of the play, too, Othello cannot accept Desdemona's separate existence. See *Disowning Knowledge in Six Plays of Shakespeare* (Cambridge: Cambridge University Press, 1987), chap. 3, "Othello and the Stake of the Other," 125–42. "Nothing could be more certain to Othello than that Desdemona exists; is flesh and blood; is separate from him; other. This is precisely the possibility that tortures him. The content of his torture *is* the premonition of the existence of another, hence of his own, his own as dependent, as partial" (p. 138).

16 Melanie Klein's 1956 lecture, "A Study of Envy and Gratitude," in *The Selected Melanie Klein*, ed. Juliet Mitchell (New York: Free Press, 1987), 211–29, is relevant to *Othello* at many points and provides an especially interesting gloss on Welles's interpretation of 4.2.: "What the envied breast has to offer is unconsciously felt as the prototype of creativeness, because the breast and the milk it gives is felt to be the source of life" (p. 219). "If it [i.e., envy of the breast] is strong ... hatred and anxieties are transferred to the female genital" (ibid.).

17 The confusion between self and other intimated by the passage may be felt in a syntax that reverses the subject-object relation implied by the paired verbs *discard* and *keep*. If Othello himself is what is "discarded," he is also what is "kept"—befouled but retained—by Desdemona. In Klein's terms the passage suggests the reintrojection of the object spoiled by envy: Othello identifies himself as a contaminated part or effluent of a maternal body.

18 The emphasis on the failure of the beloved's eyes to return an anxious gaze in a reassuring way may draw on Welles's memory of his dying mother's eyes. As Charles Higham retells Welles's description of his mother's last days, when Orson was nine years old, Beatrice Welles's eyes were a salient part of that memory:

> Beatrice spoke to him of her approaching end, quoting Shakespeare, her shining eyes appearing dark by the light of the candles on his birthday cake. Eyes that had been green were now almost black with suffering; her flesh was yellow and flabby with sickness. She told Orson to blow out all the candles on the cake, and as he did so, for there was no other light in the room, it became utterly dark. In this charged and symbolic way, she told him what death was, and he may never have recovered from that terrifying moment.

(*Orson Welles: The Rise and Fall of an American Genius* (New York: St. Martin's Press, 1985), 44.

19 See Heinz Kohut, "Thoughts on Narcissism and Narcissistic Rage," in *The Psychoanalytic Study of the Child* (New York: International Universities Press, 1973), 27: 360–400.

20 The world-as-prison motif may also be related to the psychological patterns that underlie the mirror images in the film. See especially Melanie Klein's discussion of the fantasy of being imprisoned *within the mother's body*, which she associates with the wish for revenge for the withholding of nourishment. *The Selected Melanie Klein*, 186 and notes.

21 One may contrast Welles's positioning of the spectator with Baudry's statement of the way in which the grandiose "eye" of the spectator is constituted in conventional film:

> If the eye which moves is no longer fettered by a body, by the laws of matter and time, if there are no more assignable limits to its displacement—conditions fulfilled by the possibility of shooting and of film—the world will not only be constituted by this eye, but for it. The movability of the camera seems to fulfill the most favorable condition for the manifestation of the transcendental subject.

Baudry, "Ideological Effects," 43.

22 Hector St.-J. de Crevecoeur, *Letters from an American Farmer* (New York: Dutton, 1971), 172–73.

23 See, for example, Marius Bewley, "The Cage and the Prairie: Two Notes on Symbolism," *Hudson Review* 10, no. 3 (1957): 405–8. "Horrible facts are self-purgating. The mind casts them out for its better health. But here the caged Negro acquires a symbolic status and will not be exorcised. The image of a caged man is not in itself capable of assaulting the imagination in this way, as Marlowe's Bajazet can prove" (p. 407).

24 The displacement of physical pain is consistent in the film. Othello never brandishes his sword as in so many other versions; we do not see him kill himself; the knife that kills Emilia and the one that kills Roderigo enter without our seeing them. And as we have seen, sharp edges and pointed barbs often frame the action but seldom appear *in* the action.

25 See Barbara Leaming, *Orson Welles* (New York: Viking, 1985), 329–30, citing a Welles radio speech:

> I was born a white man and until a colored man is a full citizen like me I haven't the leisure to enjoy the freedom that colored man risked his life to maintain for me. I don't own what I have until he owns an equal share of it. Until somebody beats me and blinds me, I am in his debt. And so I come to this microphone not as a radio dramatist (although it pays better), not as a commentator (although it's safer to be simply that). I come, in that boy's name, and in the name of all who in this land have no voice of their own. I come with a call to action. (p. 330)

Welles took courageous, self-risking stands on civil rights, and his efforts to put himself in the place of the oppressed and to speak for them are often moving. But can it be said that his attempts to speak for the pain of others were free of grandiose posturing, or that they did not displace and subtly disempower those he claimed to speak for?

26 Baudry, "Ideological Effects," 46.

"Haply for I Am Black": Liz White's Othello

Liz White's film of *Othello*,[1] the only film in this study never commercially released, is a remarkable example of independent black filmmaking and offers a powerful reading of Shakespeare's text in which the play's treatment of race is transformed by its reproduction within an all-black milieu. The film is entirely the work of black people—from director, cinematographer, and cast to technical crew. The story of how the film came to be made is closely interwoven with its approach to Shakespeare, for this is an *Othello* in which the historical experience of black Americans plays a central role.

The director began her career in the 1932 Broadway musical *Brown Sugar*, starring Canada Lee, and subsequently worked in the WPA Federal Negro Theater. In the following years, with parts for black actresses scarce and highly stereotyped in Hollywood and on the stage, White turned to work in wardrobe and stage managing, becoming a "star dresser" for Judy Holliday, Jennifer Jones, Lauren Bacall, and others. And she founded her own repertory company on Martha's Vineyard, the Shearer Summer Theater.

The Shearer estate, inherited from White's grandfather, a former slave who had settled in the religious community of Oak Bluffs after the Civil War, was her summer home as well as a resort for black vacationers. The Shearer company had been in existence for over a decade before their first attempt at Shakespeare, an *Othello* with substantially the same cast as the film, performed on the Vineyard in 1960 and 1961 and in

Harlem in 1960. The production drew excellent reviews, including a full-page article in the Manchester *Guardian* (December 15, 1960).

It was from this production that the idea of a film emerged. After some experimentation with a bulky sound camera and a Hollywood-style shooting schedule, White met Charles Dorkins, a prominent documentary filmmaker, winner of the Sidney Hillman and other international awards for his films of the war in Angola, and a happy collaboration began. Synchronized sound was sacrificed to flexibility and spontaneity. The use of a lighter Arriflex camera enabled Dorkins to follow the action over fairly rough terrain: on the beaches and cliffs at Gay Head, through woods, and up and down stairs in the indoor locations.

The film very successfully blends amateur, part-time, and fully professional talent. Most of the cast held other jobs (policeman, dentist, dressmaker, member of the Massachusetts legislature) and donated their time to the project over four summers, 1962–66. Some were also members of the family: Liz White herself plays Bianca (with a lively Jamaican accent); her son, Richard Dixon, plays Iago; and his wife, Audrey Dixon, Desdemona. Without pressing the significance of these off-screen ties too much, it is important to the film that it was made by a close-knit group of devoted friends and relations, that the director appears in the film as a locus of frank sexuality and *joie de vivre*, and that the villain and the victim were played by her son and daughter-in-law. Yaphet Kotto, who has since pursued a successful career in films (perhaps most notably in *Blue Collar* and *Alien*), plays Othello in his first film role. The film, whose final production costs exceeded $200,000, was financed personally by Liz White.

After its completion, White turned to other projects, and her *Othello* had to wait until 1980 to premiere at Howard University. Part of the reason for the delay was White's reluctance to market her *Othello* as an "art" film. In the wake of the so-called blaxploitation films of the 1970s, White tried to interest Warner Brothers and other studios in distributing the film, with no success. Since its first showing at Howard, White has shown *Othello* at a number of film festivals and museums, including the Museum of Modern Art, the Donnell Library, and the Dorothy Arzner International Film Festival at Harvard in 1986, but the film is still not available for general educational rental.

Shakespeare's *Othello*, of course, posits a contrast between Europeans and the Moorish (or "black") general who has married the daughter of a Venetian senator. In Liz White's version, though the "Venetians" are costumed in Renaissance dress, the ethnic contrast is construed differently. Yaphet Kotto (photo 5.1) plays Othello as a young, passionate, and emotionally sensitive African, while the rest of the cast, most of them New Yorkers and lighter in skin color, sustain a tone of urban American sophistication (photo 5.2). Othello, who claims at one point to be "of another race, another clime," only imperfectly understands the social world he has married into and in which he is a respected commander. Yet that world, though not free of skin color prejudice (Brabantio dismisses Othello at one point as a "blackamoor"), is not white, and therefore the contrast between the outsider and his new community is muted. The film everywhere softens the stark black/white conflicts of the text, both in language and in the portrayal of cultural dissonance, and this softening helps to make the stark last act viable as tragedy. Because Othello is ethnically close to the rest of the cast without really being one of them, the eruption of mistrust and rage is especially poignant: in rejecting Othello, the "Venetians" are rejecting a part of themselves, a link to their origins. In falling prey to suspicion, Othello too denies the claims of consanguinity and disavows a shared history.

The film was shot at Cobbleclose Farm, an elegant stone country mansion in the Gothic style in New Jersey (photo 5.3); in the pinewoods of Oak Bluffs (a former burial ground of Liz White's neighbors, the Wampanoag Indians); at the Shearer estate, which for generations had served as a resort for blacks when they were excluded elsewhere; and on the nearby beaches and cliffs of the Vineyard (photo 5.4). These are locations of striking beauty and function in the film in several important ways, isolating the characters from any sense of busy civic or military reality while emphasizing those promptings of the text (closely associated with Othello's

Photo 5.1

Photo 5.2

Photo 5.3

Photo 5.4

own idealizing imagination) that evoke a world, human and natural, of harmony, beauty, and peace. That the film was shot almost entirely in locations belonging to people of color is important in this connection. As with the casting, the complex interplay of self-reliance and response to exclusion that informs the social context of the production becomes part of the meaning of the film. Into this lovely and idyllic world, sequestered from white society, conflicts and self-negations whose origins lie in the absent white culture emerge—at first through Iago and then in Othello himself.

Kotto, whose ancestry is part Kikuyu and part Panamanian, is very dark, and the film at first privileges the authentic blackness he instances and its association with African origins. He wears either a plain white tunic open to the waist that displays his skin, or colorful tribal robes, and he is often accompanied by Zulu music on the soundtrack.

When Desdemona senses that she is losing Othello's trust, she exchanges her low-cut European gown for more modest, distinctly African clothing. The scenes that take place on the beach, notably the "temptation" scene, show Iago in loin-cloth. Much of the film was shot after midnight: rich brown skin tones contrasting with the impenetrable blackness of the background. Textual excisions and emendations support these choices: the worst of Iago's racial slurs are cut; the whiteness of Dian's visage is replaced by the brightness of the desert sand as a simile for Desdemona's "name." There is no aestheticized squeamishness about getting blood on alabaster statuary—no sense, which in the text even black Othello comes to share, that whiteness, in its association with moral virtue and religious rite, is sacrosanct. In this version "haply for I am black" is altered to "happily, I am black," and becomes a prideful assertion of identity and of a stricter sexual code than what Othello has discovered in "Venice."

The decision to celebrate African culture and to display and authenticate skin color was a deliberate choice on the director's part. In connection with that choice, White remembers her reaction to a moment in the Sergei Yutkevich *Othello* film (USSR, 1955) in which Sergei Bondarchuk dipped his hand in water at one point and some of his dark brown make-up came off. With work for black actors so scarce worldwide, this seemed a miscarriage not merely of realism but also of justice, and the experience contributed to White's desire to do an *Othello* film that would demonstrate black expertise and draw on black experience in its interpretation. In reviewing a print of the Yutkevich film, I found that Liz White was right about the shortcomings of the makeup work: in several places—especially in the dimly lit murder scene—Othello's color is inconsistent and uneven. But we never actually see it wash off. White may have conflated several scenes in her memory, for in a pair of matched sequences shot at a large fountain, Iago, not Othello, stirs the water with his hand, fragmenting his own image.[2] Later, when Othello begins to believe that Desdemona may despise him because he is "black," he rushes to the same fountain to ponder his self-image. But in this sequence the reflected face remains whole. Othello rejects the possibility that his color is the cause of Desdemona's supposed infidelity.

The opening sequence of White's *Othello* can be read as a response to this moment in the Soviet film, more complex and nuanced in its treatment of color. If White takes ethnic pride and the cultural pro-Africanism of the 1960s as her point of departure,[3] she explores ethnic questions in more complex and ambivalent ways as well. In the opening shot we see a young man briskly walking down a road, sidelit in total darkness, laden with five or six pieces of brightly colored baggage. This is Iago carrying Othello's "necessaries," and this way of introducing him establishes his isolation as well as his position as the general's manservant or valet. As he approaches the camera at an angle, there is a cut to a close-up of his hand in the water of a fountain, then a tilt up to his face as he begins his reproachful account of Othello's decision to promote Cassio: "but I, of whom his eyes had seen the proof ..." He seems to be weeping, tears staining his cheeks, as he stares downward at the water below the frame (photo 5.5). Unlike the comparable moment in the Yutkevich film, what Iago sees in the water is withheld from us. The tilt isolates the speaker from the object of his gaze; we don't know whether his words are addressed to a reflection or to the dark surface of the water, only that he is meditating on himself, a self devalued by an intimate betrayal. In the next moment Iago lifts a handful of water from the fountain and wets his face to wash off the dirt of the road. As he does so, his expression changes from pain at being passed over to wicked pleasure as he begins to plot Othello's downfall. This gesture retrospectively complicates our assessment of his feelings: we see him transforming pain into hatred but cannot now be sure that what we saw at first were real tears or Iago's simulation of tears using water splashed from the fountain before the shot began. Self-disclosure and masking merge; access to Iago's "real" feeling, like his reflection in the water, is barred from us—and perhaps from himself. "Knavery's plain face is never seen till used." As it casts doubt on the authenticity of Iago's self-presentation, however, the face-washing establishes authenticity of another kind: unlike Bondarchuk's, Richard Dixon's

Photo 5.5

Photo 5.6

ethnic representation can't be washed off. But that it cannot is not merely a cause for celebration, as perhaps it is in the case of Kotto's Othello. For Iago, here played as an American black and a servant, blackness has another set of associations besides beauty and the pride in origins the film so successfully invokes. Authenticity shades into indelibility; blackness is also the mark of oppression.

It is, further, the mark of a relationship Iago expects Othello to honor: the "proof" Othello's eyes have seen or should have seen is not only that of tested martial valor but also of personal affection and ethnic kinship. The passing over of Iago in this version is a crucial failure of sensitivity, a blind place in the relations between a confident African and his black American companion and subordinate. There is great warmth and intimacy between the two (photo 5.6), but it is taken for granted: Othello is unaware of his capacity to hurt, unconscious of Iago's ambivalence, and especially blind to the crushing effect of unfairness in matters of professional reward and promotion. Some recent criticism has stressed Iago's vulnerability and the importance of the promotion of Cassio in his motivation.[4] In this production that vulnerability is a prime motivation for the character; it is rendered more powerful by Iago's pain at having been treated inequitably by another man of color and by the paternal quality of the relationship that he considers betrayed. Othello's affection, even love for Iago is evident, but it is paternalistic and unconscious. He does not sense the pain or resentment Iago feels and cannot recognize the self-alienation at the center of Iago's personality. If we cannot know Iago fully, part of the reason, in this version, is that he has not been seen as he is by Othello.

Othello too is presented as an undervalued and unacknowledged son. This is conveyed by the film's boldest rearrangement of the text: all of Act I is cut, and the film begins in Cyprus (called merely "the island"), with Iago carrying Othello's luggage to his new quarters. The Venetian citizens and senate are gone, but much of the rest of the first act reappears as flashback or quotation later, so that the Oedipal and social mastery that the first act offers is always seen against the background of its tragic undoing. The most extended of these quotations takes place in a mirror scene in which Othello, having been shaken by Iago's manipulations, looks into the mirror and sees Brabantio there. Before examining this moment, however, we need to look more closely first at Iago's alienation and then at Othello's racial pride.

After the first sequence at the fountain, Iago's duplicitous scheming continues to be revealed to us most often in this location and in relation to darkness. The fountain is decorated with a single statue that emerges from its base, a white marble cherub often brightly illuminated in the foreground; Iago, standing behind it with his face only half visible in side lighting, discloses his plans to the camera (photos 5.7, 5.8). The strong side lighting is an insistent stylistic feature of Liz White's *Othello*, contributing much to the beauty of the film. But in its close association with Iago, side lighting is also

Photo 5.7   Photo 5.8

Photo 5.9

associated with deceit, with the masking of motives, and at the end conveys the power of the unconscious impulses that envelop Othello. As Roderigo comes under Iago's influence, he too is often filmed looking into the camera with only half of his face and plumed hat visible. Iago prepares his false self in darkness, and he makes it clear that he also regards Othello's blackness as a kind of mask. With Act I cut, it is Iago who delivers the council chamber speech, quoting it to Roderigo to instance Othello's bombast. "Most potent, grave, and reverend signiors," he intones as he drapes himself in the general's black cloak, drawing it across the lower part of his face (photo 5.9). At several points his clowning with the cloak obscures the image entirely, as Roderigo chuckles at this mocking recreation in which Othello's tale of his suffering, his enslavement, and his travels among the cannibals is presented as a self-serving display of mysterious otherness.

The film audience are not invited to share Iago's cynical view of Othello, however. Othello's dark color, African dress, and regal bearing are positives in the film, and he never uses them in the huckstering, manipulative way Iago suggests. He is a warm and generous man who loves his wife and appreciates his companions. Yet there is some hubris in the portrayal, an un-self-aware grandiosity that matches some portion of Iago's caricature, a suggestion that Othello's assertions of identity are insensitive to the self-doubt or deficiencies of others, especially in the problematic context of mixed birth and the memory of slavery. One sees a magnificent Othello but also a little bit of what Iago has found unbearable about him.

After the temptation scene, set on the beaches and cliffs of the Vineyard, where the open setting counterpoints the concealment of Iago's design, Othello retreats, shaken, to his chamber. We see him stand before the mirror in full shot dressed in African robes and fez. The sequence is quite complex, but its major features are

—The appearance in the mirror of Desdemona and Brabantio (photos 5.10, 5.11). They speak lines from Act I as Othello reviews the circumstances of his marriage in memory.

—Reaction shots of Othello intercut with shots of the mirror. As he listens, especially to Brabantio, he casts off his headwear and tribal robes in anger.

—An interrupted, gradual zoom-in to the mirror, so that by the end of the sequence the mirror frame is lost to sight and Othello's image in the mirror replaces his actual face (photos 5.12 and 5.13).

Like Edward Snow,[5] Liz White makes submission to the "displaced father's perspective" the crucial element in Othello's fall. In her version that surrender is the more impressive because the only time we see Brabantio is in this scene, remembered and apparently only now fully comprehended by his son-in-law. "Her father loved me, oft invited me ..." he muses, but the mirror shows us an angry and contemptuous light-skinned aristocrat wondering how his daughter could ever have run to the "sooty bosom of such a thing as thou." The final and crushing rejection is a word not in Shakespeare's text at this point, a cruel word, but one softened by obsolescence, standing in for the harsher racial epithets of contemporary speech: "You blackamoor!"

As in the text, the Oedipal and social resolution implied by the marriage and its acceptance by the duke breaks down, as Othello's ego cannot maintain its boundaries against paternal introjects. As in the text, the "displaced father's perspective" is also that of Iago, the unmirrored son. This is

Photo 5.10

Photo 5.11

Photo 5.12

Photo 5.13

emphasized in the film by the visual equation between Iago and an Othello who now sees himself as Iago wants him to. For the first time, during this sequence Othello, whose face has previously been evenly illuminated, is lit from the side and appears in the radically split, half-face presentation characteristic of Iago.

C. L. Barber and Richard Wheeler have recently attempted to describe Iago's project as a destruction of the image of an ideal father, and they stress Iago's complex mix of hostility and attachment to Othello. Iago's malice, in their view, is the negative expression of a longing for an adequate paternal presence.[6] But the absence of a strong and adequate image of the father in the play affects Othello as well as Iago. In classically Freudian terms paternal inadequacies hinder the identifications necessary for the dissolution of the male Oedipus complex. On this view, the crisis of *Othello* may be seen to issue from irresolvable Oedipal anxiety: the discovery of autonomous eros in Desdemona, in a context in which trust between men has broken down, elicits both the aestheticizing disavowals of the "alabaster" speech (5.2.4 ff.) and the violence of the murder.

A related dynamic is at work in White's *Othello*. The first night in "Cyprus" is staged as a kind of primal scene. In this production it is made tastefully clear that the "profit yet to come" between Othello and Desdemona actually arrives. When Othello is roused to attend to the "dreadful bell" of mutiny, he rises from a bed on which we see him and Desdemona lying asleep, evidently naked and partly covered by a sheet (photo 5.14). Just prior, Roderigo peers through a window at the pair and then opens the casement for a better look before Iago closes it again and leads him away, shaking his finger in mock reproach (photo 5.15). Later, as Iago explains to Othello the dubious practice of *amor purus* ("naked in bed, and not mean harm?"), he caresses a large-breasted naked African statue in Othello's chamber, and here too his teasing alludes, in tone and manner, to childhood interest in parental sexuality. The dangerously maternal overtones of Desdemona's affection and the complementary patterns of childlike need in Othello, frequently remarked by Snow and others, are part of the Liz White reading as well, particularly in the scene in which Desdemona attempts to bind Othello's troubled brow with the fatal handkerchief.

But the principal psychological interest of the film, as in the Barber-Wheeler interpretation, lies in the failure of father-son relationships, a failure that allows social and

Photo 5.14

Photo 5.15

Oedipal conflict apparently mastered by Othello at the outset to resurface in insane and murderous rage. That failure (Othello's insensitivity to Iago, Brabantio's rejection of Othello) is seen here as a surfacing of tragic potential in the relations between Americans of color and their African heritage, black fathers and sons. The turning point is in the mirror scene. After that Othello must recapitulate, through his illness and in his surrender to rage, the history of bondage and servitude he has ignored in Iago and the demonization projected onto "blackamoors" not only by Brabantio but by the white world, which, though absent from the casting, speaks in the comfortably acculturated voice of Brabantio in the mirror.

There are two epileptic fits in the film: the first, in Othello's chamber, triggered by the tactile earthiness of Iago's references to Desdemona's supposed infidelity with Cassio ("Lie with her, on her, what you will"). This ends with Iago straddling the Moor in triumph. Then there is a dissolve and we see Othello, evidently the next day, emerge from his room to an external staircase. At the bottom, Iago looks up to him smiling, holding his newly shined shoes. Othello descends the stairs, passes Iago without speaking, and in an agonizingly long sequence traverses the courtyard, enters another building in the complex, and struggles up several flights of stairs (photos 5.16, 5.17), fighting off an approaching fit before collapsing on a bed in a small isolated room in a corner tower. According to Liz White, Kotto, whose mother is a nurse, made a number of hospital visits to study actual seizures in preparation for this performance. The scene establishes our sympathy, in a way seldom exploited in stage productions, for a very ill and deeply suffering man and therefore makes certain kinds of compassionate identification possible in the last act. But the effect is more complex than "sympathy" would suggest. As Othello wraps his own gold chain round his chin, bites down on it, and struggles on his knees up the stairs, his personal suffering becomes a visual allusion to the chaining and confinement of slaves. And although we try to retain compassion for him, the final close-up of his chained mouth and sightless eyes (photo 5.18) is monstrous; it not only signifies his victimization but also

Photo 5.16

Photo 5.17

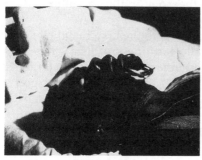

Photo 5.18

Photo 5.19

prefigures his destiny as an inhuman killer. The motif of divestment initiated in the mirror scene does not end with the casting off of African dress. It is extended, here and in the final sequences, almost to an effacement of humanity.

Yet the film finds ways of playing the end of *Othello* that grant the protagonist tragic dignity while giving full expression to outrage, not only at the loss of innocent life but at the masculine sexual obsessions that generate the crisis. The means by which this balance is effected include:

(1) *Lighting and camera distance.* The murder scene is filmed in dim blue light, mostly in full or long shot. The lighting contributes to the dehumanizing effect of the scene, and here we come closest to seeing the featureless black devil of racist projection. The "blackamoor" image of Iago's taunts to Brabantio is very much present in this scene (photo 5.19), yet the blue light makes us aware of the status of that image as a

stereotypical one, a consequence of skewed vision. The only close-ups in the sequence show us Othello as he becomes enraged and surrenders to the rage within him. The precise moment at which he loses control is rendered in a quick zoom to his face, which, in this lighting, has the effect of a sudden blackout.

(2) *A powerful Emilia, whose sanity and courage provide the last act with a moral center.* As in some recent feminist criticism,[7] Liz White's Emilia is a major—perhaps *the* major—character at the end. A crucial moment in White's presentation of her depends, like much else in the film, on a visual analogy. After discovering the murder, Emilia runs from the room, down the stairs, and turns to confront Othello (who is standing at the window of the bedchamber) from the cobbled courtyard below. This courtyard location, seen from this high angle, has been earlier established as the place of false accusation, rumor, and prurience, the place from which Iago calumniates Othello. This space is now appropriated for truth by a character whose frank sexuality and personal loyalty contrast with her husband, and whose integrity in the face of male power is heroic.

(3) *The creation of space for individual reflection on the action.* As the treatment of Emilia instances, White reverses the centripetal pattern of the text and, after the swift-paced murder, gets the characters away from one another so they can confront the significance of the action for themselves, rather than being gathered around the tragic loading of the bed. Emilia leaves the house. Othello is drawn from the bedchamber to the window of an adjoining room to hear her. The distance between them, and the evenly paced cutting between shots of Emilia from Othello's point of view and reaction of Othello from her point of view, constitute a visual dialogue in which Othello fully hears Emilia's story, accepts his guilt, and feels the unbearable weight of his misfortune. In contrast to the equally painful epilepsy sequence, he remains standing, elevated by the low angle of view and dignified by strong backlighting, used only once in the film. This is not quite tragic apotheosis, but is far indeed from the self-justification T. S. Eliot, Leavis, and their successors have found in these moments.

(4) *Intercutting.* After the murder, as Othello reenters the chamber where he will kill himself, White intercuts a series of flashbacks to moments of harmony, intimacy, and peace: brightly colored, fully illuminated outdoor shots evoking the beauty and warmth of human connection that has been destroyed.

(5) *Ellipsis.* In voice-over Othello recites his "speak of me as I am" speech by himself as he approaches the door of his room and flashbacks appear on the screen. As he opens the door, we glimpse a glint of light on the dagger he draws from under his robe, and the film ends with a freeze frame (photo 5.20). Cut are the final kiss, the suicide, and, with them, the final speech T. S. Eliot taught us to read as self-exoneration.

What the film achieves by these means is a division into good and bad not to be confused with the psychic split that takes place within Othello himself; a positive differentiation between the idealizing, almost paradisaical potentialities of the play and their dehumanizing miscarriage. Othello's monstrous revenge is not avoided or euphemized, but his grace and nobility survive his tragic error, as does his capacity for remorse and self-knowledge. Liz White's *Othello* is an altered version, to be sure (though her changes are less extensive than those Olivier made in *Hamlet*, or Welles in *Macbeth*). But it is a rich and rewarding interpretation and,

Photo 5.20

above all, one that captures the play's volatile mix of identification and repulsion. The film's historical subtext, its concern with black ambivalence toward African heritage, works finally to enrich the psychological and family dynamics of the play, foregrounding such issues as the fragility of self-esteem, the uneasy containment of masculine rage in marriage, and the consequences of inadequate connection between men. Perhaps the central insight of this fine film, and the principal use to which its cultural contrasts are put, concerns the precarious grounding of human selfhood in the mirror reflection of a kindred but alien Other. Although the film makes use throughout of the specific historical circumstances of its own production and thematizes them, it also suggests that Othello's tragedy has its source in more general patterns of misrecognition, and it implies that to withhold sympathy from Othello, even as he himself loses human feeling, is to repeat his tragic failure to recognize Iago.

Notes

1 I wish to thank Priscilla Forance of the Dorothy Arzner Festival and Churchill Films for introducing me to the filmmaker, and express my gratitude to Ms. White for discussing various aspects of the film's production with me and for her generous loan of a print of her film.

2 See above, p. 96 and photos 4.1–4.2.

3 For a useful, brief account of this cultural moment, see Robert Weisbord, *Ebony Kinship: Africa, Africans and the Afro-American* (Westport, CT: Greenwood Press, 1973), chap. 6: "Afro-America's African Renaissance."

4 Notably Madelon Gohlke, "'All that Is Spoke Is Marred': Language and Consciousness in *Othello*," *Women's Studies* 9 (1982): 157–76.

5 Edward A. Snow, "Sexual Anxiety and the Male Order of Things in *Othello*," *English Literary Renaissance* 10 (1980): 384–412.

6 *The Whole Journey: Shakespeare's Power of Development* (Berkeley and Los Angeles: University of California Press, 1986), 272–81.

7 Carol Thomas Neely, "Women and Men in *Othello*," chap. 3 in *Broken Nuptials in Shakespeare's Plays* (New Haven: Yale University Press, 1985), 105–35.

6

"Let Lips Do What Hands Do": Male Bonding, Eros, and Loss in Zeffirelli's Romeo and Juliet

Introduction

Romeo and Juliet has been the most commercially successful Shakespeare film to date, returning over $50 million on an initial investment of $1.5 million.[1] The popularity of the film is attributable, at least in part, to its sympathetic treatment of the erotic side of Romeo and Juliet's relationship. Released in 1968, the film participates in the general loosening of restrictions on the representation of sexuality on film of the period, and it seemed to endorse a number of the values of the international youth movement: pacifism, distrust of elders, and sexual liberation.

Romeo and Juliet was also, for its time, perhaps the most daring of all Shakespeare adaptations in its bringing to the surface homoerotic aspects of Shakespeare's art. In a review of the New York opening of the film, Renata Adler noted the "softly homosexual" mood of Zeffirelli's work.[2] More recently, Joseph Porter, in a scholarly study of Shakespeare's Mercutio and his antecedents and legacy, credits Zeffirelli with initiating a reversal in a long performance history in which homoeroticism, especially in the friendship between Romeo and Mercutio, had been suppressed.[3] The homoerotic side of the film seldom breaks the surface of the film or transgresses the limits of public taste, remaining as allusion, implication, subtext. Romeo and Juliet's wedding morning could be shown, in 1968, by brief and passionate embraces in the nude. Homosexual desire could not be directly represented in popular film at the same period but hovers at the edges of the film, structuring Zeffirelli's presentation of patriarchal violence, charging the separation of the heterosexual lovers with the pain of sundered male bonds, and inspiring the film's treatment of intimacy, trust, and self-reconstruction.

In preparation for a detailed reading of the film along these lines, I would like to look briefly at *Zeffirelli: The Autobiography of Franco Zeffirelli*. The life does not explain the art, but a review of several key incidents from Zeffirelli's early life may foster sensitivity to aspects of the film that have received insufficient attention.

Zeffirelli was an illegitimate son of Adelaide Garossi, a fashion designer, and Ottorino Corsi, a fabric merchant. Because both parents were married to others, the child was accepted by neither family and under such circumstances was given a name beginning with a letter of the alphabet predetermined by his date of birth, according to Florentine custom. In keeping with his mother's love for opera, the name chosen was "Zeffiretti" from the "little breezes" of Mozart's *Cosi fan tutte*. But the pen of a careless scribe transformed this airy word to Zeffirelli, an odd-sounding name to Italian ears; once registered, the mistake became permanent. A moral lapse and the failure of nurture that followed from it are reflected in a clerical error. "Nameless-ness" becomes a figure for the author's identification with the underprivileged and unknown, and later with the anonymous audiences of his popular opera and Shakespeare films. As the autobiography unfolds, the author's negotiation of a place for himself and his art comes to seem implicit in his name, and "Zeffirelli" comes to stand metonymically for the social anomaly of illegitimate birth, the importance of European high culture, the Italianness of opera, the gifts of accident and even ("the wind bloweth where it listeth") those of Grace.

Franco Zeffirelli's early life was unsettled in the extreme. He writes of having been raised by three mothers: the peasant nurse who cared for him until age two, his real mother, with whom he lived from two to six, and his Aunt Lide, who took him in when his mother died. All three "mothers" were affectionate, but "every time I offered love to one of these women I was forced to take it back and give it to another. . . . I still have difficulty trusting love when it is offered. This is something that has marked my entire life."[4] Many friendships are described in the autobiography, and the author's long-term relationship with Luchino Visconti is treated in detail, but Zeffirelli mentions being in love only once, when there was no possibility of success.[5]

If mothers changed unpredictably, father(s) too could be unreliable. Ottorino Corsi made occasional and disturbing visits during the period in which Zeffirelli lived with his mother. Corsi shared a bed with his mistress and his son on these occasions, and Franco watched, "fascinated," as his parents made love.[6] Zeffirelli's Aunt Lide also had a married lover, so in this third household of his childhood a man was also a sometime visitor.

Mourning for his mother's death and absence, grief for his own exclusion from the parental relationship when it was intermittently reconstituted, and the effort to find a place in a fragmented family leave their mark on Zeffirelli's work in film. Sometimes a connection to early experience is explicitly acknowledged, as in the case of *The Champ*, which Zeffirelli saw and was overwhelmed by just after his mother died. In the original film, starring Jackie Cooper, a young boy whose parents are separated loses his father. The film may have affected Zeffirelli deeply not only because of the loss of a parent but because of the close relationship between the boy and his father. In Zeffirelli's remake Ricky Schroeder all but replaces Faye Dunaway (the mother) in the life of an affectionate but hopelessly impulse-ridden father (Jon Voight). In *Endless Love* there is an astonishing scene in which a young couple have intercourse while the girl's mother watches in rapt wonder, "fascinated," and nearly destroyed by the experience. References to the primal scene, as well as troubled

147

family triangles, also appear, though more subtly, in *Romeo and Juliet*.[7]

Though mostly absent and then confusingly and vividly present, Ottorino Corsi had great affection for his son and provided for his education, insisting especially on English lessons from an early age. Zeffirelli's tutor, Mary O'Neill, frequently read Shakespeare aloud with Franco as part of her lesson. In adolescence Zeffirelli's link to British culture was strengthened when, fighting as an antifascist partisan in World War II, he formed close bonds with several older, artistically inclined English and American soldiers. These became mentors, confirming the future director in his developing sense of artistic vocation. After the war these friendships, memories of his English tutor, and Olivier's *Henry V* helped him to make a decisive break with his father.

Zeffirelli saw *Henry V* in September 1945 at the Odeon Theater in Florence at a time when his father, now more present in his life than in childhood, was putting pressure on him to study architecture and to belatedly assume the family name. Franco "felt that the moment had passed for the kind of father-son relationship he now wanted."[8] He had grown up as Franco Zeffirelli and had developed artistic talents that made a career in the theater a possibility. He wanted to make his own choice of career and keep what had become his own name. That choice was somehow bound up with a viewing of Olivier's film.

> The summer of 1945 dragged on in this atmosphere of uncertainty. Then in September, an event occurred which somehow cleared the air. The Entertainments National Service Association (ENSA) decided to bring over Laurence Olivier's film of *Henry V*.... Then the lights went down and that glorious film began. There was Olivier at the height of his powers and there were the English defending their honor—King Henry and all that wonderful cast of characters. Suddenly, I thought of Harry Keith, Jimmy, Sergeant Martin [war-time comrades], and I knew then what I was going to do. Architecture was not for me; it had to be the stage. I wanted to do something like the production I was witnessing.[9]

The passage shows Zeffirelli's remarkable capacity to draw sustenance from a cultural ideal, and suggests some of the ways in which this ideal offered an alternative to the losses, grief, and confusion of his relation to his actual parents in childhood. It also helps us to understand the unusual confidence concerning English culture that braced Zeffirelli's innovative direction of *Romeo and Juliet* at the Old Vic (1960), as well as his two Shakespearean films, *Taming of the Shrew* (1967) and *Romeo and Juliet* (1968).

Zeffirelli's wartime stories are marked by an insistent pattern of imagery and event in which dismemberment or the threat of dismemberment (specifically castration) is prominent. On one occasion Zeffirelli's antifascist opinions came to light at a military induction center, and he was forced to drop his pants while a gun was pointed at his genitals. Death seemed inevitable, but his father was summoned to vouch for him and subsequently revealed that the young man in charge, who had decided to spare Franco, was in fact his half-brother—another of Corsi's illegitimate sons.[10] On another, Zeffirelli was threatened with death by firing squad, this time by partisan troops who didn't believe he was one of their own, and was rescued by an older man who was apparently sexually attracted to him, a lover of theater and opera who took him home for the night.

> I woke up at dawn to find him beside me on the sofa, his shirt open, his shoes scattered on the floor, sound asleep. There, with his face hidden in a pillow and his arm around my waist, was the man who had saved my life and who had in the end been too ashamed to take the reward he desired.[11]

Perhaps one may also add to this type of story or vignette in the autobiography the visit Donald Downes and Zeffirelli paid to the mutilated corpse of Mussolini. Zeffirelli's memories of wartime violence are frequently linked in one way or another to sex, and the anxiety they provoke is often allayed by the aid or presence of an older man.

Sexual orientation becomes an explicit concern of the autobiography only when the author, in his first important "break" into the theatrical world of postwar Italy, became an assistant to Luchino Visconti. Their relationship was apparently sexual as well as professional, though Zeffirelli describes it with an odd mixture of candor and ellipsis.[12]

> Inevitably, my friends took it upon themselves to warn me of the dangers of my association with so notoriously volatile and talked-about a character. Politely but firmly I told them to spare me their advice, feeling with some justification that after two firing squads and the proximity of death on several other occasions, the attentions of a forty-year-old nobleman were hardly likely to prove uncontrollably dangerous.[13]

The sliding signification of the word "danger" creates an ambiguity: the passage can refer to the containment of the threat of a sexual connection, or it can refer to the containment, by sexualization, of a physical threat like those Zeffirelli had experienced in wartime, including threats of immediate death and castration.[14] As in Romeo and Juliet—Shakespeare's as well as Zeffirelli's—eros partly deflects and partly enacts a threatened violence.[15]

Shortly after meeting Visconti, Zeffirelli had a summer love affair with a woman (the only one mentioned in his book), and this too is discussed in relation to his entry into the theatrical world. When he later learned that the woman had become pregnant and had a miscarriage, he reflected that he had missed his "one chance" at married life.[16]

Zeffirelli's anecdotes are often weighted with the terror of symbolic or literal castration; his stories about his family often describe Oedipally resonant, triangular conflicts. Yet as Kohut and many others have suggested, Oedipal conflict and its attendant motifs of castration, disavowal, fetishization and the like can mask deeper and more fundamental fears concerning the self and its worth and coherence. One of the most interesting and moving stories in Zeffirelli illustrates this principle. Read one way, it clearly fits with the stories expressing castration anxiety. Looked at another way, it is a powerful parable of the self and its reconstruction. It is worth recounting in detail because some of its imagery reappears in the Romeo and Juliet film as a central visual pattern.

I am referring to the story of an anatomical drawing class and a visit to the morgue in early 1939. The context is the author's dawning awareness of the terrors of the imminent outbreak of war:

9 February, 1939: I didn't sleep well. I dreamt all night of the little white hand that we drew yesterday in our anatomy lesson.... It was such a fine, delicate hand and Professor Fazzari had adjusted the fingers in a natural position as if they were about to pluck a flower or a butterfly.... What troubled yet fascinated me was that the hand finished at the wrist where it had been cut. Professor Fazzari, perhaps aware of the gruesome effect a cut hand would have on us, had placed it so that it came out from a piece of light blue cloth. But I was constantly aware of the missing arm, indeed of the entire body that was supposed to be behind the hand and wasn't there. I was aware of the woman—or of the girl—to whom that hand had belonged, a person who was alive only a few hours before. Her face, her voice, alas, lost. As I was drawing I wasn't thinking of anything else. My mind was elsewhere when Professor Fazzari told me to change subjects so I asked him to let me try the hand again. I tried and tried, but I couldn't draw it. I was constantly getting the wrong proportions (and I have always been very good at drawing hands). It was as if I had gone back to elementary school. So the two hours went by wasting one sheet of paper after the other.

Even after the hand had been "sent back to the hospital to be joined to the rest of the body," Zeffirelli could not rest until he found out where it had gone and made a visit to the municipal morgue.

I wanted to see to what face and body that little hand had belonged.... In one simple coffin in a corner there was the body of a little girl, all alone, except for a very small old woman who was there to keep her company for the last hours. It must have been her grandmother. Seeing me looking with wide eyes at her granddaughter, she smiled at me and asked me if I knew her, knew her little girl. I nodded and said yes, I knew her very well. I couldn't take my eyes away from the hand that had now joined the other, both of them holding a little mother-of-pearl spray. The hand I had been trying to draw all the day before was now back with the other one.[17]

As he retells this story many years later, Zeffirelli understands it as a confused response to the fear of impending war. From a psychoanalytic point of view it may seem a response to adolescent sexual anxieties as well—perhaps even specifically to fears about masturbation and its feared punishment.[18] But it is important to note the reparative or restorative aspect of this story, the narrator's powerful wish to see the dismembered part in relation to a whole person, and the role he plays as compassionate fellow mourner in the morgue. The story begins with the author striving for mastery of an artistic skill—the drawing of the severed hand—and reaches beyond the given terms of the assignment to troubled but compassionate identification with the personal and social reality the artistic exercise implies.

It is interesting that the reassembly of the fragmented body—the *corps morcelé*, as it is called in Lacanian parlance—is held by Baudry and Metz as well as other recent film theorists to be the specific artistic and social project of realist cinema.[19] The claim is made that the unified point of view created by the camera organizes the disparate details of experience into a whole in a way that is analogous to the way in which, for the human infant, the mirror or the mother's mirroring response reflects a unified image of a self that would otherwise be experienced as fragmented, incoherent, in pieces. For such theorists this function relegates cinematic realism to the realm of the "imaginary," and they prefer the "knowledge effect" of a more Brechtian, alienating, and experimental film practice to what they consider the complicity of mainline cinema in the deceptions of bourgeois ideology. Zeffirelli is an enthusiastic and unrepentant cinematic realist, and although his emphasis on wholeness, on the restoration of the body, of the self, and of society are consonant with his political conservatism, it is also possible to trace his stylistic preferences to the psychological strategies by which he mastered the anxieties of his early life.

Patriarchy and Homosocial Desire in Zeffirelli's *Romeo and Juliet*

Patriarchal Structures

> The feud … is the primary tragic force in the play—not
> the feud as agent of fate, but the feud as an extreme
> and peculiar expression of patriarchal society, which
> Shakespeare shows to be tragically self-destructive. The
> feud is the deadly *rite de passage* that promotes masculinity
> at the price of life.   —Coppélia Kahn[20]

Although his work was independent of and earlier than the
generation of feminist Shakespeareans who have transformed our understanding of the play, Zeffirelli locates the
tragedy of *Romeo and Juliet* in the patriarchal values and
pressures of Shakespeare's "Verona," and especially in the
destructive workings of misogyny and its corollary, male fear
of intimacy with other men. Fathers rule in Shakespeare's
Romeo and Juliet, and their rule is sustained by an ideology
requiring young men to assert their masculinity by violence,
devalue women, and defensively distance themselves from
them. These tenets of patriarchal ideology are not merely
ground rules or taken-for-granted assumptions in the play:
we see them transmitted, taught, imposed, and resisted.
"Destiny" may seem to come from the heavens or from
nature, to "hang in the stars," but the play also points to its
status as a social construction. Zeffirelli is acutely sensitive to
ways in which gender ideology shapes the play, and his
visual design extends Shakespeare's critique.

"My Naked Weapon Is Out"

A central feature of the sex-gender system in place in
Shakespeare's text is the obsessive verbal equation of erect
penis and sword. "Me they shall feel while I am able to
stand" (1.1.27); "Draw thy tool" (1.1.31); "My naked weapon
is out" (1.1.33)—double meanings of this kind resonate
throughout the text, even, for example, in the nurse's

admonition to the sobbing Romeo to "stand if you be a man; for her sake rise and stand." In the film the young Capulets are equipped with obvious codpieces with bright stripes emphatically standing out from the pattern of their hose. They first appear in waist-down medium shot, hands on sword hilts; then a tilt-up shows their faces. Tybalt's entrance is even more emphatically phallic—first his feet, then a tilt that pauses abruptly at his crotch; then his face (photos 6.1, 6.2).

The camera does not merely replicate the verbal texture of anxious phallic wordplay: it also displays the men's bodies as objects of an engrossed, sensual appreciation. The young men are all trim and attractive (especially Tybalt, played by Michael York): they are presented, to use Laura Mulvey's useful phrase, "to-be-looked-at." The tilts that connect male genitality and aggression momentarily interrupt narrative, as analogous displays of women's bodies often do in mainstream film.[21]

The male body is "anatomized" here, seen in parts or as a whole at the discretion of a selective and intrusive camera. Extreme close-ups, rapid camera movements, and zooms show us parts of bodies, not only displaying them to the gaze but also, disquietingly, prefiguring the danger and terror of the street fights that quickly follow. In those fights the same techniques combine with unsteady hand-held camera work, the dust of the street, and a chaotic din of voices to convey a different but perhaps related fragmentation of the human image. The spectator cannot see exactly what is occurring; bodies appear in pieces even as the swords of the youths threaten to cut them into pieces. "Hie thee home, *fragments*" is Tybalt's manic boast, spoken in extreme close-up as he stabs Benvolio in the face, perhaps in the eye.

The motif of the body in pieces as it is used in the opening scenes of *Romeo and Juliet* draws attention to the phallic character of the feud, announces interest in men as objects of pleasure-giving display, and, once the brawl begins, works to dislodge the spectator from a position of control, involving him or her at close range in the anarchy of the street.

As in the text, Mercutio is the most enthusiastic of the phallic jokesters. His line about the "bawdy hand of the dial"

154

upon the "prick" of noon is delivered with an abusive "fuck you" gesture directed to the nurse (photo 6.3), and when he "stops in his tale [/tail]," he emphasizes the text's bawdy play on words by thrusting his fist through the crooked arm of his companion in another variant of the Italian "figs." His fatal encounter with Tybalt takes place when he is cooling off waist-deep in a fountain—at "here is my fiddlestick" his rapier point suddenly appears from beneath the water in phallic similtude (photo 6.4).

Romeo is an exception to this pattern, abstaining from sexual jokes. His dark doublet reaches below the waist to

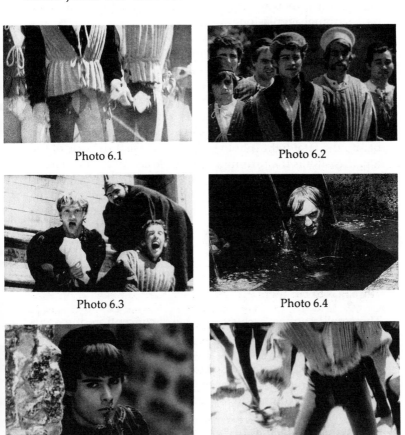

Photo 6.1

Photo 6.2

Photo 6.3

Photo 6.4

Photo 6.5

Photo 6.6

matching hose, displaying his figure but not his phallus. His entrance, in a long shot accompanied by a lyrical musical cue followed by lingering close-up, shows him carrying a mint blossom plucked on his morning walk, a delicate spike of tiny white florets (photo 6.5). This flower is the first of several to appear in close-ups of Romeo and (especially in the context of late 1960s antiwar sentiment) connotes nonaggressive, pacific masculinity. When in the later nude love scene Romeo is photographed only from behind, Zeffirelli uses the back view, perhaps required by the limitations on display of male genitals, to emphasize Romeo's beauty, tenderness, and vulnerability in ways that distinguish him from the male pack's frontal aggression.

There is only one moment—a crucial one—in which the film presents Romeo in terms of the sword/phallus metaphor. After the death of Mercutio, Romeo, unarmed, runs after Tybalt and pushes Mercutio's bloodied handkerchief into his face. Someone throws Romeo a sword, and there is a cut to a close-up of his midsection, juxtaposing the caught and extended rapier and the codpiece in a brief, still tableau before the fatal fight (photo 6.6). In the visual rhetoric of the film this shot is the turning point of the action. Romeo enters the feud at the moment when the penis-sword association is reasserted in a new, emphatic way. With rapier and phallus tightly framed in one shot, the analogy between them is more directly asserted than in the earlier puns,[22] and the tragic potential of the metaphor comes to the surface.

"Thy Tears Are Womanish": Virility as Defensive Misogyny

The corollary of an exclusively phallic conception of masculinity is the devaluation of women and of traits (like sensitivity, tenderness, emotionality) thought to be feminine. Misogyny and phallic assertion are connected from the first scene of the text, when the Capulets threaten to "thrust" the Montague women "to the wall," and to "cut off the heads of the maids" or their "maidenheads." Mercutio's insistent charge that Romeo has become feminized by his tenderness, pacifism, and love of women is another instance of the defensive construction of maleness as that which is not female.[23] But the values of the male cohort echo beyond their circle: for the friar and the nurse, tears in the male are "womanish," making Romeo an "unseemly woman in a seeming man" (3.3.110–13); locating him "in my mistress' case" (3.3.84) and calling forth the inevitable reference to anatomical destiny so deeply inscribed in the play: "Stand up, stand up, stand and you be a man" (3.3.88).

In the film Zeffirelli concentrates much of his critique of misogyny in the figure of Mercutio, studying the antifeminine obsession in one character almost as if it were an illness. The devaluation of women in the banter of the young men—especially allusions to rape and sexual assault—is cut from the speeches of the other youths and stands out clearly as a special preoccupation of Mercutio. For example, in the scene in which the nurse seeks Romeo with a message from Juliet (2.4), Mercutio uses the approach of the nurse as an occasion for an array of caricatures, obscene gestures, and physical assaults. When asked the time, he answers in a voice meant to mime the "gossip" of old women and pretends to be embroidering his handkerchief with an invisible needle,[24] then lowers his voice to a threatening growl and clenches his fist, thrusting it up under the handkerchief—the needleworking hand has become the "prick" of noon (photo 6.3). He lifts the nurse's skirts, crying "a bawd, a bawd" when she announces her wish to have some "conference" with Romeo, and falls backward, overcome with mock disgust, into the arms of his friends; he snatches the nurse's veil and parades around with it bunched to his chest in burlesque of women's breasts (photo 6.7). Finally he pushes her

Photo 6.7

157

over onto the stone steps of the piazza, to the delight of all of the young men except Romeo. This clowning is connected closely to his mockery of Romeo in the same scene: Romeo's courtship of Juliet is "French slop" and elicits a mimicry of Gallic effeminacy. Zeffirelli acknowledges and even exaggerates the misogynistic basis of Mercutio's wit, presenting it as a desperate attempt to retain Romeo's by keeping him loyal to the values of the male pack.

This is evident in the Queen Mab speech in 1.4 where Mercutio, in sharp contrast to performance tradition, is *not in control* of his copious verbal improvisations; he is manic and desperate; and as the tale-spinning proceeds, his emotional distress becomes disquietingly obvious to his friends. Amplifying his fantasy of Queen Mab, he runs ahead of the group in the torch-lit dark of the courtyard. His words begin to echo wildly as his auditors fall to concerned silence. At the same time, the misogynist content of the speech comes to be seen as the cause of his breakdown, as his angry gestures become more violent while he enacts Queen Mab's lessons for women:

> This is the hag, when maids lie on their backs,
> That presses them and learns them first to bear,
> Making them women of good carriage.
> This is she—

The ellipsis in the test is replaced in the film by repetition of the phrase "this is she," as Mercutio runs out of manic energy and realizes that he has become a spectacle. His final, sad "*this* is she" suggests a partial awareness that his inventiveness and improvisation mask an identification with the (devalued) women his discourse and antics invoke. He himself is Queen Mab: she arises from his own pain and confusion. Romeo's response—"thou talk'st of nothing"—is transformed in the film from a reproach to an expression of compassion and concern, as the foreheads of the young men touch in an intimate two-shot (photo 6.8). The moment is brief, and as the camera pulls back, a gap widens between the pair, and Mercutio is gently led out of the frame by other friends while looking back at Romeo (photo 6.9).

Photo 6.8

Photo 6.9

The scene thus balances a critique of misogyny with an empathic presentation of what, as psychic defense, the "wit" of the play so often denies or suppresses: tenderness and intimacy between men and sadness at the loss of loving connection.

Coming early, even before Romeo and Juliet have met, this scene establishes the severing of male bonds as the paradigm of loss and anguish in the film. It is the first in a series of painful partings (Mercutio's death, Romeo's banishment, Juliet's dismissal of the nurse, the tomb scene), and the later ones are linked to it by visual echo and allusion (see below, pp. 170–71, 173–74, 178–79).

Recently Joseph Porter has argued[25] that Shakespeare's Mercutio embodies a tradition in which phallicism, male bonding, and "antivenerealism" or the dispraise of heterosexual love were combined. According to Porter, the character of Mercutio instances Shakespeare's undefensive, nonjudgmental acceptance of homosexuality. In contrast, Porter finds that later Shakespeare moves toward prescriptive heterosexuality and that, in the preformance history of the play, Mercutio's challenge to heterosexist norms tends to get suppressed. For Porter Zeffirelli's film initiates a reversal, restoring to the friendship between Mercutio and Romeo its intimacy and erotic charge. Like Porter, I see the interplay of hetero- and homosexual eros as central to the play and the film, but in my view Zeffirelli's Mercutio is more confused and troubled than Porter's confident and fraternally phallic one and, despite his love for Romeo, is more deeply implicated in the misogyny and disavowals that structure the social world of the play.

Mercutio is ambivalent: as Porter argues, the play's homo-erotic allusions collect around him. In Zeffirelli's version he is played in terms that make him seem at times not merely Romeo's friend but his (former) lover, cast off when the latter opts for women. Yet Zeffirelli's Mercutio is also the locus for the film's most explicitly *anti*homosexual discourse. Mercutio expresses affection for and tenderness toward Romeo, but he also reacts violently to accusations or im-agined imputations by others of "unmanly" contact. In fact, it is the possibility of a homoerotic pun ("Mercutio, thou *consort'st* with Romeo," 3.1.45) that precipitates his challenge to Tybalt, and it is a related ambiguity in Romeo's speech that cues his fatal repetition of that challenge. Romeo's unaccountable professions of "love" for Tybalt (he has just married Tybalt's cousin) strike the young men as an elabo-rate joke, and Tybalt treats Romeo's warm handshake as a revolting taint to be washed off. Only Mercutio senses something unironic (and ignoble) in Romeo's gesture:

> Romeo: ... And so, good Capulet, which name I tender dearly as mine own, be satisfied.
> Merc. O calm, dishonorable, vile submission!

"Consort," "be satisfied" (compare "what satisfaction can'st thou have tonight," 2.2.126), and "submission" are all terms which, in this play's insistent linking of the terms of sex and swordplay, taint friendship and peacemaking with the stigma of the devalued feminine role in courtship, marriage, and sexual intercourse.[26]

"Fatal Loins": Oedipus and Exogamy in Verona

In the Freudian account rivalry between fathers and sons is normally resolved by identification (of son with father), substitution (of wife for mother), and deferral of the wish to enjoy the father's power and privileges. Whether psycho-logical or social pressures are more important in creating such a pattern, Oedipal family dynamics and patriarchal patterns of succession and exogamy would seem to reinforce and reflect each other.

In these terms the rigid separation between families in Shakespeare's Verona is merely an exaggerated instance of the boundaries required for the resolution of Oedipal tension and the redirection of the threat of incest outside the primary family. In its very rigidity the relation between the families suggests an obsessive concern or anxiety about who is part of one's family and who is not—the kind of anxiety the principle of exogamy and the prohibitions of incest exist to allay as well as provoke. The prologue speaks of the lovers taking their birth "from forth the fatal loins of these two foes" (pro. 5), as if there were only two parents rather than four and the antagonists were husband and wife; as if, that is, Romeo and Juliet were brother and sister.[27]

Images of the merger of the houses, as in the prologue, or in the irenic imaginings of the friar, coexist with the more obvious emphasis on their difference.

There are other indications that the feud has its origins in anxieties that arise within the family and which are projected outward onto the relations *between* the families. Shakespeare makes it clear that the feud was begun by the fathers, "bred of an airy word/By thee, old Capulet and Montague," and suggests that for the fathers (especially Capulet) the feud permits indulgence in fantasies of youthfulness, potency, and control at the expense of younger male rivals. The young men fight on behalf of the fathers ("Montague!" "Capulet!") in the streets, and the young people of both sexes *also* serve as vicarious representatives of their parents in courtship and erotic assertion.

Zeffirelli establishes several triangular relationships among characters that develop and explore this aspect of *Romeo and Juliet*.

"The earth hath swallowed all my hopes but she: she is the hopeful lady of my earth": Capulet, who can no longer manage a sword (his wife suggests that a crutch would be more appropriate) and for whom the day when he could tell a fair tale in a young lady's ear is "gone," looks to Juliet (and therefore to her husband) as the inheritor of his land, but also, more romantically, as the Petrarchan "lady" whose presence gives meaning to an empty world. Zeffirelli works out, in visual terms, Shakespearean indications that

Capulet's overinvestment in his daughter and her marriage possibilities compensates for a bad marriage. The first appearances of Juliet and Lady Capulet, which occur during Capulet's attempt to promote the marraige with Paris, are filmed from Capulet's point of view and are powerfully matched to convey the substitution of daughter for wife that underlies the scene. Capulet opens a window and shows Paris Juliet playing with her nurse (photo 6.10) as she stands at a window across a central courtyard ("woo her, gentle Paris"). When Paris pleads for haste ("younger than she are happy mothers made"), Capulet glances out the window to see his wife across the way. The shot is closely analogous to Juliet's introduction, but a quick zoom to Lady Capulet's unhappy and rejecting face accompanies Capulet's reply to Paris—"and too soon marred are those so early made"—and then the wife coldly closes the shutters to her husband's gaze (photo 6.11). This sequence shows us Juliet as her father sees her and as he has positioned her in relation to her mother; she has her own, more independent introduction shortly thereafter, when the nurse calls for her. "Juliet!" echoes through the palazzo as the camera shows the courtyard from the nurse's high-angle point of view, then with a quick tilt, pan, and zoom, finds Juliet's bright, responsive face ("Who calls?") shown close-up at a second-story window (photo 6.12) and tracks with her energetic run to find the nurse. This is the sequence in which Juliet's vitality and joy are first displayed, and this way of shooting it suggests that, when seen apart from her father's gaze, she comes alive. Though enmeshed in the triangular structures of feud and the generational displacements of patriarchal marriage brokerage, she seems to have the possibility of her own life, her own space.

For Capulet the marriage plans, the brawling of the young men in the streets, and the excitement of the masked dance are all means to share in or appropriate the energies of youth and to retain his daughter at least symbolically. But he is also part of another kind of triangle in the Zeffirelli film—a very direct competition with Tybalt for dominance in the family. This rivalry is textual: "Am I the master here or you?" is Capulet's recognition of the threat (1.5.78) to his dominance when Tybalt discovers Romeo in the Capulet house and wants to

Photo 6.10

Photo 6.11

Photo 6.12

confront him. His "flesh trembles" at the intimacy of the greeting Juliet gives the intruder, and a kind of cousinly jealousy seems appropriate and is often portrayed in production. To this Zeffirelli adds an even more directly Oedipal flirtation with Lady Capulet: he dances with her, they share a *sotto voce* confidence, she can coyly control his behavior when her husband cannot, and she reacts appreciatively to his presence. Thus an erotic coloration is added to the intergenerational conflict, and because Tybalt is the most aggressive of the young men and the principal sustainer of the feud, the roots of that feud are connected to a family dynamic in which the struggle for dominance among the males again, though in a different way, involves conflict for or over women.

The pattern created by Tybalt's jealous and angry reaction to Juliet's interest in Romeo is especially significant, for here, as with Tybalt's entry during the brawl, the overtly violent competition between men is shown in a way that alludes almost comically to an erotic alternative. The overt triangle is centered on Juliet, with Tybalt as stand-in for the forbidding Oedipal father. But another relationship is suggested by the substitution of Tybalt for Juliet at crucial moments during Romeo's meditation on the as-yet-unknown Juliet's beauty.

163

The sequence begins with a substitution of objects: Romeo is searching the faces of the guests looking for Rosaline, but as soon as he catches sight of her, Juliet—who is much shorter, much prettier, and dresses in a striking red gown—emerges dramatically from behind her in the dance. A change in the music and a forward motion of the camera emphasize her replacement of Romeo's former "love." An alternation between close-ups of Romeo and Juliet follows as Romeo reacts to his first sight of Olivia Hussey's Juliet; at first unaware of his gaze, she notices him, appreciates his attention, and returns his glance (photos 6.13, 6.14). But at two points of particularly hyperbolic praise ("so shows a snowy dove, trooping with crows/As yonder lady o'er her fellows shows," 1.5.48–49; "I ne'er saw true beauty till this night," 1.5.53) Tybalt replaces Juliet in a medium-to-close shot, recognizes Romeo, and bites his lip in anger (photo 6.15). Part of the effect is to establish the temporal ironies of tragic nemesis: even before the lovers have actually met, the conflict that will lead to Romeo's banishment and then to the death of the lovers is set in motion. But Tybalt, gorgeously costumed as a Renaissance prince, is striking enough so that the unintended reference to his beauty is not only ironic and funny but also appropriate. These cuts, like the matched

Photo 6.13

Photo 6.14

Photo 6.15

164

point-of-view shots of Juliet and Lady Capulet earlier, intimate a substitution. Romeo is unaware of Tybalt's angry gaze and, of course, also of the shot-countershot editing that makes his lover's discourse apply also to Tybalt. Along with the irony and comedy, then, we may perceive a kind of homoerotic utopian impulse that hovers beyond the characters' awareness: the sequence divides attention between male and female beauty as it does elsewhere and suggests, as do the first shots of Tybalt in the film, that if this attractive and dangerous young man could be brought wholly under the power of an erotic gaze, his violence would be neutralized.[28]

"[Men's] Eyes Were Made to Look": Visual Pleasure and the (Bi-)Sexual Gaze

The gaze in the ball sequence thus resists and contests the patriarchal rule of the Capulet household. Aligning itself initially with the well-known conventions of romantic film, it admits the play of unconscious and unconventional alignments, provokes watching in unexpected modes, and registers subtle shifts in spectator placement in regard to sex and gender. Zeffirelli's camera involves us in fresh and inventive ways as watchers of male as well as female beauty; in addition, it uses and revises cinematic traditions governing the gaze to underscore Shakespeare's treatment of Juliet as an active, desiring subject.

At the Capulet ball and on the balcony Juliet is the more active of the two lovers, and her desire, expressed as gaze, enhances her presentation as self-directed and self-possessed. At first meeting Romeo and Juliet *exchange* looks; when they lose eye contact they search for each other, moving and looking in shots that are carefully matched. When they touch and kiss, each is presented to the spectator in close-up. In the balcony scene too looks alternate, and although Romeo assertively climbs up to the parapet to be with her, once he is there Juliet dominates, taking the lead and setting the pace both verbally and physically. As in Zeffirelli's stage production,[29] the parapet provides a runway for an energetic interpretation, a space in which Juliet displays her confident balancing of personal integrity and self-giving, of sexual desire and its deferral not only by what she says but by her control, almost stage direction of Romeo and her firm negotiation of distance from and closeness to him.

This is not to say that conventional gender roles are abandoned in regard to either physical activity or gaze. If Juliet takes control after Romeo's approaches, he remains the initiator, and there are differences in the gaze pattern to note. Romeo's extended, gazing meditation at the ball initiates the contact between the two—she returns the look at first directly, then more demurely and certainly more briefly— and, at the moment of first eye contact, *Romeo is half-masked.*[30] He wears a particularly attractive, unthreatening, feline mask which obscures only the top half of his face and through which we can always see his bright eyes (photo 6.13), but it grants him the privilege of looking without being fully seen. Romeo also remains hidden in the opening moments of the balcony sequence while Juliet speaks her flattering revery of him, with its fantasied exchange of his name for her "self" ("And for that name which is no part of thee, take all myself"). As she joyfully wraps herself in her own arms, imagining them to be Romeo's, he is looking at her in her low-cut, tight nightdress (photos 6.16–6.18); again, the scene begins with a privileged, protected, incipiently voyeuristic positioning of the male. However, as at the ball, this conventional arrangement of male gaze and female "to be looked at-ness" yields to a more complex pattern. It is complicated by the striking day-for-night close-ups of Romeo, which function not only as reaction shots but as displays of *his* youthful beauty and by alternation of point of view once Romeo reveals his presence. As in the text, Juliet is more conscious of sex than Romeo: the prospect of "satisfaction" Romeo proposes alarms her because she cannot dismiss from the word connotations of sexual consummation, whereas Romeo has in mind merely an exchange of faithful vows.

Shakespeare's Juliet has a generous measure of robust sexual energy. It is she who has "bought the mansion of a love,/But not possess'd it" (3.2.26–27), who thinks of her wedding night as losing a "winning match,/Play'd for a pair

Photo 6.16 Photo 6.17

Photo 6.18

of stainless maidenhoods" (3.2.12–13), and who asks the fiery-footed steeds of day to "gallop apace" (3.2.1), bringing in the night upon whose "wings" Romeo will lie, "whiter than new snow upon a raven's back" (3.2.18). And if, with some commentators, we hear the almost mandatory Elizabethan pun on dying as a reference to orgasm, she imagines their climax as a kind of explosion, showering "little stars" (3.2.22) upon the "face of heaven." As in the case of most of the longer speeches, Zeffirelli substitutes visual correlatives, translating Juliet's self-assertion in love into physical activity and, using film's special capacity for representing this aspect of human interaction, by emphasizing her desiring look. Her gaze, together with her quick wit and energetic physical command of herself and of the scenes in which she appears, implies parity between genders, as Zeffirelli moves away from the conventions of mainstream cinema and toward a more reciprocal and unpredictable treatment of sexuality.

In the film's central love scene the camera's interest in male beauty—established independently of Juliet earlier in the film—and Juliet's loving gaze are brought together. The scene begins with a close-up of Romeo and Juliet sleeping, their heads close together on a pillow, as sacred-sounding organ music plays (photo 6.19). The shot looks like a freeze

Photo 6.19   Photo 6.20

frame. Then the camera pulls back and pans slowly over Romeo's nude body. He is lying on his stomach in a prostrate pose, at once "artistic" and erotic, his right arm embracing Juliet (photo 6.20). She is covered to below the breasts by the sheets and further covered from the look of the spectator by Romeo's arm. At the point at which Romeo is fully seen, there is a cut back to the original two-shot, and we see Romeo wake beside Juliet (who remains asleep), arise sleepily and go to the window, the camera partly repeating its discovering movement back and over the bed, then following him to the window until he is seen in three-quarter shot from the rear standing at the casement (photo 6.21). This is followed by a cut to the original camera position a little farther back from the bed (photo 6.22). We see Juliet wake, cover what shows of her breast with the sheet, glance over to where we know Romeo to be, and smile (photo 6.23). The first point-of-view shot in the sequence follows, a shot identical to the rearview three-quarter shot of Romeo while Juliet was still sleeping. That it is exactly her point of view is confirmed by a backtracking movement that brings the pair together in the frame (photo 6.24). As Romeo falls back on the bed struggling into his pants, the backward movement of the camera reveals Juliet still looking appreciatively at his body. (Her line of sight is shown here, though now, because we see her in profile at medium distance, her reaction or response is not emphasized.)

Thus the film's only nude sequence emphasizes the male as object and is shot *a tergo* from a point of view first closely associated with and then identical to Juliet's. By contrast with this first part of the scene, the shots that follow, in which the lovers proceed to embrace on the bed and then part, are briskly edited. Juliet is briefly seen with bare breasts, but she is in rapid motion, and the narrative urgency of Romeo's flight competes with our fleeting sight of her body: there is no lingering "to be looked at-ness." Romeo is on screen naked for more than seventeen seconds in three shots, during which he is the sole object of attention: Juliet's nude "scene" lasts less than a second.

Yet it is not enough to say that Zeffirelli offers a feminine gaze for our identification that is analogous to the customary male look at the female as object of sexual desire. The gaze here is and is not Juliet's; again, as in Romeo's praise of beauty which the camera diverts from Juliet to Tybalt earlier, we have a use of the gaze that invokes a literally unconscious dimension. Juliet is asleep during the first two nude shots of Romeo, and her unconsciousness means that what we see, though anchored in and representative of her experience of Romeo, is also partly independent of her. This gaze draws for its effect on our memory of Tybalt's entrance, of the lovely introduction of Romeo as he is seen by Benvolio, of the close-ups of the singer at the ball, of the moments of

Photo 6.21

Photo 6.22

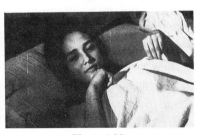

Photo 6.23

Photo 6.24

tenderness between Romeo and Mercutio, and of the powerful undercurrent of *macho* denial of feeling between men in
the text which Zeffirelli has conditioned us to read as
disavowal. Although Romeo is the only male present in the
scene, the camera work creates a homoerotic connection even
as it portrays heterosexual love. The scene evokes earlier
instances of male bonding in the film and can be read as a
surfacing of the erotic potential of those moments.

Making use of heterosexual film conventions governing
the deployment of the male gaze, as well as on his own
contrary or complementary presentation of men as *objects* of
an admiring gaze, Zeffirelli creates a spectatorial position
neither simply male or female nor simply identificatory or
detached. The bisexual identifications suggested by the
camera position also work to inscribe a sense of loss in the
presentation of heterosexual intimacy.

Because the narrative point of view has by this point in the
film acquired homoerotic associations through its treatment
of the male body and of Mercutio's grief at the loss of Romeo,
and because the scene itself restates the homoerotic theme by
its treatment of the male nude, the *aubade* offers a rich
interplay of sexual perspectives and of the feelings that have
come to be associated with those perspectives. The lovers'
pleasure and passion is presented in a way that evokes the
pain of sundered male bonds that has made it possible and
perhaps at a less conscious level, the pain and longing of
childhood exclusion from the primal scene.[31]

It is possible to understand this approach to the love scene
as a "passive" Oedipal triangle in which the camera replaces
the woman in an erotic configuration with the man. A related
pattern shows up in several of Zeffirelli's other films: as in
Endless Love and *Otello* it is the nude body of a young man
that receives most attention.[32] These scenes recall the remarkably candid passages in Zeffirelli's *Autobiography* in which
he describes watching "fascinated" as his parents had sexual
intercourse.

But although Freudian terms seem helpful in understanding this scene, they may belie the delicacy of Zeffirelli's
mediating intrusion. As in the *Autobiography*, the film's
passive Oedipal dynamics, its evocation of homosexual eros

at the site or scene of heterosexual intercourse, convey a sense of loss and even renunciation.[33] The homoerotic or androgynous positioning of the spectator works to inscribe the pain of loss and separation even in the film's most intimate moments. Our identification with the lovers is balanced by awareness of their privacy, of our exclusion from it, and by the memory of the first painful scene of parting in the film, that between Romeo and Mercutio. The sense of exclusion of the spectator, of Mercutio (perhaps also of the direct representation of homosexual lovemaking even in the "liberated" climate of 1968) works to enrich the feeling of loss in the scene, as the married couple awake not only to the memory of sexual pleasure but to the impending reality of exile.

Private Spaces and the "Public Haunt of Men"

The aubade or love scene takes place in Juliet's bedroom in the Capulet house, and the newly married couple enjoys privacy that is reasonably secure until the household awakes. The sense of intimate or private space that is conveyed here builds on earlier sequences in which Zeffirelli creates moments of intensely focused personal interaction in the midst of a busy and threatening social world. Using close-ups, extreme close-ups, and selective shallow focus Zeffirelli transforms the parting of Mercutio and Romeo before the ball, the meeting of Romeo and Juliet that follows, and the dying moments of Mercutio into intimate personal exchanges, private moments never wholly removed from the bustle and danger of "Verona" and its prevailing ethos of Oedipal rivalry, violence, and forced growth.

The first of these has been discussed already: the torch-lit nighttime setting, the alternation of long shots and tight close-up two-shots of Mercutio and Romeo help to create the important sense of intimacy in the friendship and convey the depth of Romeo's concern for this friend's distress at the moment when a decisive parting is about to occur.

The use of shallow focus and rapid pans at the Capulet ball also creates a sense of privacy in a large, public space. The ordered circles of the dance and of the listeners gathered around the singer serve not only to establish the space within which Romeo and Juliet meet but also provide a visual image of the larger social world into which the love and marriage of the couple *might* be integrated but for the feud. Long shots of the hall in which one can see the pattern of the dance contrast with extemely tight close-ups of the lovers (photos 6.25, 6.26). Rapid, shallow-focus pans indicate how they search only for each other, maintaining intimate contact through the gaze as the other participants in the swirling dance merge in a blur.[34]

Later, when Mercutio and Tybalt duel, similar techniques echo the masked ball scene. Here the private, secret moment that takes place in the larger space gives Mercutio his death wound. As at the ball, a large circle forms within which the two principals perform a more private action while appearing to conform to the expectations of the group (photo 6.27). In the Capulet house Romeo and Juliet transact their very private and illicit contact in the midst of the dance and the song, and without breaking the surface of the highly patterned social occasion. Only Tybalt notices, and he is forced by Capulet into acting as if nothing had happened. In the duel Mercutio and Tybalt appear to all to be fencing in jest, with no more than a "scratch" at stake; as the wounded Mercutio staggers and begs for aid, all believe he is carrying on the joke, even when he lies dead. Only when Romeo removes the handkerchief Mercutio clutches to his hidden wound is the truth revealed. In this scene, as at the ball, there is intercutting between the duelists in close-up and the circle of onlookers. The audience is closer to both Tybalt and Mercutio than are the spectators in the street; we can see fear

Photo 6.25

Photo 6.26

Photo 6.27

and confusion beneath the brave and joking pretense of their duel. As the fight enters its fatal phase, the group moves into the central square ("the public haunt of men"). Selective focus, rapid pans, and zooms make the film audience privy to the danger. The death stroke is presented in a rapid zoom to Tybalt's bloody sword point, which the young men watching the fight do not see, followed by Tybalt's reaction (photo 6.28). The fatal moment is unperceived even by Romeo and is followed by a kind of reprise of the parting before the Capulet ball, with Romeo and Mercutio in tight two-shot and the others presumably unable to hear his whispered reproach—"Why the dev'l came you between us? I was hurt under your arm" (3.1.102–3; photo 6.29). This way of presenting the death of Mercutio balances, a last time, the two sides of his character as Zeffirelli portrays it—both his capacity for intimacy and his inconsistent but obsessive belief that tenderness between men is shameful and even harmful. Here the action may partly confirm his opinion: he experiences Romeo's touch rather than Tybalt's as the fatal contact.

Through these stylistic analogies the private spaces in which lovers meet or duelists fight are equated: each is beyond the control of the encirling social group. The analogy also works to inscribe the trace of the fatal danger of the street in the film's most private and secluded moments in Juliet's bedroom. The film superbly evokes both sexual privacy and civic publicity, but in Zeffirelli's visual design these two realms are disjunctive. The movement that relates private moments to the larger social realities of state and family is always incomplete; the lover's privacy cannot finally be reintegrated into the patriarchal violence of feud-

Photo 6.28   Photo 6.29

ing Verona, despite the friar's best hopes, and the secret marriage is as fatal as the obscured thrust of Tybalt's rapier.[35]

"What Hands Do": The Fragmented Body and the Restoration of the Self

As focus and camera distance are essential to the interplay of private and public in Zefirelli's film, so is the emphasis on human bodies in parts (eyes, hands, legs, codpieces) and wholes. Zeffirelli's camera engages in a kind of erotic analysis or anatomy and a corresponding synthesis, selecting one part then another of the human body for pleasure-giving display, then relating parts to wholes. This corresponds to the breaking down of social units into private spaces previously discussed, and as in the case of that figure, the movement from intimate part to whole is contested between eros and violence. I have noted instances of this from the brawl scenes, in which phallic violence threatens actual dismemberment (Tybalt's "fragments").

But at the level of the body—or of two bodies—the synthetic work of the camera is more powerful and lasting than it is in the social or political dimension and intimates the capacity of the threatened self to reconstitute itself in the face of loss, separation, and hostile opposition.

In ways that recall Zeffirelli's journal entry recording his search for a young girl's hand in the Florence morgue, the human hand as visual image and repeated motif becomes the film's symbol for such recuperation. Hands, of course, acquire many other associations in the course of the film, and I want to look at some of these before discussing Zeffirelli's

174

culminating treatment of Juliet's hand in the Capulet monument.

Often photographed in frame-filling close-up, hands are associated (predictably enough) with contact between the lovers. Their first emphatic use, however, is as an index of the demanding requirements of social form. At the Capulet ball Juliet's initiation—first into the complex pattern of the dance and then into the ritual of courtship—is presented largely as a matter of using the hands. Zeffirelli has chosen several dances with complex hand gestures and shows the young people, especially Juliet, as slightly inept or off the beat with their gestures: at one point Juliet stops and tries out various possibilities, not getting any of them quite right. For the second dance (the Moresca) the dancers put on wrist-tambourines, and Juliet has to learn to wear and use them. Romeo and Juliet's mutual attraction is expressed first as an exchange of glances and then, when Romeo steps into the dance as Juliet's unauthorized partner, as a coordination of hand movements. Romeo initiates physical contact by using his hands in an even bolder way: the pair search for one another around the periphery of a large circle that has gathered to listen to a handsome young man sing a song about the passing of youth, and Romeo finds a place near Juliet behind a curtain and reaches through it to catch her hand from behind. As she is made aware of his touch, she continues to face away from him and toward the center of the circle, trying to pretend nothing has happened. But the camera—here in the tightest close-up of her face in the film, from brow to mouth—shows her eyes open in pleasant shock and close in pleasure and wonder before she turns to face Romeo, who draws her back through the part in the curtain (photos 6.30–6.32).

The hand movements intimate an interplay between artistic convention (the complex movements of the dance) and social custom (the courtship rituals the dance embodies) on one side and transgression (the intrusion into the dance, the seizure of Juliet's hand, the kiss) on the other. This parallels the text, where the first kiss follows an interchange that elaborately plays on the word "hand" (photo 6.33) and in which the lovers' dialogue, though it issues in a tragic

Photo 6.30

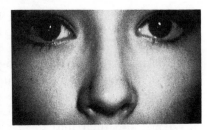

Photo 6.31

Photo 6.32

Photo 6.33

transgression, takes the form of a rigidly constrained literary form: the sonnet ("If I profane . . . ," 1.5.93–106).

Before Juliet returns Romeo's kiss she touches her fingertips to her lips (photo 6.34). It is a tiny but significant gesture but an important one: echoed later, Juliet's touching her face or her lips will convey acknowledgment of contact as well as recognition of a self changed by contact and the revival of touch in memory.

The first restatement of this motif follows quickly, when Juliet discovers Romeo's identity and reacts to the discovery: "prodigious birth of love it is to me [*touches her lips*] / That I must love a loathed enemy" (photo 6.35). Although the nurse hears these words in the text, Zeffirelli's Juliet is alone in the frame in a long shot in the first of several moments that anticipate her isolation after Romeo's exile.

Hands play an important part in the balcony scene as well. For the film, as in Zeffirelli's stage versions, the inaccessible balcony becomes an outdoor terrace to which Romeo climbs on a tree. It ran the length of the stage in the theater, and often fills the width of the frame in long shot in the film. It sets the lovers free to make contact and to display their youthful energy and vitality in physical as well as verbal terms, as they traverse the space from the point at which Romeo gains entry to the far-off door to Juliet's chamber, crossing and recrossing it, joining and separating with each verbal exchange.

The hand motif accompanies this pattern of joining and separation and caps it in the final moments of the sequence. At the outset it is Juliet's hand against her cheek that inspires Romeo's approach ("would I were a glove upon that hand that I might touch that cheek"); and when he has climbed onto the terrace, the hand is used again to intimate the internalization of the physical touch of love, the revival of that touch in memory, and the commitment it entails. This happens in the sequence that follows Romeo's "But wilt thou leave me so unsatisfied?" Here, even more than in a conventional stage production where Romeo and Juliet cannot touch, Juliet may well be startled at what she hears as a request for sexual satisfaction and breathes a visible sigh of relief when she learns that "satisfaction" means in Romeo's still somewhat idealizing vocabulary—an exchange of vows ("I gave thee mine before thou did'st request it / And yet I would it were to give again.") Before Juliet speaks these lines, she looks at her palm—the site of their first touch, the "holy palmer's kiss" of 1.5—smiles, and holds it out to him again (photo 6.36; compare 6.33). The "vow" he seeks is for her already implicit in the tactile memory of having joined hands.

After the many goodbyes and returns for one last embrace ("Romeo!—I have forgot why I did call thee back ..."), the

Photo 6.34   Photo 6.35

Photo 6.36

last shot begins as a close-up of their hands clasping, as Juliet leans over the terrace wall and Romeo descends. The camera slowly pulls back as the hands part but remain extended toward each other in farewell, the lovers' eyes fixed as they slowly back away. Juliet draws her hand along the edge of the wall, as if continuing the touch by tracing the space she has now shared with Romeo. The camera frames the pair as they part in a slow backward track and then, as the distance becomes greater, in a slow backward zoom until the couple, almost invisibly tiny, appear at the top left and lower right of the screen, the entire width and height of the space within which the scene has been played (photos 6.37–6.39). It is as if their union survives, traversing in thought the distance between them. Yet an even longer shot follows as the camera follows Romeo after he turns his back: we follow him as he runs madly joyous through the meadow outside the orchard, and then the camera pulls back for a sweeping view of the hills and fields of the region (photo 6.40). The extreme long shot in the dawning mist suggests the way his love for Juliet opens out on an expansive and joyous new world—in contrast to his previous love for Rosaline, which made him a solitary and melancholy wanderer.

Filmed this way, Zeffirelli's balcony scene foregrounds Shakespeare's suggestions of a connection between the achievements of infancy and those of adolescent love and sexuality. The principal locus in the text for this connection is the nurse's speech implicitly comparing Juliet's learning to walk (and falling) to the excitement as well as the "falling backward" that marriage will entail.[36] In the film Juliet is not only very young (Olivia Hussey was fifteen at the time of filming) but is played as a girl still vividly in touch with certain aspects of early childhood experience; her spontaneity is part of this but also her "startle" reactions, her pouting, and her recourse to dependent clinging to the nurse and finding comfort in her arms. With this repertoire of engaging childlikeness well established in the film, the balcony sequence may be thought of as a replay or evocation of certain aspects of the childhood separation-individuation process. As the child's autonomy increases with the acquisition of the ability to stand and walk, a new kind of relationship to the mother or primary giver of care becomes possible, a relationship in which distance and separateness can be accepted because repeated testing (parting and rapprochement) have shown that connection can be reestablished. The child acquires an internalized confidence in the reappearance of the mother. Margaret Mahler refers to this testing period the practicing subphase of the separation-individuation process,[37] and it is particularly to this phase of infant-mother relations that the first great adolescent love for someone outside the family circle can recur. The good experiences of

Photo 6.37

Photo 6.38

Photo 6.39

Photo 6.40

that time with a mother, nurse, or (more rarely still) father provide a basis for the more decisive move away from the family in adolescence and for the recreation with a maturely loved partner both of the joyous quality of the original mother-child dyad and of the acceptance of loss, change, and absence within that relationship.

Thus the reaching, touching, and parting hands of this sequence evoke the self-recognition of infants in the presence of the mother—and the toleration of absence on which such self-recognition depends. The style of first love is regressive, a regression in the service of development—the extension of the mother's first love into the capacity to entrust the self to another in a self-risking commitment outside the family.[38]

The powerful affirmations of this scene are balanced by a tragic prefiguration. Across the meadows disclosed at the end of the sequence stretches the tree-lined road to Mantua, which the friar's tired donkey will be unable to traverse in time to bring news of Juliet's feigned death (photo 6.40). The private space created by the joining of hands and extended by the reach of hands and the gaze of love, cannot finally become or replace the larger space of the film, which remains dominated by the tensions and imperfections of the adult world. In the developmental theories I am using to gloss this scene, the achievements of individuality and confidence in the separation process of the early years depend on adequate parental support, on what D. W. Winnicott called the "good enough" mother or the "facilitating" or "holding" environment of the family.[39] Similarly, the second separation process of adolescence depends on an adequate social context, on the possibility of finding in appropriate adult social roles and connections an analogue to the holding environment of infancy. The suggestion here—as in Shakespeare—is that in "Verona," and perhaps in any society in which male aggression plays so large and distorting a role, the younger generation cannot find such a nourishing environment.

After Romeo's banishment, Juliet's reaching hand is seen again, first in her parting from Romeo after their wedding night (a moment that closely repeats a portion of the first parting at the orchard wall) and then in a particularly

Photo 6.41 Photo 6.42

childish gesture reaching for the friar's potion to forestall the marriage to Paris (photos 6.41, 6.42). Like Romeo's gesture of self-destruction in the friar's cell, this first reaction to the potion is intemperate and rash, its spontaneity a sign of immaturity. Yet by the time Juliet actually drinks the liquid, her act will be shown as heroic and powerful, a token of her further growth in Romeo's absence. In the interim she manages a decisive separation from the nurse (who wants her to marry Paris), uses her childlike qualities to feign obedience to her parents in order to gain time, and is able to act alone.

The various associations that have accrued to the human hand in the film recur at the close. Just before the tragic conclusion, we see the friar entrust to a courier the letter explaining the feigned death of Juliet. In a slow farewell he grasps the messenger's hand, draws him near, and covers the handclasp with his other hand. This gesture is reciprocated, and we see four hands clasping as a sign of the weight of personal trust that has been conveyed, too late, to too slow a messenger.

In the tomb in the final scene, Romeo's dying words ("Thus, with a kiss, I die") cue a close-up kiss of Juliet's hand (earlier, in the balcony scene, she had kissed his hand). The shot of this kiss follows his drinking of the poison (staged so as to recall Juliet's "drink"). As he drains the vial, there is a close-up pan left along his dark cloak, until Juliet's hand appears resting on her bodice as she lies on her slab of funerary marble. Romeo's fingertips are already in the frame at the extreme left as her hand appears, and his whole hand moves rightward into the frame to cover hers, and then his lips replace his hand in the final kiss. The shot is a curious one, for we have seen Juliet lie *to his right*. The pan left to something that is spatially right has the feel of a flashback— not that we are literally in another time, but perhaps we entertain just below the level of conscious awareness the possibility that, if movement through darkened space shows us Juliet's hand where we know it is not, a past time is suggested or alluded to. Understood this way, the hidden cut makes this meeting of hands evoke earlier moments in the film, and the more so because it is followed by a replay in miniature of the vertical parting of hands we have seen in the balcony scene and after the wedding night: Romeo falls from Juliet to the floor, their hands parting at the edge of the marble as they had parted at the terrace wall.

Next, the friar enters, but Zeffirelli cuts him out of the crucial first moments of Juliet's awakening by presenting her alone in the frame. An extreme close-up of her still hand begins the sequence. The hand slowly opens, then shuts briefly in a firm fist, then moves, the camera moving with it, along the marble and along her body and veil until it reaches her lips and cheek (photos 6.43–6.46). Only then does she

Photo 6.43

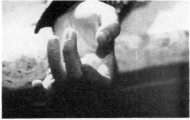

Photo 6.44

Photo 6.45

Photo 6.46

open her eyes and speak: "I do remember well where I should be—/And there I am." Zeffirelli presents this poignant moment in the text as a reintegration of the self in which a reawakened sense of touch precedes sight.[40] The gesture of touching her lips recalls earlier moments: her first kiss and reaction to it, the "palmers'" kiss and her repetition of it in the balcony scene. Here the gesture is also charged with our awareness, beyond her conscious knowledge, of Romeo's last kiss.[41]

The end of *Romeo and Juliet* can be read, and is often played, as a working out of the tragic impetuosity of character of the young lovers. Both act quickly, and the symmetry of their deaths may suggest that it is only an accident that Romeo takes his own life in response to a feigned death and Juliet to a real one: either would have done the same in the other's place. Yet critics and directors struggle for a less distanced reading of the end in which the "tragic flaw" of youthful rashness may be balanced by a sense that the lovers have achieved something full and complete, and die in possession of the knowledge of that achievement and of the impossibility of its finding a place in the social world of the play. Perhaps no presentation of the last act of the play is wholly satisfactory, but Zeffirelli's reading—and especially his summative use of the motif of the hand as the agent of the re-membering of fragmented experience—aligns itself with those interpretations that see the end as the completion of a process of growth through love. Juliet's awakening revives not only her sense of bodily and psychic wholeness but also her tactile memory of the love, risk, and painful experience of separation through which she has grown in the course of the film.

And in Zeffirelli the value of that growth is registered in its effect on the families who have resisted it. In an ending that reads Shakespeare's ending unironically, Zeffirelli shows the Montagues and Capulets joining in shared grief for their children, filing past the camera in pairs as the final credits roll.

In this study I have tried to suggest how intensely personal the terms of Zeffirelli's adaptation are, and at the same time to point to the continuing relevance of the film to contemporary concerns. Its critique of patriarchy, its use of homoerotic or bisexual perspective to deepen the play's sense of exclusion and loss, its inventive enactment of Shakespeare's sense of the resilience of the self in its power to give, to change, to remember, and to reassemble after separation and injury—all these contribute to a fresh and vital reconception of *Romeo and Juliet* for our time.

Notes

1 *Zeffirelli: The Autobiography of Franco Zeffirelli* (New York: Weidenfeld and Nicolson, 1986), 229.
2 "The Screen: Zeffirelli's *Romeo and Juliet* Opens," *New York Times*, October 9, 1968, 41.
3 Joseph A. Porter, *Shakespeare's Mercutio: His History and Drama* (Chapel Hill: University of North Carolina Press, 1988), 190–93. See also Porter, "Marlowe, Shakespeare, and the Canonization of Heterosexuality," *South Atlantic Quarterly* 88, no. 1 (Winter 1989): 127–38.
4 *Zeffirelli*, 9.
5 "Since my break from Luchino, I had led a pretty carefree life with occasionally a deeper commitment, but now I had made the classic error of falling in love where there was no possibility of its being returned. This is a humiliating, wretched feeling most of us experience at some time" (p. 217).
6 *Zeffirelli*, 6.
7 See especially the later discussion of the love scene and of triangular erotic relationships (Tybalt-Juliet-Romeo; Mercutio-Romeo-Juliet).
8 *Zeffirelli*, 60.
9 Ibid., 60–61.
10 Ibid., 40–41.
11 Ibid., 59.
12 Ibid., 68–75, 86, 109–10, 217.
13 Ibid., 72.
14 Ibid., 39.
15 See below, pp. 164–65, 172–73.
16 "Observing the theatrical world I had just joined, I knew that the possibility of marriage and family was not for me. Anita had been my one chance and I had rejected it. Whatever longing I had for children would have to be satisfied elsewhere" (*Zeffirelli*, 75).
17 Ibid., 20–21.
18 That the hand is feminine may strengthen such a speculation,

for in the orthodox Freudian view castration anxiety is closely related to the knowledge of sexual difference and the infantile sexual theory of female castration.

19 See Jean-Louis Baudry, "Ideological Effects of the Basic Cinematographic Apparatus," *Film Quarterly* 28, no. 2 (Winter 1974–75): 39–47; Christian Metz, *The Imaginary Signifier: Psychoanalysis and the Cinema*, trans. Celia Britton et al. (Bloomington: Indiana University Press, 1982).

20 *Man's Estate: Masculine Identity in Shakespeare* (Berkeley and Los Angeles: University of California Press, 1981), 84. For other feminist and related work on *Romeo and Juliet*, see Marianne Novy, *Love's Argument: Gender Relations in Shakespeare* (Chapel Hill: University of North Carolina Press, 1984); Edward Snow, "Language and Sexual Difference in *Romeo and Juliet*," in *Shakespeare's "Rough Magic": Renaissance Essays in Honor of C. L. Barber*, ed. Peter Erickson and Coppélia Kahn (Newark: University of Delaware Press, 1985), 168–92. My discussion of the film is also indebted to Eve Kosofsky Sedgwick's *Between Men: English Literature and Male Homosocial Desire* (New York: Columbia University Press, 1985).

21 See Laura Mulvey, "Visual Pleasure and Narrative Cinema," in *Feminism and Film Theory*, ed. Constance Penley (New York: Routledge, 1988), 57–68 (originally published in *Screen* 16, no. 3, Autumn 1975).

22 We may compare this shot with Mercutio's "here is my fiddlestick" gesture, where the verbal connection is mediated through a third term and the water obscures both the sword hilt and Mercutio's lower body. The nasty wit of the male cohort depends partly on indirection and concealment; Romeo's phallic violence is direct and tragic.

23 This insight nourishes much of the feminist literature on Shakespeare. For a central and influential account of the roots of these attitudes in patterns of early child care as they intersect with basic Western attitudes toward gender difference, see Nancy Julia Chodorow, *The Reproduction of Mothering: Psychoanalysis and the Sociology of Gender* (Berkeley and Los Angeles: University of California Press, 1978).

24 When Mercutio encounters Tybalt in the next scene, he is washing his handkerchief in the public fountain and caricaturing women's work with his exaggerated gestures. In fact the handkerchief may function as a kind of fetish in Mercutio's clowning. At one point he wears it over his head so that it obscures his face. As "woman's" kerchief—cloth to be embroidered, laundry to be washed—it is associated with femaleness. As he uses it in banter with Romeo it becomes a "French" affectation, an emblem of effeminacy. As it covers both his head and his phallicized fist, it may intimate a disavowal or veiling of maleness. When he dies, he clutches it to his wound, and

only when it is pried from his chest by Rome is the clowning stopped and his death recognized.

25 In *Shakespeare's Mercutio* and "Marlowe, Shakespeare."

26 Although Porter is right to emphasize the homoerotic element in Shakespeare's Mercutio, he is less sensitive to the ways in which the "antivenerealism" of Mercutio's discourse shades into contempt for homoerotic feelings or acts, as in the remark that Romeo, in his submission to love, had been "cleft with the blind bow-boy's butt-shaft" (2.3.16). Porter's defense of this line against Kahn's charge that it hints at the subjugation of women is unconvincing (Porter, *Mercutio*, 153; Kahn, *Man's Estate*, 90). The line implies that to fall in love with a woman is the emotional equivalent of a debasing sexual penetration, thus devaluing not only women but some men.

Alan Bray has recently argued, in *Homosexuality in Renaissance England* (London: Gay Men's Press, 1988), that a distinctive homosexual identity only became a possibility in England in the early eighteenth century. The Renaissance period was characterized by a mix of theoretical execration of sodomy and other crimes "against nature and God" and practical toleration of what would later be considered homosexual activity. In such circumstances it was possible for certain kinds of close, even physical relationships between men to coexist—even in the same person—with vigorous condemnation of "sodomy" and other sometimes vaguely defined forbidden acts. One way of understanding Zeffirelli's Mercutio might be to say that the contradictions he embodies arise from a reading of his part *through* modern categories. Zeffirelli reads Mercutio's mix of desire and contempt for male intimacy not as evidence of cultural heterogeneity but as dissonances and confusions within an individual psyche struggling with the issue of sexual identity.

27 Zeffirelli's Lady Capulet and Lady Montague are very similar in appearance, height, voice, and costume.

28 A related dynamic occurs in Zeffirelli's *Autobiography*, in which threats of violence, sometimes specifically of castration, are contained by sexualization. See the section on "Sex and Danger."

29 See review in *Saturday Review*, March 3, 1962.

30 Part of the effect of this sequence comes from the rhythm of the exchange of glances the editing establishes: at one point, Romeo begins to nod in greeting and there is a quick cut to Juliet's acknowledgment of his salutation—so brief that the following shot shows us Romeo finishing his nod. This is a visual analogue to the linguistic pattern of coordinated response Edward Snow has noted in the play, an example of which is the sharing of a single line of verse between the lovers while Juliet is still unaware of Romeo's presence in the orchard:

Romeo: ...
  O that I were a glove upon that hand,
  That I might touch that cheek!
Juliet: Ay me!
Romeo: She speaks!
  O, speak again, bright angel ... (2.2.24–26)

31 Theorists like Mulvey and Metz have emphasized too exclusively the connection between the erotic gaze in cinema and sadistic fantasies of power and control associated with the dynamics of the primal scene. For Mulvey visual pleasure is male, hegemonic, and inevitably patriarchal. Gaylan Studlar, following Jean Laplanche, has developed the analogy between the film spectator and the child-watcher of the primal scene in another direction, perhaps more fruitful for the present inquiry, stressing the helplessness and exclusion entailed in looking on. See Christian Metz, *The Imaginary Signifier*, trans. Celia Britton, Annwyl Williams, Ben Brewster, and Alfred Guzzetti (Bloomington: Indiana University Press, 1982), 59–63; Gaylan Studlar, "Masochism and the Perverse Pleasures of the Cinema," in Bill Nichols, *Movies and methods, Vol. 2* (Berkeley and Los Angeles: University of California Press, 1985), 602–21; Jean Laplanche, *Life and Death in Psychoanalysis*, trans. Jeffrey Mehlman (Baltimore: Johns Hopkins University Press, 1981). For Laplanche the position of the child spectator at the primal scene is like Odysseus tied to the mast, or like that of Tantalus (p. 102; cited by Studlar, "Masochism," 612 and n. 45).

32 See above, p. 147. The triangular dynamics of the relations among father, son, and mother in Zeffirelli's version of *The Champ* are also relevant here.

33 At this point it may be helpful to recall Zeffirelli's sense that entering "the theatrical world" and Visconti's household entailed a renunciation of marriage and family, as well as his earlier account of how the loss of his "mothers" made it permanently difficult for him to accept love.

34 In the 1962 Old Vic production in New York, the proscenium curtain was dropped at the moment at which the lovers touched, isolating them from the rest of the dancers. See Walter Kerr's review in the *Herald Tribune*, February 15, 1962.

35 See the stimulating discussion of Romeo and Juliet's private or secret world in Novy, *Love's Argument*, 106–9.

36 See Katherine Dalsimer's excellent discussion of the nurse's speech and its bearing on the "second individuation process" in *Female Adolescence* (New Haven and London: Yale University Press, 1986), 85–90, and her citation of Peter Blos, "The Second Individuation Process in Adolescence," *Psychoanalytic Study of the Child* 22 (1967): 162–86; and compare Snow, "Sexual Difference."

37 Margaret S. Mahler, Fred Pine, and Anni Bergman, *The Psycho-*

      logical Birth of the Human Infant (New York: Basic Books, 1975), 65–108.

38 Zeffirelli's own "mothers" are described as unreliable and confusing; his own first heterosexual love was "renounced" in favor of a theatrical career; and his relationship with Visconti, though close, is described as mutually calculating (see *Zeffirelli*, 72).

39 D. W. Winnicott, *The Maturational Process and the Facilitating Environment* (New York): International Universities Press, 1965), *passim*.

40 Zeffirelli's treatment of the moment of awakening illustrates the quality of "self-coincidence that is both arrival and return," which Edward Snow finds in Juliet's speech (see "Sexual Difference," 181–82).

41 It is striking how closely details of Zeffirelli's journal entry for February 9, 1939, recorded at such length in his *Autobiography* only to "show the confused way that the heady events of the time were absorbed into my self-centred teenage world"—are recapitulated in the final sequences of *Romeo and Juliet*. The dead hand of a young girl, severed for a drawing class; now the hand of Juliet, who lies in a deathlike sleep, isolated from the body by the frame line. The Florentine morgue; the Capulet tomb. A reassembly, or making whole, of the *corps morcelé*. A shared grief or mourning.

7

Disseminating Shakespeare: Paternity and Text in Jean-Luc Godard's King Lear

Even while it keeps the texts it culls alive, this play of insemination—or grafting—destroys their hegemonic center, subverts their authority and their uniqueness

—Derrida[1]

Introduction: Shakespearean Descent

A film programmatically suspicious of names, Jean-Luc Godard's *King Lear* nonetheless claims the title of a Shakespeare play and endows the playwright with an unhistorical male descendant, William Shakespeare Jr., the Fifth. Godard's film is a modernized, fragmented, constantly self-interrupting work, only part of which—a fraction of the dialogue and the subplot involving "Don Learo," a retired Mafia chief and his daughter, Cordelia—derives from Shakespeare's text. There is no Edmund in this free adaptation, but the film itself takes on aspects of his character, asserting filial rights despite illegitimacy, by turns denying paternity and appropriating the riches of the paternal text. Godard's *King Lear* is like Edgar too: trifling with despair, toying with madness, disguising itself, enacting redemption in burlesque, cognizant of its diminishment, deeply injured, quirkily loyal. It is a distant and debased copy of its model but, like Gloucester's devalued son, sometimes establishes

189

sudden, intimate connection to its parent while dissembling its filial relationship.

Shakespeare had no male heirs and, according to Samuel Schoenbaum, devoted himself in his last years to acquiring real estate in Stratford to leave to his descendants in the female line, which, however, failed in the third generation with the death of his granddaughter in 1670.[2] Shakespeare's King Lear has no male children, divides his land among daughters, and lives to see his line end with the death of Cordelia. Like Shakespeare, Godard is interested in patrilineal descent and its vicissitudes; his *Lear* is about how paternal inheritances tend to disperse, to get lost in transmission; about how links between fathers and children break down and have to be restored; about the special challenge to male authority occasioned by female inheritance. The film, like the play, is partly about a virtuous, recalcitrant daughter who will not serve as a passive mirror or echo to a grandiose father. But for the film fatherhood is also a metaphor for the relation between authors and texts, arists and disciples, cultural traditions and their influence. In these relations too filiation is problematic and dispersive: in this insistently metacinematic work Godard addresses the limits of his control over his work. Authors cannot foreclose the play of unruly texts; artistic precursors, including Shakespeare, cannot determine how their works will be used or even the meanings those works may have for later artists and audiences.

But, perhaps unlike Shakespeare, Godard's film posits no "natural" bond or link by which we may measure breach or inauthenticity in the connection of father to child, artist to work, "source" to adaptation. What seems an organic connection may be arbitrary *bricolage*; filiation (from *filius*, a son) may be merely filature (from *filum*, a thread), a stitching or stringing together.[3] Adaptation is, inevitably, pastiche. Yet in stretching the limits of Shakespearean ascription, in scattering and recomposing the paternal body of the text of *King Lear*, Godard reveals how fully the play of dispersal is already at work *in* that text and acknowledges Shakespeare as precursor, even ancestor, of his own deconstructive artistic practice.[4]

Godard himself is not literally a father, but (especially since he began to collaborate with Anne-Marie Mieville in 1973) he has often spoken of his films as children, as in this exchange with Laura Mulvey:

> Mulvey: In your more recent projects there's more and more of an emphasis on children.
> Godard: Of course. Because now I'm probably too old to have children. I'm looking at a real creation ... pictures, or books, or music are creations ... from nothing. But they have a relationship. In the old days I very often spoke of my movies as babies. And for me to try to run a small production house is like Anne-Marie with the children.[5]

The script of *The Story*, an unfinished Godard film of the late 1970s, also presses the analogy between the begetting of children and artistic creation:

> There's a story between us. As with other people, the story comes out of *him* and goes back home into *her* [*rentre chez elle*]. And there, inside, you lose track [*on perd sa trace*]. And then the story reappears, a child is born, and you find that outside, in the outer world. And there, you can see again the *story*.[6]

Here narrative originates in a kind of insemination and is perfected by a process obscurely analogous to sexual reproduction. The seed is male, but only proximately so, "returning" to a prior female source before reemerging as child/story. And even that proximate male origin must be (temporarily) forgotten: one must lose track. Watching a Godard film, the spectator too may "lose track," yield to bafflement, experience a loss of mastery. From the perspective of *The Story*'s reproductive narratology, the disruptions, ellipses, and inconsistencies of Godard's style may be taken as enactments of the discontinuity and self-oblivion the director associates with fatherhood, and perhaps as attempts to master the anxieties occasioned by those aspects of filmmaking (a bigendered, collaborative activity) most like fatherhood. This is particularly true of *King Lear*, in which, under the influence of Shakespeare's text, Godard's metacinematic and psychological concerns are directly related to the arch-metaphor of troubled paternity.

This essay will pursue some of the transmutations of that metaphor in Godard's *Lear*. In doing this there is a risk of imposing a factitious unity on a work that flaunts its *lack* of unity and closure. But the film may be more coherent than its disjointed narrative suggests, and its metaphoric, free-associative play on the theme of fatherhood may offer its most valuable commentary on *King Lear* precisely at those points at which Shakespeare seems to have been forgotten.

The Frame: Cordelia's Three Fathers

The story of Godard's *King Lear* begins at Cannes in 1986, when Menahem Golan, representing Cannon Films, Godard, and Norman Mailer signed a contract written on a napkin for a film version of Shakespeare's play. Godard was to be director, Mailer was writer and star, and Woody Allen was the Fool.[7] But as Godard's voice-over narration says at the beginning of the film that was actually made, contracts are words, and "words are one thing, and reality is another thing, and between them is *no* thing." Mailer wrote a script in which Lear was transformed into a contemporary gangster, and he and his daughter Kate, who was to have played Cordelia, flew to Switzerland to begin work with Godard. Their work on the film lasted only a day, and they returned to America. Because the story of their departure in some measure replicates the first act of *Lear*, Godard used footage from the day's shooting as an introduction to the completed film, which, as an intertitle ("A PICTURE SHOT IN THE BACK") informs us, never recovered from Mailer's betrayal and the Cannon group's crass pressure for a return on their investment. We see Mailer, in brief takes that are replayed several times, smugly enjoying the prominence he had given himself in the original script ("Mailer!—O, that's a *good* way to begin," he reads); sitting on a hotel bed with Kate; drinking orange juice with her on the terrace of the hotel and proclaiming the wisdom of his "Mafia" updating of

Shakespeare. Godard's voice, oddly distorted, accompanies these images explaining the failure of their collaboration. Mailer challenged every directorial decision beginning with the first (I said, "O.K., let's go." The great writer said, "Why don't you say *action?*") and including such details as whether he was to kiss Kate or she him and what was to be in the glasses from which they drank. The shooting had to be stopped, and "they went back to America first class—Norman and his daughter; daughter's boyfriend—economy." A grandiose father like Lear, Mailer precipitously cancels his own plans when his will is thwarted, though in this case it was not so much the resistance of the daughter as conflict between men that caused the break. Godard's commentary shows how the projects of fathers, or father-artists, collapse under the weight of their own overdetermination:

> It was not Lear with three daughters. It was Kate with three fathers: Mailer as a star, Mailer as a father, and me, the director.

Fatherhood is multiple and metaphoric.[8] Lear's part, as in the main action of the film, which contains several competing and alternating father figures including Godard playing an eccentric inventor as well as Shakespeare himself, is distributed among several voices, one of which speaks with doubled authority like the Jacobean Lear, king and father. Yet paternal care tends to get lost in the male struggle for dominance, to dissipate in metaphor and multiplicity. There are three "fathers" but no father. Godard's account also displaces the conflict onto Kate Mailer, as if her fragility or lack of sophistication caused the break: "In the end it was too much for this young lady from Provincetown." Although it was Norman Mailer who quit, this line rhetorically recoups Godard's position at Kate Mailer's expense, reversing the direction of Lear's banishment of Cordelia, sending Kate *from* France to an imagined provincial exile on Cape Cod, and perhaps also restoring, in fantasy, a daughterless harmony between the "fathers." Godard's narrative voice is not exempt from the arrogance he depicts in Mailer or from the blind self-excuse and testy centrality of Shakespeare's Lear.

Gods and Titans: Goya's Chronos and the Pantheon Directors

At this point Godard's role as disembodied voice-over narrator begins to be shared or parceled out among other voices, the first of which belongs to Peter Sellars (William Shakespeare Jr., the Fifth). He appears alone in the image in close-up but is not introduced at first as a character: he speaks as continuator of Godard's exploration of the relation between fatherhood and artistic production. As his character unfolds, Sellars will profess complete ignorance of cinema, and even of the meaning of the word "image," yet, inconsistently, here he speaks for Godard with intimate knowledge of the great directors, pondering the filial relations between artistic "fathers" and sons as black and white photographs of Auguste Renoir, Jean Renoir, Luchino Visconti, François Truffaut, Pier Paolo Pasolini, Fritz Lang, Orson Welles, Sasha Guitry, and others fill the screen—first as if summoned by his ruminations and then, as the shots widen to show him seated at a hotel dining table, as close-ups of the pages of the photo album he holds. The sequence juxtaposes images of young directors with the angry, suffering, or visionary selves they would become, and with the Lear-like old men their mentors had been (photos 7.1, 7.2, 7.3). Somehow a paternal mystery linking art and age and touching Lear's need for love is intimated: thinking of the relation between "Jean Renoir and his father Auguste, and between Luchino and his artistic father Jean," Sellars understands "why they were so keen on young girls." Was this need somehow passed down, as if in discipular succession, from artistic father to son, along with the mysteries of the art? There are suggestions of erotic or incestuous needs here, particularly in the Auguste Renoir-Jean Renoir sequence. An image of a Renoir nude flashes momentarily on the screen and is dismissed: "no nudity, please, I'm on duty ..." Godard's meditation on the transfer of artistic powers evokes, then suppresses the archetypal sensuality of the elder Renior's art, and it may also allude to the hints of the sharing of women between father and son that play about the story of Jean Renoir's childhood and early adulthood.[9] It is also important to the effect of this sequence

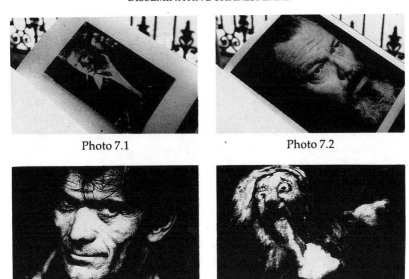

Photo 7.1   Photo 7.2

Photo 7.3   Photo 7.4

that it brings close to the surface, only to ignore, other potential disturbances of the regular partrilineal succession it posits: several of the directorial "Lears" were homosexual or bisexual; others failed as artists in old age; Pasolini was killed in a brutal murder. On the surface this section of the film presents the passing on of artistic creativity as male mystery in which young women play a mediating role connecting older men to their disciples—and through them, the sequence of photographs suggests, to their own past selves. Beneath the surface of this narcissistic myth of male regeneration, suggestions of incest, homosexuality, and the misuse of women connect patrilineal artistic descent to the subject matter of (Greek) tragedy. The concluding image of the sequence, a vivid still of Goya's *Chronos Devouring His Children* (photo 7.4), brings the hints of paternal violence and transgression to the surface, relating the pantheon directors and their legacy to *Lear* at yet another point of connection, evoking "the barbarous Scythian/Or he that makes his generations messes/To gorge his appetite" (1.1.116–118).[10]

Shakespeare's Text as Gnostic Gospel

The principal plot of *King Lear*, a search for Shakespeare's lost works, is a Gnostic or mock-gnostic quest in which Shakespeare's text is the lost light—scattered in debased contexts but recoverable and potentially redemptive. The action is set in an indefinite future time referred to as "after Chernobyl," which for the film means after an apocalyptic nuclear accident far more widely devastating than the actual nuclear accident referred to. "It was after Chernobyl, and everything had disappeared." This voice-over glosses the first appearance of Goya's Chronos, relating *King Lear* to twentieth-century apocalypse, locating the threat of nuclear holocaust, through *King Lear*, in an excess of paternal will and appetite threatening future generations. The worst has occurred, and the work of reconstruction is beginning.[11] "Things" have begun to reappear—hotels, cars, guns—but "meaning" and "culture" are more elusive.

As part of the recovery of meaning, William Shakespeare Jr., the Fifth, a bright, literal-minded employee of the Cannon Cultural Division and Her Majesty's Royal Library, has been sent to Europe to search for the works of his famous ancestor. The redemptive text has been forgotten and cannot be directly recalled. It can, however, be *collected*, identified, and reassembled. Peter Sellars carries a notebook and seems to be equipped with a kind of matching memory: unable to reproduce the text unassisted, he, like the true hero or Arnoldian critic, knows the authentic text when he hears it, and writes it down. He comes upon a famous line in Denmark ("To be or not to be ..."), struggles by trial and error to remember the simple title, *As You Like It*, and has now settled in the Swiss town of Nyon (Godard's birthplace, though the film never says so), where he begins to hear passages from *King Lear* spoken by an elderly American (Burgess Meredith, Mailer's replacement) and his daughter (Molly Ringwald) in the hotel dining room (photos 7.5 and 7.6).

It is possible to read this part of the film as a debunking of the pretensions of the secular literary canon, and of the preeminent place Shakespeare increasingly enjoys in it, by raising bardolatry to the level of Gnostic or Kabbalistic

Photo 7.5   Photo 7.6

mysticism while giving Lear's lines to a gangster. But the effect is not so simple. The relation of canonical text to profane context is not altogether unlike that posited between *The Odyssey* and the corrupt milieu of Hollywood movie deals portrayed in *Le mépris* (1963). In both works the mindless worship of "culture" is certainly satirized, and textual idolatry is seen to go hand in hand with vulgar misprision (Odysseus as neurotic; naiads as synchronized swimmers). But the great text survives its transformation into a cultural commodity, and may even be reenergized by dispersal. Even hostile critics of Godard's *King Lear* have noted how Shakespeare's lines acquire unexpected resonance in their new settings, new poignance by the fiction of their having been forgotten and newly identified. In Godard's handling, this play of oblivion and recollection stages Shakespeare's text as, above all, a source of *nourishment* available, at least in parts, for new modes of assimilation, after dismemberment.

As he listens to Cordelia's refusal of her father's demand for love, which follows Shakespeare fairly closely at this point, Sellars cannot remain a wholly disinterested observer and enters into a low-key but distinctly Oedipal rivalry in relation to Meredith, lighting Cordelia's cigarette and interrupting Learo's monologue. Reacting to Cordelia's interest in Shakespeare Jr. and noticing that everything said is being transcribed into his notebook, Don Learo makes the first (not altogether unShakespearean) bad joke of the film, associating theatrical scholarship and *eros*: "Young man!—are you making a *play* for my daughter?" Put off but not defeated, Sellars remains in the dining room as father and daughter exit.

197

Referring to the personal eccentricity of the pair, as well as to their potential value in his project of literary reclamation, Sellars judges Meredith and Ringwald "characters!" in Pirandellian exasperation.

Mafia Shakespeare: Lear as God(ard)father

The choice of a retired Syndicate gangster as the film's equivalent to Shakespeare's Lear may have been suggested by Mailer (who announces in the opening minutes that "the Mafia is the only way to do *King Lear*"), but it also accords with Godard's long-standing interests in American gangsters, evident in his early criticism and in the many references to Hollywood gangster films from *A bout de souffle* on. Since the mid-sixties this preoccupation of Godard's has often combined with a Marxian critique of society that regards organized crime as systemic, the expression of the underlying violence of American imperialism.[12]

Godard's most searching exploration of this subject is to be found in his script for *The Story*, the uncompleted film of the late 1970s I mentioned earlier in connection with its metaphoric association between insemination and narrative creation. The film was to have been about the impossibility of producing works of art that tell the truth about the connections among crime, entertainment, and government in America. The film's narrative centers on a young filmmaker named Frankie, the renegade son of a Mafia family, who tries to make a film documenting the influence of the crime Syndicate—and especially of Bugsy Siegel, the gangster-entrepreneur who developed postwar Las Vegas—on the Hollywood film industry. Assisting him in the film are Robert DeNiro as cameraman and Diane Keaton, who plays DeNiro's separated wife, a radical professor of film history, who rejoins him on this project at Frankie's request. The couple already has a child, a blind eight-year-old girl, and the project holds promise of their renewed collaboration as parents as well as artists. But as the film nears completion, organized crime and government agents learn of it, and both Frankie and the DeNiro character are killed. Thinking De-

Niro has abandoned her, Keaton returns to their child, closing the picture with a bleak gesture of sexual and political withdrawal, snapping her thighs shut while bathing with her blind daughter to illustrate "how to keep guys from screwing you."[13]

A far less dispirited work, Godard's *King Lear* takes over from *The Story* an interest in the Hollywood-Mafia connection and its ultimate influence on the making of Godard's own films. It also develops the implied analogy between chastity and resistance to aesthetic and political corruption. Like *Bugsy*, *King Lear* is "a picture shot in the back" by the system, as a repeated intertitle informs us. Alternating with this title card, a "close up" still of a Raphaelesque angel whose expression of sudden distress makes it look uncannily like a victim of gunfire (photo 7.7), associates the film with the martyrdom of the innocent, anticipating Cordelia's association with Joan of Arc later in the film and the striking conclusion, in which she is apparently shot in the back by Lear.

In *King Lear*, however, the figure of the gangster-patriarch (present only through his agents in *The Story*) comes to occupy the center of attention, rather than being refracted through a narrative centering on a rebellious son and a blighted couple. With this shift Godard moves away from social criticism and modernist satire toward tragedy—or at least toward a fragmented and burlesque form of tragedy, for despite his faults and the bizarre premises of his story, the father's suffering is presented as resonant and meaningful.

Like Lear and Goya's Chronos, Meredith's Don Learo is a violent, transgressive father: now retired, he glories in the

Photo 7.7

memory of his association with the great figures of the Syndicate of the 1940s—Meyer Lansky and the brutal Bugsy Siegel. Unlike King Lear but like Mailer, he is a writer, a producer of texts engaged in writing his memoirs, an epic chronicle of the passing of a formative era in American history when the Syndicate was formed and its central institution, the luxury casino, later to influence all of American culture, was established. Cordelia serves as unwilling scribe, a modernized version of Milton's daughter, refusing, as Shakespeare's Cordelia does, her father's demand for unconditional love ("my heart is not in my mouth") and responding to his grandiose ruminations with bordeom and challenge.

Don Learo's visionary epic-in-progress is ironized and fragmentary: it may never be completed. But although we see the writing of the book as something in process, in one sense it is already completed: its text is a pastiche of two already written texts, *King Lear* and Albert Fried's *The Rise and Fall of the Jewish Gangster in America*.[14] Fried's book is present in the film as a prop (we see Meredith reading it; photo 7.8);[15] but it is also the text he is dictating: lengthy passages are borrowed from it as Don Learo develops his theme and attempts to textualize his history. Godard's choice of Fried's book as a source for the dialogue is significant because in his account of the "gangster-capitalist," Fried portrays Siegel and Lansky as visionary founders not only in their development of Las Vegas but in their initial steps toward a national "entertainment" empire, enmeshed with Hollywood and bringing the underworld and upper world of American culture together.

Photo 7.8

Photo 7.9

The book was not published until 1980, but its view of the relationship between postwar American hedonism as exemplified by the casinos and the larger structures of American capitalism accords with Godard's view, expressed in the screenplay of *The Story*, of the crucial role of the entertainment industry and of organized crime in American society.

Godard's direct borrowings from Fried are extensive. Perhaps the longest single extract is this passage describing the "Las Vegasization" of America:

> "Entertainment" conglomerates like MGM today own the largest establishments in Las Vegas. Bugsy Siegel's Flamingo is now the Las Vegas Hilton. And as the newspapers tell us daily, the rush is on in Atlantic City, one "entertainment" conglomerate after another—Bally, Playboy, Hilton, Caesar's Palace, Holiday Inn—having already staked its claim to this reborn Eldorado on the sea. Will New York City be far behind? Will other tourist and entertainment centers across the land? The point need not be labored. America is embracing Bugsy Siegel's vision; his martyrdom was not in vain.[16]

With these references to Siegel, whose influence on Hollywood in the 1940s was to have been the subject of the film within a film of *The Story*, organized crime and film history intersect: Hollywood, for Fried as for Godard, is the point of intersection (*convergence* is Fried's term) between the "upper" and "underworlds" of American culture. Godard's repetition of Fried's mythopoeic pop history is more personal and poignant than the original. Meredith suffers and broods, wringing his hands and glancing at his daughter for a response as he searches for words for Siegel's fate: "No, not death: his *martyrdom*" (photo 7.9). But Godard's version is simultaneously more comic and self-conscious, inflating Fried's glamorizing prose to absurdity through wordplay, imagining an America in which all the centers of illicit pleasure and organized crime are "linked together by *Learo* jets!"

Yet despite ironizing misquotation, much of Fried's analysis of American society is endorsed. In sentences the film repeats, for example, Fried pays tribute to the power of the capitalist system to contain and transform gangsterism:

> In the end, the system swallows up the gangsters in its gigantic maw, leaving behind only the traces of their errant careers.... And even if Lansky is as awesome as he is reported to be he is by now scarcely more than a lonely isolated old man on the criminal landscape of America. He bears the mark of Cain and knows no peace.[17]

Godard slightly revises these lines: "Even if Lansky *and I* are as awesome as *we* are reputed to be ..."; "*I* bear the mark of Cain ..." Don Learo is compounded of King Lear and Fried's mythic version of Meyer Lansky, never either one in any simple way but always Lear's shadow, Lansky's double. He claims a part in the exploits of the Syndicate, but his daughter is skeptical. Like Burt Lancaster in Louis Malle's *Atlantic City*, he may be a mere underling, trying to write himself into gangster history after the fact.

Fried's gangsters are creative individualists whose energies and innovations are resisted and then coopted by capitalism. In this sense they allegorize the relation of the independent filmmaker, including Godard, to the Hollywood "system." Isolated, conscious of the power of the system, and resentful of his lack of recognition in a changing world that has profited by his efforts, Godard's own persona as narrator overlaps with Fried's Lansky and with Don Learo.

In assessing the mix of pathos and burlesque with which Godard treats his central character, it is important to keep in mind how frequently Godard reminds us that what we read as "character" is an effect of *texts*. Don Laero is presented as *writing* the very text he is *reading*: as he composes his memoir, he holds in his hands a copy of the book from which Godard borrowed many of his lines; he keeps in his pocket a scrap of paper on which Meyer Lansky inscribed his philosophy of life in his own hand; as he struggles for words to express his feelings, we recognize them as quotations or misquotations from Shakespeare already written in our texts and immediately transcribed by Peter Sellars for publication in a future edition. At the end of the film Sellars, outpacing

Meredith, has somehow gotten beyond him in writing out the text, and when Learo is at a loss for words, he refers to Sellars' notebook, which has now become a working script.

The motif of textualization, like the other alienating and ironic strategies of the film and their equivalents in Shakespeare, are impossible to confine in either a deconstructive or a recuperative mode. They contribute to a powerful *fragmentation* of the image of the father/artist, whose traditional claim to uniqueness, singleness of being, self-presence, and centrality is undercut by disjunctive presentation. Yet they also oddly enhance the affective power of Meredith's performance. There is pathos in the spectacle of an old actor with a touch of greatness that might carry him through an impressive portrayal of a major tragic role, having to be fed lines by Peter Sellars in a bizarre science fiction metacinematic version of Shakespeare that proclaims its own absurdity and failure with obsessive frequency.

Perhaps the most important of these distancing or fragmenting techniques—one common in Godard's other work but put to special use in *Lear*—is disjunction of soundtrack and image, a stylistic constant in Godard's work which here contributes to the dispersal of Shakespeare's text, and especially Lear's lines, into multiple voices. The foregrounding of text and script is a part of this effect (Learo's voice is not his own but that of Shakespeare or Fried), but other techniques contribute as well. Often Lear's lines are spoken in voice-over, sometimes by Meredith, sometimes by Sellars, sometimes by a (disembodied, nondiegetic) woman; sometimes one voice overtakes another so that different parts of the same Shakespearean speech, spoken by voices of different ages and genders, interfere with one another and blend into unintelligibility. At the end of the film Lear's final words are murmured, his back to the camera, and they cannot be made out.

The descent into noise may be felt as a dismantling of Shakespeare's canonical poetry, or, alternatively, as an attempt to find a cinematic equivalent to Shakespeare's portrayal of Lear's suffering as he slips into madness.[18]

A closer look at Godard's adaptation of one particular exchange in *King Lear* may help to illustrate how Godard's disjunctive style works at once to fragment Shakespeare's text and to enact the fragmenting play *of* that text, as Lear's self-division spreads outward, creating fissures in the unity of the spectatorial position from which we perceive him.

In Shakespeare Lear responds to Goneril's criticism of the behavior of his "insolent retinue" with a question: "Are you our daughter?" (1.4.218), making identity dependent on obedience. Goneril's reply employs a related strategy, making her father's self-possession and self-coincidence depend on its accord with her wishes, as she beseeches him to "put away/These dispositions which of late transport you/From what you rightly are" (220–22). Lear speaks:

> Does any here know me? This is not Lear.
> Does Lear walk thus? Speak thus? Where are his eyes?
> Either his notion weakens, or his discernings
> Are lethargied—Ha! Waking? 'Tis not so.
> Who is it that can tell me who I am?
> *Fool.* Lear's shadow.
> *Lear.* I would learn that; for by the marks of sovereignty,
> knowledge and reason, I should be false persuaded I had
> daughters. (230–34)

Lear's self-negations blend ironic reproach (Lear can't really be here—he would be treated better), his rising fears of annihilation, and metatheatrical critique ("Does Lear walk thus?"). The fool's reply, "Lear's shadow," may answer the question, "Who is it that can tell me who I am?" in which case the shadow is a *memento mori*, a reminder of the contingency of all human identity. Or it may answer the implied question, "Who am I?" pointing to a diminishment of the self in age or to the "shadowing" of Lear by the actor who plays him.[19] Lear's repeated "I" in the last three lines momentarily wards off the knowledge he has begun to absorb concerning the precarious grounding of his regal self-conception, already deeply fissured by psychological, ontological, and metatheatrical paradoxes which the disrespect of his daughters merely bring to the surface.

Influenced by Jean Jacquot, Anne Barton, and Robert Weimann, I find those productions of Lear most powerful in which the theater itself is dramatized as a special site for this diverstiture of self, in which, for example, "Does any here know me?" interrogates the audience as well as Lear's on-stage auditors; or in which, later in the play, the answer to Lear's question "Am I in France"—"In your own kingdom, sir" maps Lear's senile disorientation onto the protean space of the playhouse, now experienced as the dominion of the mad player-king.[20]

In Godard's adaptation the self-disintegrating play of the text of the self is multiplied by several specifically *cinematic* tropes of disjunction: voice is set against image; speeches spoken by one character are dispersed among several voices and "textualized" by being read with exaggerated deliberation or by the appearance of source texts on screen. Peter Sellars reads Lear's lines in voice-over as we watch Don Leato leaning on the hotel balcony in a brooding, *silent* meditation (photo 7.10). "This is *not* Lear" in this presentation sounds either like a decision on the part of Shakespeare Jr. that he has not found the right postnuclear avatar—maybe this old man is not a repository of some of Shakespeare's lines. It also voices the recognition, not localized in Sellars' fictitious consciousness, that the film is not *King Lear* but an unworthy imitation, and perhaps refers as well to the doubtful status of all theatrical or cinematic representation. Even if Shakespeare's play were historically accurate and Godard's film a faithful adaptation, Lear would still not be present on the screen, any more than would those images the naive soldier in Godard's *Les carabiniers* (1963) mistakes for real people in his first experience of cinema. The negation of fictitious identity is one of the staples of Godard's armory of

Photo 7.10

Photo 7.11

alienation effects, as in the famous opening of *Deux ou trois choses que je sais d'elle* (1966), in which actress Marina Vlady is introduced twice—as herself and as Juliette Janson, the character she plays. Here Lear's self-negating words are shared—partly spoken about him, partly spoken by him—as Meredith continues Shakespeare's text where Sellars' voice-over leaves off: "Who is it that can tell me who I am?" In answer to this double question, a young woman emerges from the hotel from *behind* Lear, places her hand on his shoulder, and answers, not so much to him as to the camera: "Lear's shadow" (photo 7.11).

The parceling out of the very questions which serve in Shakespeare to maintain identity even while it is being questioned is accompanied by metatextual and metacinematic play more complex and copious than Shakespeare's allusions to the stage. Meredith holds in his hands one of the texts (*The Rise and Fall of the Jewish Gangster in America*) that could "tell him" who he is (if he had finished writing it). In addition, at the beginning of Sellars' recitation, it is not Meredith but Godard himself who appears—bizarrely disguised yet clearly recognizable by his voice and sunglasses—for the first time on the screen (photo 7.12). "Does any here know me" can thus refer to the partly hidden author of the film. Or, considering that in his character as "the professor" Godard is reciting sonnet 138 ("When my love swears that she is made of truth,/I do believe her, though I know she lies"), the line may refer to Shakespeare as author of the words being spoken and Godard's precursor in the field of double negation.

Thus the "I" Don Learo seeks knowledge of is shifting

Photo 7.12

Photo 7.13

from the start, migrating from Sellars to Godard to Shakespeare to Shakespeare's Lear, and thence to Burgess Meredith. Yet the film, zestful as it is in its mocking revisionism, undermines "Lear's" centrality in a way that preserves or recasts his pathos. The suffering of fathers—even of the burlesqued, fractured, and fictional Don Learo—is privileged, not for Godard, because his grandiose claims to centrality and authority are valid but because paternity now is the paradigmatic site of the deconstruction of the unified self.[21]

Godard as Magus: The Reinvention of the Image

At one point in his search, Sellars/Shakespeare is told that someone else in the town of Nyon has been engaged in a search similar to his own, and this turns out to be "the professor," sometimes called "Pluggy" after the high-tech shamanistic costume he wears, capped by mock-Rastafarian dreadlocks fashioned from RCA cords, dogtags, and Christmas ornaments (photo 7.13).[22] The professor is not only played by Godard but is linked to the autobiographical voice of the frame narrative by the distorted voice he affects, which we now see as a result of his speaking out of only one side of his mouth, an affectation or speech defect that accords with his distrust of words.[23] When Sellars has found his way to the professor's house ("he hates the outdoors and natural light"), the professor rises and fakes a fart in greeting, and distant thunder sounds. This is interpreted by one of his pretty female assistants as cosmic resonance: "When the professor farts, the moon changes!" If Don Learo represents Lear's political power, the professor subsumes some of Lear's role as sacred king, able to invoke the upper and lower gods, his inner life enmeshed with the storm.

The professor is trying to invent something that will turn out to be cinema, and, preferring images to words, he is deeply skeptical of Shakespeare Jr.'s quest of verbal recovery. His own theories are difficult to follow; their exposition is obscured by noise, interrupted by numerous other voices on the soundtrack, and undercut by his own deep skepticism concerning anything said or named. Nonetheless, a theory of sorts emerges through his discourse, and after a while Sellars begins to echo it and continue its exposition in voice-over, applying its privileging of sight over sound, silence over voice, to the plot of *King Lear*, with its emphasis on Cordelia's silence and the transformed "sight" of Lear.

The theory has several tenets including mistrust of all names and words; a preference for visual over auditory experience; an aesthetic in which "found" images are juxtaposed to create a new effect; and a belief that "image" and "reality" are equivalent terms. As the theory unfolds in voice-over, some of the professor's experiments appear on the screen, and several of these should be noted.

1   The theory of juxtaposition is illustrated by a two-frame slide show in which two contrasting images are shown in increasingly rapid alternation. One is a female figure in flowing white robes lifting a torch, a recognizable signifier of Liberty as a sacred cultural ideal. The other is a cartoon frame in which an animal cartoon character (a Tex Avery wolf) faces the spectator, somehow devouring and extruding himself like the mythic uroboros,[24] his legs disappearing into his mouth and his arms and hands emerging from his ears (photos 7.14 and 7.15). The images contrast in several ways: imploding versus open form; popular art versus high culture; farce versus epic. As they alternate, the two images begin to seem part of one rhythm, perhaps miming the systole-diastole of a natural process like the beating of a heart, or alluding to the infamously less natural rhythm of (male) masturbation,[25] with the self-enfolding of the cartoon seeming to *produce* the erect torch of liberty as, to use a phrase from Godard's early critical writing, "the cinema plays with itself."[26] Is it "truth" that has been found when these images alternate, as the professor insists, or an instance of the cinema's arbitrary, wilful, and perverse power? Alternatively, has the professor, though scornful of Shakespeare Jr.'s search, unwittingly furthered the rediscovery of Shakespearean mixed and indecorous dramatic practice in which (especially in *Lear*) cheap tricks and bawdry jostle with numinous truths?

Photo 7.14

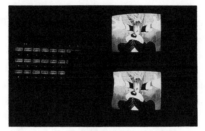

Photo 7.15

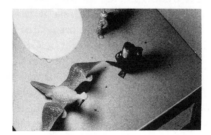

Photo 7.16

2   Before attempting to reinvent the cinematic image on a
large screen, the professor experiments with a proto-
cinematic effect in miniature, swinging a light bulb behind tiny plastic dinosaurs in a carboard box with a hole
cut in one end for a projection window (photo 7.16). The
elementary effect of shadow play is created, and in this
case the spectacle evokes Apocalypse: the tiny creatures
teeter and slide in the eerie, naked light as Godard tips
the box back and forth and intones, *The Last Judgment!"*
Again, Godard demonstrates—with Shakespeare's Edgar,

who convinces his father that a flat stage is a steep cliff —that an oddly powerful effect can be generated with the silliest and least impressive of means. Yet that effect—with its metaphor of earthquake, its association of Darwinian and Scriptural epochal shifts, its allusion to the film's "after Chernobyl" setting and to the malicious sport of the gods, the "promised end," and "image of that horror" in Shakespeare—depends heavily on "names," despite the professor's theory, and on the complex cultural significances that have accrued to each element of this miniature, fake holocaust either in wider cultural usage or in the course of the film.

3 The professor unveils his invention in a small auditorium. We never see what is on the screen, but, again, at a crucial juncture the figure of the artist is doubled. Just as the quest for Shakespeare's works turns up a second quester, the professor, "working along parallel lines," so the professor's own cinematic quest is doubled by that of another researcher, Professor Kozintsev, who has come from Siberia to share in the presentation, somehow, of the first film. In fact the film Don Learo, Shakespeare Jr., and Cordelia file in to watch must be Grigorii Kozintsev's 1970 film of *King Lear*, for we hear part of Yuri Yarvet's response to the Russian Cordelia and can make out at least one word of his, a repetition of hers: "nichevo?" ("nothing?"). What had been prepared for as the moment of founding originality is belated, imitative, and repetitive in every sense: the cinema has already been invented, as we watch a burlesque of its reinvention by a character who shares a voice and body with the director of the film we are watching. The purported core of Godard's film, and the only part of it we can hear (not see), is borrowed from an earlier, highly successful cinematic adaptation of *Lear*, and the word chosen is one signifying "nothing" in Russian, meaning nothing in English, and quoted by Lear from Cordelia. Even the name of the new invention is hedged and untranslated from French; Professor "Kozintsev" calls it "L'image ... mais je ne sais pas que c'est le mot juste."

Sowing/Sewing the Text: The Death of the Author and the Voice of *The Waves*

At this point in the film, the project of reclaiming Shakespeare's text and that of creating the first "image" have become closely intertwined with each other and with the story of Learo and Cordelia. In fact Cordelia becomes as necessary to the success of Professor Pluggy's project and to that of Shakespeare Jr.'s as she is to her father's, and because this is the case, all of these masculine endeavors are tainted with Lear's exploitation of his daughter and with the transgressive "needs" suggested in the meditation on artistic fatherhood in the opening minutes of the film.

As Sellars' investigation of Learo and Cordelia proceeds, he is led to the hotel bedroom, which (perhaps) Cordelia shares with her father.[27] Lifting up the bedspread, he uncovers blood-soaked sheets. We are kept from taking this clue very seriously by a troop of mime performers who swarm over the bed performing a rite of purification, swinging censers and chanting the names of Mao Ze-dong, Che Guevara, and other revolutionary leaders in mock litany. But however canceled and however inconsistent this sequence is with the narrative that follows, it invokes the murder-incest associations of the opening. This is the blood of a primal paternal transgression, like Chronos' infanticide, Lansky's murder of Bugsy Siegel, or the murder of Che Guevara. At this point Sellars has become quite uncertain that he is on the track of the real Shakespeare. Perhaps "this" is "not Lear" at all. Professor Pluggy proposes a test: if a fireworks sparkler that burns with a yellow light in Sellars' hand glows pure white when held by Molly Ringwald, "then her virtue is true and her name is Cordelia." When the sparkler is passed to her, it does glow white (photo 7.17), not only validating Sellars' quest but also improving Pluggy's "invention," for when installed in his carboard shadow theater instead of a tungsten bulb, it (apparently) provides the proper color temperature for projection (photo 7.18).[28]

However, in establishing Cordelia's "virtue" and authenticity, Sellars must shed his role as detached researcher and become, at least momentarily, her persecutor and inquisitor.

211

Photo 7.17

Photo 7.18

Alone in her room, Cordelia holds herself apart from the men's various projects, Sellars' quest, Learo's epic, and the professor's cinematic experiments. Sellars intrudes on her as she turns the pages of a book of Gustave Doré reproductions (in which female nudes and threating, Satanic male figures alternate)[29] and begins to question her about her "voices" and "visions," and particularly about how she can tell whether the "apparitions" she sees are male or female. "You shall not have that from me," she replies, and prophesies that "in seven years the Americans shall lose all they have in France, in a great victory God is giving to the French." What has happened is that Cordelia's French exile in Shakespeare's play has aligned her with Joan of Arc—both to the historical Joan, from whose trial these words are adapted, and (as the ultra-close-up style used here suggests) to that of Carl Dreyer's *Passion of Joan of Arc*. Thus the daughter of an American gangster has somehow come to stand for France-as-colony in its resistance to Americanization.[30]

At the same time, the privileged male madness of Shakespeare's play drifts toward the female, in a pattern that will be developed further, as female voices usurp the poignant lines in which Lear recognizes the approach of madness. The cooperation or cooptation of the resisting, victimized, and heroic female is necessary for the success of the men's artistic enterprises. Yet at this point too Sellars suddenly and unaccountably spreads his arms in the cruciform pose of the "wounded angel" (photo 7.19; refer to photo 7.7) that is perhaps the film's most insistently repeated image of itself. "Martyrdom" (Bugsy Siegel's death was also a "martyrdom," the founding event in Don Learo's/Albert Fried's

212

Photo 7.19

American epic) begins to dominate the final minutes, though its form and meaning vary according to gender. The men die (one is reborn), and their works are scattered (and only partly reassembled); the death of Cordelia provides the film with its nearest approach to closure in a powerful, repeated tableau accompanied by an even more emphatic voice-over conclusion.

As the recovery of Shakespeare's text and the professor's reinvention of cinema proceed, Godard denies the spectator any firm sense of closure by juxtaposing intimations of completion with images of dispersal, interruption, and death. After the screening of the first film (which we never see), Sellars declares that he has recovered "ninety-nine percent of the lines [of *King Lear*]; perhaps all of them, thanks to the professor, the old man, and his daughter." But we have heard only a small fraction of the lines of this well-known play, and in the sequence in which Sellars proclaims the imminent completion of his labors, he is seated on a rocky beach where the roar of the surf drowns out his words and a breaking wave washes over him and his notebook-script. This image is paired with a shot of the same beach, with the waves lapping over a book, perhaps washed to shore, whose title is clearly visible—it is *The Waves*, Virginia Woolf's masterpiece, in a recent paperback edition (photos 7.20, 7.21). As he finishes his work, Sellars cedes control of it: "I had reinvented the lines: now it was up to the characters.... All I knew was that I could no longer control them; perhaps they were controlling me." The obliteration of his voice by the waves is one aspect of this letting go, and the appearance of *The Waves* as text signals another, for this book will to

213

Photo 7.20 Photo 7.21

some extent supplant *King Lear* as the script of his "characters." As with *The Rise and Fall of the Jewish Gangster*, the literal appearance of this text potentially reveals the point of origin of the film text. If Shakespeare's text is present "after Chernobyl" only in scraps and must be reconstituted through immense labor, Fried's text (the history of the father-as-criminal) and Woolf's (the woman's text) are materially present in contemporary editions.

Professor Pluggy's work also disperses as it concludes. When Sellars tries to thank him for his role in helping to restore Shakespeare, he finds Pluggy (or part of him—the extreme close-up shows only hands at first) attempting the creation of yet another image: the reassembly of scattered flower stems and petals into a spring bouquet as Easter bells ring. The bouquet complete, Sellars canonizes Pluggy as a source of Scriptural widsom: "through his words I understood St. Paul's words that the image will appear in the time of resurrection." Yet the miming of organic creation by human hands is transparently fake, for the effect is achieved by a very old and thinly disguised technique: the camera is cranked in reverse while a hand pulls petals off a flower. Then Pluggy dies clutching a gerbera daisy, his head wreathed by the cords of his electronic headdress. His last words as he looks skyward are "Mr. Alien." Then Sellars too appears to die, shot by Edgar. As he falls, he spreads his arms in the precise gesture of the falling angel "shot in the back" which has been the icon of the film itself since the beginning (photo 7.22); yards of film are seen to unwind in a pile in the field, and the lid of a film cannister drifts downstream in the river.

214

Photo 7.22

In the final sequences of the Lear narrative, images and words from Virginia Woolf compete with and supplant those of Shakespeare. To initiate the close, Godard uses a long take of several characters sitting on the rocks. Sellars is writing, as usual, in his Lear notebook; "Virginia," Edgar's girlfriend, is reading *The Waves*; and Edgar is cleaning or playing with his rifle. Meredith enters the frame from the upper right, playing with a butterfly net in token of his madness ("we two will . . . laugh at gilded butterflies"), and Cordelia enters from the woods in the upper center of the image, dressed in white and leading a white horse (photo 7.23). By this point apparently Sellars has outdistanced his characters in composing *King Lear*, so when Meredith stumbles over his own lines, he borrows Sellars' text to read them. Meredith exchanges his net for Edgar's gun and follows Cordelia out of the image (photos 7.24 and 7.25). As they move through the woods to the shore, Virginia's silent reading accompanies the image in voice-over and we hear the magnificent final paragraph of *The Waves*:

And in me too, the wave rises. It swells; it arches its back. I am aware once more of a new desire, something rising beneath me like the proud horse whose rider first spurs and then pulls himself back. What enemy do we now perceive advancing against us, you whom I ride now, as we stand pawing this stretch of pavement? It is death. Death is the enemy. It is Death against whom I ride with my spear couched and my hair flying back like a young man's, like Percival's, when he galloped in India. I strike spurs into my horse. Against

215

you I will fling myself, unvanquished and unyielding, O Death![31]

The actual death of Cordelia is elided, not shown. But we conclude that Lear has shot her "in the back," for the final tableau of his narrative strand shows her stretched out on the rocks in a reprise of the "angel shot in the back" posture, with Learo holding the rifle and looking out to sea (photo 7.26). We cannot hear Lear's final words, mumbled while the surf roars.

The text of *The Waves* has many resonances and associations that contribute to the close. It is, first, a woman's masterpiece, now part of the secular canon in which we paradigmatically locate "meaning" and "culture." Then it seems partly an interior monologue of Cordelia, a restoration to voice of some part of her story left unwritten by Shakespeare, for whom her last moments and words are not heard ("her voice was ever soft,/Gentle and low, an excellent thing in woman," 5.3.273–74). And like Godard, the passage combines epic heroism with a dispersal or decentering of the

Photo 7.23

Photo 7.24

Photo 7.25

Photo 7.26

216

self. Drawing on medieval romance (Percival), *Don Quixote*, and perhaps the Cuchulain legend of a battle with the sea, Woolf imagines a heroic self poised and ready for battle that seems to set itself apart and against death as enemy, even while acknowledging death's presence within as the rising wave. This is also a passage in which genders cross. In Woolf these are nominally the words (or thoughts) of a male character, Bernard. Yet his is the closest approach to an authorial voice in the novel. His hair "flying back" like a "young man's" is male by simile yet irresistibly authorial and female as well. Elsewhere Bernard speaks as androgyne ("For this is not one life, nor do I always know if I am man or woman"). *The Waves* is also a *locus classicus* for the modernist dispersal of self in text ("this is not one life . . ."). Woolf's six "characters" share thoughts, share exposition, share a story without speaking; it is "their" story rather than the story of conventionally and more clearly bounded individuals. Finally, at this point in the text Godard has supplemented Lear's madness with the madness of women, and perhaps alludes in the process to Woolf's actual and tragic mental illness. Many of Lear's lines expressing his fragmentation are spoken in voice-over by female voices, as Cordelia's "visions" as Joan of Arc have supplanted the hallucinations of Edgar and Lear.

The final tableau depicting the dead Cordelia and Learo with his gun is repeated several times, serving as a kind of final punctuation for the text of *The Waves*. The film allows that text an emphatic closure denied to Shakespeare's *King Lear*. Virginia Woolf's novel speaks as Cordelia is silent. The feminist novel supplies the female voice excluded from the patriarchal text, blending with the text of Shakespeare's *Lear* and that of Godard's *Lear* at the point at which those texts recognize the power of dispersal, acknowledging "the wave" as that which deconstructs the self, revealing its grounding in the terrible "nothing" Cordelia speaks in answer to her father's demand for wholeness and presence.

After this sequence, a title announces "THE END," but the film continues with the narration of Pluggy's death and the unwinding of his film. Yet this is not the end either, despite a second false title card: there is a coda in which, "twenty years

Photo 7.27

later," Sellars is back in New York in an editing room run by ("This could be no accident") Mr. Alien—actually Woody All(i)en dressed in a Picasso T-shirt. Sellars and Allen edit the professor's film expertly using a travel-size sewing kit and safety pins to make splices (photo 7.27). Images from the "film," most prominently slow-motion jump cut shots of the white horse running free, appear as Allen dubs a soundtrack consisting of a recitation in full of a Shakespeare sonnet ("Like as the waves make to the pebbled shore/So do our minutes hasten to their end."). Godard's *King Lear* does not end at all but runs through the final leader without punctuation or credits.

In *King Lear* Godard burlesques, disperses, interrupts, and disconnects Shakespeare's text, displaying in the process most of the deconstructive and distantiating techniques for which he has become known. But he also acknowledges Shakespeare as a decisive precursor in these very techniques. *King Lear* is not merely a text to be demystified: for Godard it is the locus, in the Western cultural tradition, of the self-critique of patriarchy and of the totalizing aesthetic and psychological assumptions that support it. The deconstruction of "the father" as source, authority, and hegemonic center is already under way in Shakespeare's *Lear*, as is the unruly interplay of selves and texts.

The Western cultural inheritance, as Godard receives it, is a tainted one, compromised by the "pleasant vices" of the father in which the sons are implicated. For Godard these vices are not so much Shakespeare's as those of Western patriarchalism, and especially the artistic variant of patriarchy, in which women are necessary as subject matter, inspiration, and support for male creation. As part of its critique of patriarchy in political and cultural life, Godard's *King Lear* attempts to redress certain aspects of the exclusion, objectification, and commodification of women, sharing male roles of the play with female voices, infiltrating Shakespeare's text with words by women writers, foregrounding the process by which the propagation of male culture entails the subordination of female bodies and female images. This aspect of the film is far from being completely successful, and perhaps even recoups or excuses the male arrogance that is the subject of its critique.[32] But Godard's experiments in the "feminine" reinscription of patriarchal texts are a central and important feature of his reading and reproduction of *King Lear*.

Whatever the successes of this controversial and in some ways certainly unsuccessful work, Godard has used Shakespeare to attempt a self-decentering, a displacement of the father-artist into his child-texts, accepting (or coming as close as he can to accepting) their wayward independence, their failure to mirror the grandiose intentions of their author, their denials of origins (which repeat the father's, or the artist's *own* denials), and their strangeness.

As the film opens itself to the text of *The Waves* and the voice of the woman, to the posthumous mess of the editing room, to the conveyance of the master's works into the hands of Woody Allen—competing *auteur*, aggressively parodic American, and perhaps the murderous "Mr. Alien" himself—Godard embraces one version of *King Lear*'s teaching, accepting limitations on his control and acknowledging the dangerous, chaotic, and contingent future that attends his (and our own) attempts at self understanding and creation.

Notes

1 Jacques Derrida, *Dissemination* (Chicago: University of Chicago Press, 1981), 344.

2 Samuel Schoenbaum, *William Shakespeare: A Compact Documentary Life* (New York: Oxford University Press, 1977), 319.

3 French *fils* does for thread and son; I borrow this play on words from Barbara Johnson's translation of Derrida's "Plato's Pharmacy" in *Dissemination* where she writes of "filial filaments" (p. 84). In the preface she plays on sowing/sewing as an English analogue to these French and Latinate paternal homonyms. In the final moments of Godard's *Lear* the unraveled film text is gathered and edited—by being sewn together.

4 Godard's practice as a filmmaker and philosophical and literary-critical deconstruction are closely related. A copy of Derrida's *De la grammatologie* appears on screen in *Le gai savoir* (1967), a film in which, like many to follow, Godard's own developing aesthetic seems directly influenced by Derrida's formulations. See Julia Lewis Lesage, "The Films of Jean-Luc Godard and Their Use of Brechtian Dramatic Theory" (unpublished Ph.D. thesis, University of Indiana, 1976), 23–25. In his *King Lear* Godard seems particularly close to the imagery and strategies of *Dissemination*, and some of the parallels will be noted here, but the aim is not to establish that the film is programmatically Derridean. I am principally concerned with Godard's deconstructive "reading" of *Lear*, a reading that nearly coincides in time with the belated emergence of Derridean deconstruction in Anglo-American Shakespeare studies in the work of Jonathan Goldberg, Margaret Ferguson, Marjorie Garber, and others.

5 Colin MacCabe, Mick Eaton, and Laura Mulvey, *Godard: Images, Sounds, Politics* (London: Macmillan, 1980), 103.

6 "Il y a une histoire entre nous. Comme pour tout le monde, l'histoire sort de chez *lui* et rentre chez *elle*. Et là, à l'intérieur, on perd sa trace. Et puis elle ressort, un enfant est né, et on trouve ça dehors, à l'extérieur. Et là, on voit de nouveau l'histoire." As cited and translated in ibid., 164–65. Fuller extracts from the screenplay are printed in Alain Bergala, ed. *Jean-Luc Godard par Jean-Luc Godard* (Paris: Cahiers du Cinéma-Editions de l'Etoile, 1985), 418–41.

7 Richard Corliss, "Mad Monarch as Gang Lord," *Time*, February 1, 1988, 71.

8 Perhaps all paternity is metaphoric. "But what is a father" is Derrida's question put to Plato's *Phaedrus* in "Plato's Pharmacy," an inquiry into the founding connections in Western tradition of fatherhood, speech, writing, and metaphor (see especially *Dissemination*, 75–94). A speaker, as author of (his) words, stands behind them as a father does his son, authorizing them. Yet there is no fatherhood without speech, without the logos that seeks out the occult connection between a man

and his offspring. "Father of the *logos*" is therefore not merely a metaphor—perhaps not a metaphor at all—but the "hearth" or origin of all metaphor. In Derrida's view the Western tradition privileges speech over writing because speech has a "father" who can vouch for it; writing is devalued because it is "a bastard" whose connection to its source is more problematic. Such metaphors of legitimate and illegitimate filiation play continually through Godard's *King Lear*. Lear's insistence on hearing, his command that his daughter's love be fully present in their speech, is countered by the film's constant textualization, marking speech as quotation. The use of intertitles, the frequent surfacing of the *script* from which apparently spontaneous dialogue is read, and the narrator's theorizing about the cinematic image as a kind of bastard "text" are all implicit replies to Lear's (and "Learo's") fearful need for full presence.

9 Jean Renoir was raised by one of his father's beautiful models (his cousin Gabrielle) and married another, Catherine Hessling ("Dédé"). In *My Life and My Films*, trans. Norman Denny (New York: Athenaeum, 1974), Jean Renoir refers to Hessling as "the last present given to my father by my mother before her death.... Dédé adored my father, who returned her love" (p. 47). According to John Gielgud, Sasha Guitry, another of the directors in this sequence of stills, also inherited a mistress from his father (PBS interview with Sir John Gielgud, aired January 1989).

10 The expression "pantheon directors" is Andrew Sarris's, but it derives from the 1950s *Cahiers du cinéma* practice of ranking films and directors in which Godard played a part. Having shared in and helped to initiate the secular worship of these Olympian *auteurs*, Godard now ponders their relation to the more violent artistic traditions their practice derives from. Shakespearean drama and post-Renaissance painting constitute, for the film, the Titanic prehistory of the cinema.

11 In kabbalist terminology, this is *tikkun*, or "raising of the sparks," the reconstitution of the light lost in *shephireth ha'kelim*, the "breaking of the vessels."

12 Other contemporary film versions of *King Lear*, including Kurosawa's *Ran* (1985) and Kozintsev's *King Lear* (1970), also relate family tyranny to the working of an oppressive social system, expanding on the brilliant but fragmentary social vision Shakespeare's Lear gains through his suffering and madness.

13 MacCabe et al., *Godard*, 30–33; Bergalá, *Godard par Godard*, 418–41.

14 New York: Holt, Rinehart & Winston, 1980.

15 The title of the book is never easily legible on screen—we see it either in long shot, or when it is shown in close-up, part of the title falls below the frame line (at least when properly masked

for projection). This partial display of a textual source contrasts with the treatment of *King Lear* and with the still different use of *The Waves* later in the film, where we can read the whole title clearly but may not identify it as the source for subsequent voice-over extracts.

16 Fried, *Rise and Fall*, 280.

17 Ibid., 281.

18 Tadashi Suzuki's 1988 theatrical production of *The Tale of Lear* used a chorus of conflicting voices speaking scraps of verse in a related way to represent the aural hallucinations the text suggests at several points.

19 Compare Ann Righter [Barton], *Shakespeare and the Idea of the Play* (Westport, CT: Greenwood Press, 1977; first published, London: Chatto and Windus, 1962), 133:

> [The Fool] answers Lear's wild query "Who is it that can tell me who I am" (i.iv.229), with a term customarily associated with the actor: "Lear's shadow" (i.iv.230). In resigning his kingdom to his daughters, Lear has reduced himself to that absurd condition which Alencon described in *Henry VI, Part One*; a king whose authority has been given up, he is now "as a shadow of himself." (*Henry VI, Part One* 5.4.133–37)

Righter also cites *King Lear* 1.4.229–30 to instance the way in which the "loss of political place finally entails the dissolution of the self" (p. 40).

20 Lear's question and its answer are frequently repeated in voice-over in the film, where the play of geographic indeterminacy is dizzying. Nyon is not in France, nor are Boston, Cambridge, and Somerville, where I watched prints of the film. Yet "France" or "the kingdom of France" is in some sense the fictional location, as the film inconsistently announces. "Am I in France?" has been an important question for Godard throughout his life, and perhaps the best answer to it has been: "In your own kingdom, sir."

21 I am suggesting that Godard's fragmentation of Lear within the diegesis, and of the spectator's experience *of* the film, may be understood not simply as a modernizing trope on *Lear* but as a tribute to and reproduction of a splitting of the subject already present in Shakespeare's theatrical practice. As Francis Barker, Catherine Belsey, and others have argued, Shakespeare's stage, unlike its medieval and post-Restoration counterparts, "disrupted" the factitious unity of the spectator:

> In the period between the precarious unity offered by the moralities and the stable, transcendent unity of the Restoration stage, from 1576 when Burbage built the Theatre to 1642 when the playhouses were closed, the stage brought into conjunction and indeed into collision the emblematic mode and an emergent illusionism. The effect was a form of drama capable at any moment of disrupting the unity of the spec-

tator. Not, of course, that it could compel this disruptive reading. No form can unilaterally determine the response of the audience. The moralities could not guarantee their emblematic intelligibility; the scenic theater could not insist on a humanistic reading.... None the less, it is possible to identify, especially in the public theatres of the late sixteenth and early seventeenth centuries, a form of staging that can be read as withholding the certainty which offers to unify in different ways both the medieval and the Restoration spectator.

Catherine Belsey, *The Subject of Tragedy: Identity and Difference in Renaissance Drama* (London: Methuen, 1985), 26.

22 This headdress is also a tribute to the bells and baubles of the Fool's motley in *Lear*. There is no fool proper in the film: Woody Allen was to have taken this part in the original plan, but in the finished work Godard, to a certain extent, is his own fool.

23 Until this point he is a disembodied voice-over narrator and thus occupies the hidden point from which the film in enunciated. By localizing this strange voice in a grotesque body, and especially by revealing the source of its mysterious speech as a mouth afflicted by (actual or fictional) paralysis, whatever sense of mastery this voice may have accorded the spectator is further undermined.

24 I mean the ancient cosmic serpent, pictured as devouring its tail. This cartoon descendant of the self-consuming, self-producing deities of the ancient world echoes and answers Goya's "Chronos." Art, as the professor tells us, "*Is* born from what it destroys."

25 See Derrida's discussion of Rousseau and masturbation as the "dangerous supplement" to nature in *Of Grammatology*, trans. Gayatri Chakravorty Spivak (London and Baltimore: Johns Hopkins University Press, 1976).

26 Tom Milne and Jean Narboni, eds., *Godard on Godard* (New York: Viking, 1972), 21; Bergalá, *Godard par Godard*, 76. These collections reprint Godard's review of Rudolph Maté's *No Sad Songs for Me*, which first appeared in *Cahiers du Cinéma* 8 (January 1952).

27 This is also the bed on which Norman Mailer embraces his daughter Kate.

28 Cordelia is also thus associated with the slide-show image of Liberty and her torch.

29 These images too echo the opening of the film. Godard symbolically connects Lear's tyranny with the sexual exploitation of women, but that exploitation is never directly represented in the diegesis of *King Lear*. The mysterious blood on the sheets suggests it but is bracketed off from the rest of the narrative and never referred to by the characters. The major references to the sexual use of women are the stills of female nudes by canonical

post-Renaissance artists. In the virginal ambience of late Godard, these images acquire the force of a cultural critique comparable to the explicit treatment of violent sex and prostitution in earlier Godard, or to the use there of women's images from popular magazines (see MacCabe et al., *Godard* chap. 4, "Images of Woman, Images of Sexuality," 77–104). The way Western "high culture" has traded in erotic images is now emphatically included in Godard's critique of the commodification of women. Cordelia seems dazed, perhaps disgusted, by what she sees, as if understanding in a new way the demands made on her.

30 This scene, like Learo's self-questioning on the balcony of the hotel, is one of the most moving in the film. In these cases the incessant play of allusion, cross-reference, and erasure does not block identification, as in the more strictly Brechtian mode of early Godard. Rather, the pathos seems somehow deepened by the bizarre overlaying of character-texts. The characters seem to suffer most intensely precisely at points at which their construction out of cultural and textual quotations and traces is most evident. For Godard's cinematic transformation of Brechtian principles, see Lesage, "Films," 29–71, 238–62, and *passim*.

The scene also illustrates Godard's disturbance of linear chronology. At the start the image of Chronos is connected to the album of filmmakers in many ways. One of these is the fact that, in editing a film, a director "holds in his hands the past, the future and the present." Shakespeare's play was written after Joan of Arc yet is culturally remote from the myth of her as sanctified national redeemer (compare Shakespeare's treatment of her in *Henry VI*); it was written before fears of universal nuclear destruction gave point to its images of doom. Yet, for Godard *King Lear* subsists in the play of traces—retained or anticipated—of other times, other contexts, other stories.

31 Virginia Woolf, *The Waves* (London: Hogarth Press, 1972), 211.

32 The desexualization of Cordelia and the idealizing of her "silence" seem to me issues around which the critique of Godard's quasi-feminism might be further explored. Such a critique, which might also apply to *Hail Mary*, might follow the lead suggested by Derrida in relation to Rousseau:

Since they both scorn writing, Rousseau and Levi-Strauss both praise the range of the voice. Nevertheless, in the texts that we must now read, Rousseau is suspicious also of the illusion of full and present speech, of the illusion of presence within a speech believed to be transparent and innocent. It is toward the praise of silence that the myth of a full presence . . . is then deviated. (*Of Grammatology*, 140)

In developing Professor Pluggy's theories and applying them to *King Lear*, Peter Sellars is aware, in a way closely coincident with Kaja Silverman's *The Acoustic Mirror* (Bloomington: University of Indiana Press, 1988), that Lear (or Learo) demands his daughter's voices because they "enfold" the female body: "he wants to hear their bodies stretched out against their voices." Yet the idealization of Cordelia as Joan of Arc, and the praise of her "violent silence" in Sellars' discourse, may be a version of Lear's demand in which woman still plays the role of guarantor of male wholeness; just as, in the text, Lear's demand for Cordelia's obedience is succeeded at the end of the play by his fantasy (phasally inappropriate for Cordelia, who would thereby be condemned to celibacy) of himself and his daughter as "God's spies."

Filmography

Henry V, U.K., 1944. 137 min. A Two Cities Film, released by United Artists. Technicolor. 35mm.
Producer, Director: Laurence Olivier
Screenplay: Alan Dent and Laurence Olivier
Cinematography: Robert Krasker
Music: William Walton
Cast: Laurence Olivier (Henry V); Robert Newton (Pistol); Leslie Banks (Chorus); Renee Asherson (Princess Katherine); Esmond Knight (Fluellen); Leo Genn (Constable); Felix Aylmer (Archbishop of Canterbury); Ralph Truman (French Herald); Harcourt Williams (Charles VI); Ivy St. Helier (Alice); Ernest Thesiger (Duke of Berri); Max Adrian (Dauphin); Francis Lister (Duke of Orleans); Valentine Dyall (Duke of Burgundy); Russell Thorndike (Duke of Bourbon); Michael Shepley (Gower); Morland Graham (Sir Thomas Erpingham); Gerald Case (Earl of Westmoreland); Janet Burnell (Queen Isabel); Nicholas Hannen (Duke of Exeter); Robert Helpman (Bishop of Ely); Freda Jackson (Mistress Quickly); Jimmy Hanley (Williams); John Laurie (Captain Jamie); Niall MacGinnis (Captain MacMorris); George Robie (Sir John Falstaff); Roy Emerton (Bardolph); Griffith Jones (Earl of Salisbury); Arthur Hambling (Bates); Frederick Cooper (Corporal Nym); Michael Warre (Duke of Gloucester); Brian Nissen (Court); Vernon Greaves (English Herald)

Hamlet, U.K., 1948. 153 min. Two Cities Films, released by J. Arthur Rank. Black and white. 35mm
Producer, Director: Laurence Olivier

Cinematography: Desmond Dickerson
Sets: Roger Furse
Music: William Walton
Cast: Laurence Olivier (Hamlet); Eileen Herlie (Gertrude); Basil Sydney (Claudius); Jean Simmons (Ophelia); Felix Aylmer (Polonius); Norman Wooland (Horatio); Terence Morgan (Laertes); Harcourt Williams (First Player); Patrick Troughton (Player King); Tony Tarver (Player Queen); Peter Cushing (Osric); Stanley Holloway (Gravedigger); Russell Thorndike (Priest); John Laurie (Francisco); Esmond Knight (Bernardo); Anthony Quayle (Marcellus); Niall MacGinnis (Sea Captain)

Throne of Blood, Japan, 1957. 105 min. Toho. Black and white. 35mm
Producer, Director: Akira Kurosawa
Screenplay: Akira Kurosawa, Shinobu Hashimoto, Ryuzu Kikushima, Hideo Oguni
Cast: Toshiro Mifune (Washizu); Isuzu Yamada (Asaji); Takashi Shimura (Ogadura); Minoru Chiaki (Miki); Akira Kubo (Yoshiteru); Takamaru Sasaki (Tsuzuki); Yoichi Tachikawa (Kunimaru); Chieko Naniwa (The Forest Spirit)

Othello, U.S.A., 1951. 91 min. Mercury Productions, released by United Artists. Black and white. 35mm
Producer, Director: Orson Welles
Cinematography: Anchise Brizzi, G. Araldo, George Fanto
Music: Francesco Lavagnino, Alberto Barberis
Cast: Orson Welles (Othello); Micheál MacLiammóir (Iago); Suzanne Cloutier (Desdemona); Robert Coote (Roderigo); Hilton Edwards (Brabantio); Michael Lawrence (Cassio); Fay Compton (Emilia); Nicholas Bruce (Lodovico); Jean Davis (Montano); Doris Dowling (Bianca)

Othello, U.S.A., 1980. 115 min. Eastmancolor. 16mm
Producer, Director: Liz White
Cinematography: Charles Dorkins
Music: Jonas Gwangwa
Cast: Yaphet Kotto (Othello); Richard Dixon (Iago); Audrey Dixon (Desdemona); Lewis Chisholm, Jr. (Cassio); Olive

Bowles (Emilia); Douglas Gray (Roderigo); Liz White (Bianca); Benjamin Ashburn (Montano); Jim Williams (Brabantio)

Romeo and Juliet, U.K./Italy, 1968. 139 min. B.H.E. Productions. Verona Productions. Dino De Lauretiis Cinematografica. Released by Paramount Pictures. Technicolor. 35mm
Producers: Anthony Havelock Allan and John Brabourne
Director: Franco Zeffirelli
Screenplay: Franco Brusati, Franco Zeffirelli, Masolino D'Amico
Cinematography: Pasquale De Santis
Music: Nino Rota
Cast: Leonard Whiting (Romeo); Olivia Hussey (Juliet); Michael York (Tybalt); John McEnery (Mercutio); Pat Heywood (Nurse); Natasha Parry (Lady Capulet); Robert Stephens (Prince of Verona); Bruce Robinson (Benvolio); Laurence Olivier (Narrator); Milo O'Shea (Friar Laurence); Paul Hardwick (Capulet); Antonio Pierfederici (Montague); Roberto Bisacco (Paris); Esmeralda Ruspoli (Lady Montague)

King Lear, U.S.A., Switzerland, 1988. Cannon Films. Color. 35mm
Producers: Menahem Golan, Yoram Globus
Director: Jean-Luc Godard
Screenplay: Jean-Luc Godard
Cinematography: Sophie Maintigneux
Sound: François Musy
Cast: Burgess Meredith (Don Learo); Peter Sellars (William Shakespeare Jr., the Fifth); Molly Ringwald (Cordelia); Jean-Luc Godard (The Professor); Norman Mailer (The Great Writer); Kate Mailer (Herself)

About the Author

Peter S. Donaldson is Professor of Literature at the Massachusetts Institute of Technology and Fellow of the Royal Historical Society. He has written numerous articles on Shakespeare and other Renaissance topics and is the author of, among other works, *Machiavelli and Mystery of State* (1988).

Index

A bout de souffle (film), 198
Abelin, Ernest, 29
Adelman, Janet, 28
Adler, Renata, 145
Allen, Woody, 192, 218–19, 223
Althusser, Louis, xiv
Andrew, Dudley, 26, 28
As You Like It, 4, 196
Asherson, Renee, 9, 12
Ashworth, John, 63
Avery, Tex, 208
Aylmer, Felix, 50

Bacall, Lauren, 127
Bach, S., 29
Ball, Robert H., xi, xiv
Banks, Leslie, 30
Barber, C. L., 137–8
Barker, Francis, 222
Barton, Anne [Righter], 204, 222
Battenhouse, Roy, 25
Baudry, Jean-Louis, xii, 74, 93, 94, 105, 112, 122, 125, 126, 152, 185
Beckett, Samuel, xiv
Belsey, Catherine, 27, 222–3
Benjamin, Jessica, 28, 29, 30
Berger, Harry Jr., xiii, xv, 73, 90
Bergman, Anni, 29, 187
Bewley, Marius, 125
Billington, Michael, 28–9
Blos, Peter, 29, 30, 65, 187
Bock, Audie, 89
Bondarchuk, Sergei, 113, 131–2
Bray, Alan, 186
Brown, Ivor, 63
Brown Sugar (musical), 127
Bulman, J. C., xv
Burch, Noel, 71, 74, 89, 90
Burland, J. A., 29
Burge, Stuart, 122

Carabiniers, Les (film), 195
Cavell, Stanley, 122, 124

Champ, The (film), 147
Chodorow, Nancy, 28, 185
Coleridge, S. T., xiii
Confessions of an Actor, 24
Cooper, Jackie, 147
Corliss, Richard, 220
Corsi, Ottorino, 146–9
Cosi fan tutte (opera), 146
Cottrell, John, 30, 64
Coursen, Herbert R., xv
Cross, Brenda, 65–6

Dalsimer, Katherine, 187
Davies, Anthony, xv, 28
De Crevecoeur, Hector St-J., 119–21, 125
De Niro, Robert, 198–9
Derrida, Jacques, 189, 219–21, 223, 224
Deux ou trois choses que je sais d'elle (film), 206
Dixon, Audrey, 128
Dixon, Richard, 128, 132
Dollimore, Jonathan, 25, 26, 90
Donaldson, Peter S., 29, 64
Doré, Gustave, 212
Dorkins, Charles, 128
Downes, Donald, 149
Drakakis, John, 26
Dreyer, Carl, 212
Dunaway, Faye, 147

Eaton, Mick, 220
Eliot, T. S., 141–2
Endless Love (film), 147, 170
Erickson, Peter, 185
Erikson, Eric, 107
Esaki, Kohei, 90
Eyes on the Prize (documentary), 120

Ferguson, Margaret, 220
Foucault, Michel, xiii–xv
Forance, Priscilla, 143

Ford, John, 70
Forbes-Robertson, Sir Johnston, 25
Fried, Albert, 200–2, 212, 222
Freud, Sigmund, xii, xiv, 29, 31–5, 38, 55, 57, 62–3, 159
Furse, Roger, 50, 66

Garber, Marjorie, 220
Garossi, Adelaide, 146–7
Geduld, Harry, 10–11, 15, 27–9
Genn, Leo, 30
Gielgud, Sir John, 29, 221
Godard, Jean-Luc, xii
Gohlke, Madelon, 143
Golan, Menahem, 192
Goldberg, Jonathan, 220
Gourlay, Logan, 29
Goya, Francesco, 195–6, 199, 223
Greenblatt, Stephen, xv, 25
Greenson, Ralph, 29
Griffith, D. W., 71
Grunberger, Bela, 64
Guevara, Che, 211
Guitry, Sacha, 194, 221
Guthrie, Tyrone, 31, 67

Hail Mary (film), 225
Halio, Jay, 63
Halperin, David, 30
Hamlet, 105
Hannen, Nicholas, 30
Harari, Josue, xv
Heald, Rev. Geoffrey, 22, 25, 35
Herlie, Eileen, 31, 37, 48
Hessling, Catherine (DéDé), 221
Higham, Charles, 124
Holderness, Graham, 28, 90
Holliday, Judy, 127
Howell, Jane, xv
Hussey, Olivia, 164, 178

Jacquot, Jean, 204
Joan of Arc, 199, 212, 224, 225
Johnson, Barbara, 220
Jones, Ernest, xiv, 31–3, 41, 47, 49, 62–4
Jones, Jennifer, 127
Jorgens, Jack, xi, 76, 90
Jardine, Lisa, 27

Kahn, Coppélia, 26, 28, 153, 185–6
Keaton, Diane, 198–9
Keith, Harry, 148

Kernberg, Otto, 64
Kerr, Walter, 187
Kiernan, Thomas, 29
Klein, Melanie, 107, 124–5
Kliman, Bernice, xv, 63
Kohut, Heinz, xii, 64, 107, 125, 150
Kotto, Yaphet, 97, 121, 127–30, 133, 139
Kozintsev, Grigorii, 210, 221
Kurosawa, Akira, xiii, 221

Lacan, Jacques, 94, 107, 123
Lady from Shanghai (film), 105
Lancaster, Burt, 202
Lang, Fritz, 194
Lansky, Meyer, 200, 202, 211
Laplanche, Jean, 187
Laurie, John, 30
Lax, R. F., 29
Layton, Lynne, 64
Leaming, Barbara, 125
Leavis, F. R., 141
Lee, Canada, 127
Leigh, Vivien, 36
Lesage, Julia, 220, 224
Levine, Laura, 27
Lévi-Strauss, Claude, 224
Lide ("Aunt Lide", Franco Zeffirelli's aunt), 147

MacCabe, Colin, 220, 221, 224
Mahler, Margaret, 29, 107, 179, 187
Mailer, Kate, 192, 193
Mailer, Norman, 192, 193, 198, 223
Malle, Louis, 202
Manvell, Roger, 90
Maté, Rudolph, 223
McDevitt, J. B., 29
Meltzer, Annabelle, xv
Mépris, Le (film), 197
Meredith, Burgess, 196–201, 203, 206–7, 215
Metz, Christian, xii, 123, 152, 185, 187
Mieville, Anne-Marie, 191
Mifune, Toshiro, 88
Milton, John, 200
Mizoguchi, Kenji, 71
Moshinsky, Elijah, xv
Mulvey, Laura, xii, 154, 185, 187, 191, 220
Mussolini, Benito, 149
My Life and My Films, 70

Neely, Carol T., 143
Nichols, Bill, 187
Novy, Marianne, 123–4, 185, 187

Odyssey, The, 197
Olivier, Agnes, 20, 22, 35–6
Olivier, Gerard, 20, 22–3, 25, 35–6
Olivier, Lord (Laurence Olivier), xii, xiv, 105–6, 122, 148
Olivier, Richard, 20, 23–4
Olivier, Sybille, 22
O'Neill, Mary, 148
Orgel, Stephen, 27
Otello (film), 170
Ovesey, Lionel, 65

Parker, Barry, xiv
Pasolini, Pier Paolo, 194–5
Passion of Joan of Arc, The (film), 212
Paul, St., 214
Penley, Constance, 185
Pine, Fred, 29, 187
Plato, 220
Porter, Joseph, 145, 158–9, 184, 186

Rabkin, Norman, 25
Renoir, Auguste, 194
Renoir, Jean, 70, 194, 221
Righter, Anne, *see* Barton, Anne
Ringwald, Molly, 196, 198, 211
Rise and Fall of the Jewish Gangster in America, The, 200, 206
Robey, George, 30
Rothwell, Kenneth, xiv–xv
Rousseau, J.–J., 224

Sanderson, Michael, 30
Sarris, Andrew, 221
Schapiro, Barbara, 64
Schoenbaum, S., 190, 220
Schroeder, Ricky, 147
Schwartz, Murray M., 26
Sedgwick, Eve Kosofsky, 185
Sellars, Peter, 194, 196–8, 202–3, 205–7, 211–15, 218, 224
Settlage, C. F., 29
Shakespeare on Film, xi
Shakespeare on Film Newsletter, xi
Shakespeare on Silent Film, xi
Shepley, Michael, 30
Siegel, Bugsy, 198, 200–1, 211–12
Silverman, Kaja, 224–5

Silviria, Dale, 28
Sinfield, Allen, 25, 26, 90
Smith, G. R., 25
Snow, Edward A., 28, 104, 122–4, 136, 143, 185–8
Something Like an Autobiography, 69
Sprengnether, Madelon, *see* Gohlke Madelon
Studlar, Gaylan, 187
Suzuki, Tadashi, 222
Sydney, Basil, 57

Taming of the Shrew, 22, 35, 148
Terry, Ellen, 25
Thorndike, Sybil, 22
Truffaut, François, 194
Twelfth Night, 4

Vertov, Dziga, 94
Visconti, Count Luchino, 147, 150, 184, 194
Vlady, Marina, 206
Voight, John, 147

Walton, William, 50
Waves, The, 213–15, 217, 224
Weimann, Robert, 5, 26, 204
Weisbord, Robert, 143
Welles, Beatrice, 124
Welles, Orson, xiii, 142, 194
Wentersdorf, Karl P., 25
What Happens in Hamlet, 43
Wheeler, Richard, 137–8
White, Liz, xii, 95–7, 101, 105, 113, 120
Wilson, J. Dover, 43, 54, 66
Willbern, David, 26
Winnicott, D. W., 107, 123, 180, 188
Woolf, Virginia, 213–17, 224

Yarvet, Yuri, 210
York, Michael, 154
Yutkevich, Sergei, 95–7, 101, 105, 112–13, 116, 131–2

Zambrano, Ana Laura, 90
Ze-Dong, Mao, 211
Zeffirelli, Franco, xiii
Zeffirelli: The Autobiography of Franco Zeffirelli, 146, 170
Zeitlin, Froma, 24